Undocumented Aliens
in the New York Metropolitan Area

An Exploration into their Social and
Labor Market Incorporation

Undocumented Aliens in the New York Metropolitan Area

An Exploration into their Social and Labor Market Incorporation

Demetrios G. Papademetriou

and

Nicholas DiMarzio

1986

Center for Migration Studies of New York, Inc.

The Center for Migration Studies is an educational non-profit institute founded in New York in 1964 to encourage and facilitate the study of sociodemographic, economic, political, historical, legislative and pastoral aspects of human migration and refugee movements. The opinions expressed in this work are those of the authors. The authors also wish to note that any interpretations and opinions expressed in this report do not necessarily represent the views of the United States Catholic Conference.

This volume contains the report to the Tinker Foundation, which funded the research project, "Profiling Unapprehended Undocumented Aliens in the New York Metropolitan Area: An Exploratory Study-Phase I and Phase II".

The co-authors of this report, Demetrios G. Papademetriou, a former CMS research associate and now free-lance researcher in Fairfax, Virginia, and Nicholas DiMarzio, Executive Director of the Migration and Refugee Services of the United States Catholic Conference, were the investigators of the project.

Center for Migration Studies
209 Flagg Place, Staten Island, New York 10304

Library of Congress Cataloging-in-Publication Data

Papademetriou, Demetrios G.
    Undocumented Aliens in the New York Metropolitan Area
    Bibliography: p.
    Includes index.

1. Aliens,Illegal — New York Metropolitan Area.

I. De Marzio, Nicholas. II. Center for Migration Studies (U.S.) III. Title.

JV7048.P37 1986 323.6'31'09747 85-23385 ISBN 0-913256-99-4

To Sigrid Papademetriou and
Nicholas A. DiMarzio, Sr.

PREFACE

The Center for Migration Studies (CMS) was among the first research institutes to focus attention of policy makers on the problem of undocumented immigrants in New York. In 1975 CMS conducted a symposium on immigration policy with the participation of many leaders of various undocumented immigrant groups.[1] In 1977 CMS organized the First National Consultation on Undocumented Migrants and Public Policy.[2] To meet the obvious need for data on this population and to move beyond the previous survey by North and Houstoun (1976), CMS, with the financial assistance of the Ford-Rockefeller Foundation's Program in Population and Development Policy Research, undertook a research project on undocumented Haitians and Dominicans in New York not in custody of immigration authorities.[3] New research on undocumented immigrants and legal policy development in this area have been a constant component of the annual National Conference on Immigration and Refugee Policy, sponsored by CMS since 1978.[4] The complexity of the global phenomenon of irregular migration was analyzed in 1984 in a special double issue of the quarterly **International Migration Review**, published by CMS.[5]

With this history in the area and through its many years of research, publications and conferences, with one of the few comprehensive research libraries on immigrants, refugees and

---

1. **Migration Today**, Vol. 3, No. 2, March 1975.

2. **Migration Today**, Vol. 5, No. 2, April 1977.

3. Charles B. Keely, **et al., Profiles of Undocumented Aliens in New York City: Haitians and Dominicans.** New York: CMS, 1978.

4. **In Defense of the Alien,** Volumes 1-8. New York: CMS, 1978-1985.

5. **International Migration Review,** Vol. 18, No. 3, Fall 1984. Pp. 401-822.

ethnic groups, with the support of many noted scholars and researchers in the field, and a network of private voluntary agencies working among the newest immigrants, in 1983 CMS sought to continue this major role in research on undocumented aliens in the New York Metropolitan Area, with special emphasis on their labor market experiences and their utilization of social services. The financial support for this project was granted through the Tinker Foundation, which has a long-standing interest on South and Central America and on Spanish-speaking people in the United States.

Data assistance for this project was provided by the Rev. Nicholas DiMarzio, Director of the Migration Office of the Catholic Community Services (CCS) of the Newark Archdiocese. This office has provided a range of services for immigrants and refugees from legal assistance with immigration problems to job placement and resettlement. During that year, nearly 6,000 persons sought the assistance of the CCS Office of Migration. An extensive questionnaire (Intake and Reporting Form, superseded the following year by Client Profile Form) was administered to each applicant. Some of the questions dealt with national origin, wages, labor force participation, public assistance status and utilization of social services. Of those interviewed, between 20 and 30 percent were classified as out-of-status aliens.

A research plan was then developed into two phases. The aims of the first phase were to ascertain the quality, size, and potential of the CCS data; to provide some preliminary and fairly large-scale data on those out-of-status aliens who seek CCS assistance; and to develop a state-of-the-art questionnaire which would serve as the centerpiece of subsequent research in this area. In December 1981, the Tinker Foundation awarded a one-year grant to CMS to carry out the first phase of the project which was completed by September 1982.

A two-year grant for the second phase (1983-1985), which sought to obtain a socio-demographic profile of undocumented aliens in the New York Metropolitan area, and assess their impact on the social structures and the economy of local communities, was awarded to CMS by the Tinker Foundation in June 1983. The final report of the project was completed by November 1, 1985.

The two investigators for this project were Demetrios G.Papademetriou and Nicholas DiMarzio. As discussed in Chapter 3 of this report, the cooperation and active participation of various voluntary agencies in the New York Metropolitan area assured the successful conclusion of this research project. The success of such a risky project, however, is due to a great extent to the Migration Offices of the Catholic Community Services of the Archdiocese of Newark and its former director, Rev. Nicholas DiMarzio, presently the executive director of the Migration and Refugee Services of the United States Catholic Conference.

To complete this research project took more than the required technical expertise and professional responsibility. The length of the project turned out to be more than double the period originally planned. In addition to the usual frustration in administering a lengthy questionnaire interview to unpredictable respondents, a problem of 200 spurious interviews, which had to be replaced, tried the endurance of the research team.

In their acknowledgements the authors already mentioned the contributions of various individuals and organizations. Sincere thanks are also due to Edna Schroder-Guerrero, research assistant during the first phase of the project, and to the following individuals and institutions for their assistance in the preparation of the questionnaire administered to the undocumented aliens profiled in this study: Vernon Briggs, N.Y.S. School of Industrial and Labor Relations, Cornell University; Wayne Cornelius, Program in United States-Mexican Studies, University of California, San Diego; Douglas Gurak, Hispanic Research Center, Fordham University; Marion Houstoun, U.S. Department of Labor; William C. McCready, National Opinion Research Center, University of Chicago; David S. North, Center for Labor and Migration Studies New TransCentury Foundation; Patricia Pessar, New York University Center for Latin American and Caribbean Studies; Edwin P. Reubens, The City College, C.U.N.Y.; Survey Research Center at the University of Michigan; and Maurice Van Arsdol, Jr., University of Southern California.

CMS owes special thanks to Martha Twitchell Muse, President and Chairperson of the Tinker Foundation and to its

Board of Directors, for the financial support of the project and above all, for their trust in our ability to carry out such an unusual venture.

Center for Migration Studies   Lydio F. Tomasi
November 25, 1985   Executive Director

ACKNOWLEDGEMENTS

When one becomes engaged in projects of the scope and magnitude of the present study, one invariably incurs substantial debts. We are no exception. Our first debt is to the staffs of the various Catholic migration offices which were the many project sites. Without their cooperation this study would not have been possible. We wish to thank especially the directors of those offices who, together with their overworked staffs, took the time to advise and assist us, while also committing their own resources - time, goodwill, and office space - to this project. George Piegaro, Peter Zendzian, Bob Wright and Frank Dominguez became as much a part of this study's rich resource reservoir as those who worked with us directly to bring this project to a successful completion.

A special note of appreciation goes to the Center for Migration Studies and its far-sighted director, Lydio Tomasi, and to the Newark Archdiocese which housed the project and made available with utmost generosity its human and material resources. Mark Schenkel offered constant support and advice; Calvin Tran helped with some of the data analysis; Bonita Couch gave us her untiring assistance, as well as her generous friendship; finally, Jim Haggerty organized the participation in the project of the New York United States Catholic Conference.

No study can be successfully completed without incurring a few very special debts. To John McTernan, Director of Immigration Services of the Newark office, the project owes such a debt. He shared with us his substantive and procedural expertise gained from 40 years experience with the INS - including a stint as Director of the Newark office. More than that, however, he became a sounding board and a facilitator for this study.

Others also gave their talents and time more directly: Martha Parmalee (Prospect Park); Juan Fernandez (Astoria), Angela DiPaola (Ridgewood), and Adalberto Acosta (Manhattan). Edna Schroder-Guerrero worked diligently in the preparation of the questionnaire; Sebastian Alexander tirelessly did all coding and data entry work; Sister Mary Leane, Louise Franciosa and Daniel Vendrell did most of the

Newark interviews; and Luis Mejia stepped in and righted the boat with his productivity and high professional standards as the study's principal interviewer.

We would also like to express our appreciation to several INS officials who were particularly helpful in allowing us to compare our results with profiles of apprehended aliens in the Newark and New York offices - especially Executive Associate Commissioner, Doris Meissner; Newark District Director, James Pomeroy; and New York District Assistant Director, J. Scott Blackman.

We have incurred our biggest debt, however, to our respondents. They trusted us, they gave freely of their time, they opened their hearts and minds to us. They are the true authors of this study.

Our last two debts are to Barbara Van Wagner, whose intelligence, patience, and good cheer were instrumental in the production of the tables and typing and production of the seemingly endless drafts of this report, and Lucy Corcoran of the Center for Migration Studies for her friendship and her work with the earlier phases of this project.

Finally, we must thank our sponsors, the Tinker Foundation. Martha Muse, Chairman and President of the Foundation, believed in the importance of this study and was willing to take a chance on a project which we all knew from the outset would have to conquer the many problems associated with conducting research on undocumented aliens. She and her staff, especially Ken Maxwell and Renate Rennie, offered us more than financial support: they offered us an opportunity to work with professionals who were supportive, sympathetic, and intellectually challenging. Without them, the project would never have left the ground.

Of course, all errors of commission or omission, as well as of interpretation, rest with the authors of this report.

TABLE OF CONTENTS

LIST OF TABLES

SUMMARY

This research has sought to accomplish a number of aims: first, to review critically and order the literature on the field of undocumented immigration both on methodological and theoretical grounds; second, to establish the conceptual parameters of and a specific methodology for building a reservoir of local labor-market studies on the manner in which undocumented aliens incorporate themselves into and impact on local communities; third, to create, test and administer a questionnaire which can be adapted to the specific needs of researchers in this area; fourth, to analyze the results of that survey with particular emphasis on a number of broad policy-relevant research areas such as the labor market characteristics of undocumented aliens, their motivational structure prior to and during their stay in the United States, their plans for the future, and the entire set of social welfare questions; and fifth, to draw out the policy implications of the research on areas where advocacy, rather than scientific objectivity, has routinely carried.

In pursuing these goals, we developed an extensive multidisciplinary questionnaire which addressed key questions in the following areas: sociodemographic characteristics; movements and socioeconomic characteristics prior to coming to the U.S.; reasons for, and methods of, coming to the U.S. (including the role of the extended household in the decision to emigrate); the process of settlement (including plans for the future); employment history (when possible, information on three jobs was obtained - first job in the U.S., job prior to the current one, and current job); participation in social insurance and benefits in the U.S. (including health benefits, unemployment benefits, SSI and AFDC); participation in payroll deduction programs; income transfers and remittance behavior while in the U.S.; and extensive information about the subject's household in the U.S. - 363 questions in all.

The results have allowed both an in-depth look at the goals and motivations of the immigrant households and the individual immigrants and a glimpse of the structural causes and consequences of international migration. Social, economic, and political conditions at home and destination are examined and considerable light is shed on the complex relationship between emigration, remittances and return by providing evidence on some of the principal components of the arguments repeatedly presented during the ongoing debate on the proposed Immigration Reform and Control Act.

The overwhelming majorities of respondents in all three samples were from the Western Hemisphere, especially the Northern rim of South America, Central America and the Caribbean. Sex and age information on sample III indicates an even distribution between men and women and our modal undocumented immigrant is between the ages of 21 and 44 years of age. The average age of these respondents is about 32.6 years.

Of the respondents in sample III (n=192) nearly two-thirds are married. The average size of the respondents' households is 3.6 members. About 30 percent of the members of these households were children, a third of whom were born in the United States. About 30 percent of all children were attending U.S. schools.

Our data on the sociodemographic and economic background of our respondents support the emerging body of surveys which indicate that undocumented immigrants in the U.S. Northeast are of middle and lower-middle class background; are mostly of urban prior residence; are typically employed prior to emigration; have high levels of education and substantial labor market skills; are able to elude the immigration authorities with relative ease; are often repeat immigrants (about one-third of our sample III respondents had been in the U.S. more than once); often experience downward mobility at home and come to the U.S. primarily to avoid economic and political insecurity at home and advance their economic status; stay on in the U.S. for indefinite periods of time and are adept at having their nuclear family join them; are economically mobile and quite successful when compared to other U.S. blue-collar households (including experiencing substantial upward economic mobility with each job change); and are travelling along well-established and smoothly functioning ethnic pathways and networks which assist them repeatedly and substantively during the entire course of the immigrant experience.

Both our respondents and the other adult members of their household (n=697) exhibit extraordinarily high labor force participation rates and unemployment rates which compared favorably with gross unemployment rates for the states of New Jersey and New York at the time of the interview, and dramatically more so with unemployment rates of blacks and Hispanics in these states.

Of those employed, the modal employment sector was manufacturing (in union shops employing under 100 workers), followed by service establishments employing between one and five persons. Over three-quarters of our respondents were asked to give their employers a social security number and most of them also had to show them some work-authorizing identification documents. The average wage for those employed was over $5.00 per hour with almost half of them earning more than that amount. The average household income was slightly under $20,000. These figures are comparable with those for recent studies of legal Caribbean immigrants in the New York area.

The depth and relative success of the economic and social incorporation of our respondents in the U.S. is reflected in their reluctance to consider returning to an environment over which they can exercise little control. In fact, nearly all of those who reported a change in plans about their likely length of stay in the U.S. (nearly three-quarters of the sample) indicated that their stay would be substantially longer than they expected when they first came to the U.S., and about two-thirds of them indicated that it was either "probable" or "very probable" that they would still be in the U.S. 10 years from the time of the interview.

The question of intended length of stay is a difficult one to address because it is often inextricably intertwined with one of the most enduring, and most elusive, of concepts: the almost universal expression by immigrants of the intention to return to their home countries. When probed, however, our respondents expressed rather clear intentions which, to a large degree, expose the often mythical nature of this concept. While a plurality of respondents were "not sure" about how long they expected to stay in the U.S. when they first came to the New York metropolitan area, only about one-fifth said that they expected to stay for as long as five years. Five years later (the average length of stay of the respondents in sample III), almost all subjects admit to a change in plans in favor of a longer stay.

When asked why they have continued to stay in the U.S. past their original projections, five conditions seem to be of particular relevance: two responses revolve around family matters - the starting of a family here and the reunification of the family in the U.S.: two other responses revolve around the continuing economic and political uncertainty at home; the final answer alludes to their success in adapting to the United States. The strength of the resolve of our respondents to remain in the U.S., and the depth of their incorporation into their adopted community, is corroborated further when a remarkable two-thirds of the sample reported that it would not return to its home country even if offered a job of comparable status and pay.

It must be emphasized that almost regardless of immigration status, there is an apparent convergence in the socioeconomic experiences of recent legal and undocumented immigrants from the Caribbean area. In comparing our respondents with legal immigrant populations of the same origin from the 1980 Census, we notice an extraordinary convergence along 11 major sociodemographic and economic variables. Subsequent comparisons of our respondents with samples of undocumented aliens in the custody of the immigration authorities in New York and Northern New Jersey, however, find substantial differences across most of the same spectrum of variables. The explanation for the insignificant differences between legal and unapprehended, undocumented immigrants is rather simple: the two groups have similar socioeconomic and educational backgrounds, are often members of a single household, and perform similar functions in the labor market. Those apprehended and in custody, however, seem to be much less successful and more recent immigrants with a less complete incorporation into the local ethnic community and labor market. These differences aside, however, the three groups report quite similar country of origin, sex, age, and ethnic characteristics.

A final area of considerable contention and policy interest is the question of payment of taxes and unauthorized utilization of social infrastructure by undocumented aliens. Of those among our respondents who are employed, virtually all had social security cards and were participants in the payroll deduction program - but, only about 70 percent filed federal or state income tax returns. With regard to their participation in income maintenance and human service programs, the highest use was for unemployment compensation, with about 5 percent participation in that program. In the areas of medical benefits and education, finally, the picture is by necessity different. Two out of five of our subjects had utilized hospital services at least once during the 12 months prior to the interview but payment has been made in at least 80 percent of these cases. Finally, about two-fifths of the children of the respondents were attending school in the United States.

Among the most important conclusions of our research are that:

* In the absence of reliable information on specific communities of undocumented aliens, the in-depth investigation of legal immigrant communities of the same ethnicity may be an acceptable (if interim) surrogate measure. We have found that legal and undocumented immigrants form not only a single community but frequently a single family;

* Our respondents appear to have fled neither abject poverty nor political supression **per se.** Their reasons are much more complex than either of these alternatives indicate and point to mixed motives which include economic uncertainty and political insecurity;

* Our subjects appear to be almost an elite when compared to the many undocumented communities studied in the Southwest - yet they are close to the profiles of similar communities studied in the Northeast. Economically, they are distributed along a wide spectrum of the job hierarchy although they are by and large concentrated in the lower end of the job ladder. Our data do not support theories which assign purely marginal labor-market positions to undocumented aliens;

* Our sample of undocumented aliens reports extended tenure in the U.S.; success in unifying their families in the U.S.; and expects to remain indefinitely - even permanently;

* The evidence suggests that our respondents are successful labor market competitors **vis a vis** both native and legal immigrant groups;

* We found no evidence of abuse of income transfer programs by our respondents - although with regard to health services and education the situation is necessarily more complex;

* In terms of the policy debate, there is ample evidence that the currently considered social security card-based identification requirements can be easily met by virtually all of our economically active respondents;

* Finally, in terms of the contemplated cut-off dates for legalization, a 1980 date would disqualify most of our respondents while a 1982 date would allow a substantial majority of them to regularize their status.

CHAPTER ONE

THE CONTEXT

Few issues are proving to be more intractable for many advanced industrial societies than international migration. The importance of this issue manifests itself in numerous ways as it seems to have a substantial impact on a state's ability to formulate and implement many domestic, regional and global initiatives.

The United States has occupied an often reluctant center stage in this human circulation as the destination of large numbers of both voluntary and involuntary (refugees) immigrants. During the past 15 years, this position has become again particularly visible as the figures for total immigration to the United States have come to parallel those of the previous high immigration period around the turn of the century. As a result, the following argument is heard with increased frequency around policy and political circles: if the immigration and refugee issues are left unattended, they will gradually undermine the ability of this nation to address important social and economic problems.

What often gets lost in this reasoning, however, is that it is the hyperbole which seems to have captured the imagination of many advocates on both sides of the immigration debate. In reality, important as the issue of immigration reform might be, it cannot be placed on the same level with the major issues of foreign and domestic policy. The importance of immigration, then, must be sought in the manner in which it impinges on the entire gamut of these policies.

The example of unemployment might suffice to demonstrate the point. To understand how immigrants might affect unemployment, one must first begin to disaggregate "unemployment" and "immigrants". Those U.S. workers who are employed either in what some economists and sociologists (See, especially Piore, 1979) call the "secondary labor market", or in what Morales (1985) and Edwards (1979) might call an eroding primary labor market, are indeed likely to be adversely affected by competition for low pay/low status/uncertain and/or seasonal duration work as most immigrants and refugees enter the U.S. labor market at those levels. Yet, economic theory predicts that the infusion of additional labor in such occupations creates additional jobs, that immigrants as consumers increase aggregate demand for goods and services, and hence more jobs, and that the elasticity in the supply of immigrants willing to work at low wages may in fact keep certain industries competitive and many jobs (such as in apparel) in the U.S. At the same time, it is in these jobs that some analysts perceive actual labor "shortages" as native workers, under certain economic circumstances and in certain settings, are presumed to avoid these positions (Papademetriou, 1983d).

The situation becomes further complicated, however, when immigration status (legal or undocumented) and conditions of local labor markets (such as those in the inner city service industry or in labor-intensive agriculture) are examined. Furthermore the longer term effects and structural nature of the competition between U.S. and foreign workers becomes even more abstruse when one considers that many inner city and seasonal establishments, as well as agricultural producers, do in fact need entry level and temporary workers if they are to continue to perform their economic function competitively.

In view of these complexities, and in light of continuing global economic difficulties (and the attendant sociopolitical problems which such difficulties often exacerbate), the United States can expect the controversy about its immigration and refugee policy to remain high. The certainty that pressures for large-scale movements of people across national borders will remain high, promises to maintain the place of international migration as one of the most challenging and stubborn policy dilemmas for the entire international community in the 1980s and beyond.

THE POLICY PROCESS

It is one of the givens of the U.S. policy process that immigration concerns would be examined within an almost exclusively domestic context. This focus defines the debate in spite of increasing awareness that the issue has both its roots and its possible resolution as much in the sending countries and the larger international political and economic system as in policy initiatives emanating from Washington. Increasingly, this awareness has found explicit formulation. Both the Final

Report of the Select Commission on Immigration and Refugee Policy (SCIRP, 1981) and a number of "alternative" pieces of legislation offered particularly by the allies of the Hispanic groups reflect this awareness. The former consciously sought to emphasize the futility of unilateral responses to the immigration issue by placing its recommendations for regional initiatives with regard to immigration on top of its long list of recommendations (SCIRP, Section I, Recommendations I A-D). The thinking and priorities of the Hispanic groups have been, in turn, reflected in the various Bills introduced by Representative Roybal, until recently the chairman of the Congressional Hispanic Caucus (See, Papademetriou, 1984c).

In spite of these initiatives, however, the tendency to view the matter almost entirely with domestic glasses remains dominant. Although Administration witnesses invited to testify before key immigration Congressional Committees almost invariably include State Department officials, the latter usually come from the Visa and Consular Affairs sections, are asked mainly technical questions, and usually play an obviously secondary role to other government witnesses. In addition, and with few exceptions, the foreign policy establishment overlooks the potential significance of the immigration issue on its agenda. And, with the exception of a small group of scholars who are working in the refugee policy area, there is almost a complete void in scholarly research on the foreign policy implications of U.S. immigration and refugee policy. The few efforts to redirect the attention of the foreign policymaking community toward viewing immigration as a salient foreign policy issue for the 1980s and beyond - especially with regard to U.S. relations with Mexico and the Caribbean and Central American states - appear so far to have failed (See, especially, Teitelbaum, 1985; Papademetriou, 1983a; and Pastor, 1982, 1985).

The reasons for this failure are numerous and complex. One might involve the very nature of the foreign policy community. By their training and experience, most members of the foreign policy community, both in their private and institutional roles, identify foreign policy relevant issues in the context of what is often called "high-politics" (See, Miller and Papademetriou, 1983a; Papademetriou, 1983a). This tradition focuses almost exclusively on government-to-government contacts especially in such matters as defense policy, East-West relations and, in general, matters which have a demonstrable influence on easily identifiable strategic U.S. relationships. These relationships usually concentrate either on other advanced industrial societies and our main political and, potentially, military adversaries, or on nations which, because of geopolitical accidents and/or equally accidental endowments with strategic resources, command the attention of the United States. It is these common, if not always obvious, denominators which usually define an issue as "foreign-policy relevant" (**See,** Katzenstein, 1976; Nye and Keohane, 1971; Holsti, 1978).

Measured against these fundamental concerns, it should perhaps not be surprising that the involvement of the foreign policy community with immigration policy has been casual and intermittent and lags far behind that of both the general public and domestic special interests. Many of the antecedent conditions for what is such an obvious "issue appreciation lag" may also be traced to the prevalent analytical traditions in the academic field of foreign policy analysis. One often overlooked but possibly important additional factor for this lag, however, is the fact that much of the post-1965 immigration to the U.S. - regardless of legal status - is of Latin American (and especially Caribbean) origin.

THE CARIBBEAN REGION

In few regions has international migration played as pivotal a role as in the Caribbean region.[6] Many of these political entities owe their existence, as well as their specific sociodemographic, linguistic, cultural and economic configuration on the migration of Europeans, Africans, and

----

6. For the purpose of this study, this region will be understood to include the 16 independent Caribbean islands and the 10 island dependencies; the nation-states of Central America which are commonly included in the designation of Caribbean Basin; Mexico; and all remaining states on the Caribbean littoral. For the significance of specific states in terms of immigration, in general, and for this study, in particular, see Tables 1 and 2.

Asians. Although these migrations occurred during the period of classical imperialism (and as such responded to the political and economic forces of that historical epoch), more recent Caribbean migrations have continued to respond to the capital and labor needs of advanced industrial societies that have played, and continue to play, a dominant role in the economy and politics of the region.

In other words, regardless of whether international migration in the Caribbean was responding to the needs of the British and French trade and financial classes, as Hobson (1939) would argue, or to U.S. territorial ambitions and agricultural, industrial, and commercial interest, as has been the case during the past 100 years, the exogenous control of the size, composition, direction, and duration of such movements is beyond dispute. For instance, large numbers of Jamaican and other island migrants were recruited by French interests to build the railroad system through Costa Rica and Panama in the third quarter of the last century. Similarly, islanders provided the backbone of the labor force both for the unsuccessful French efforts to build the Panama Canal and for the successful effort by the U.S. in the beginning of the twentieth century. Subsequently, the many ventures of U.S.-owned United Fruit Corporation in the area employed large numbers of Caribbean migrants, as did U.S. strategic interests in the U.S. Virgin Islands and the entire area during World War II (See, McCullough, 1977; McLean Petras, 1982; D. Marshall, 1983; and Kritz, 1981).

The turn of the twentieth century brought about the emergence of a definite pattern in Caribbean island population movements. It involved the migration of Caribbean island people to the U.S. mainland along both immigrant and nonimmigrant lines. The former peaked during the 1911–1920 period when nearly 124,000 such immigrants came to the U.S. and began to pick up steam again in the 1950s, when it reached a size comparable to that of 40 years earlier. The flow nearly quadrupled during the 1960s, to 470,000 immigrants, and increased by an additional 63 percent in the 1970s – to 741,000 people (INS, Annual Reports, various). By 1980, many of the Caribbean islands had substantial proportions of their populations abroad (See, Population Reference Bureau, 1984). These figures stand at about 9 percent for most of the islands but reach as high as about 22 percent for Jamaica and Barbados.

In all, about 10 percent of the population of the islands has emigrated in the last 30 years (Pastor, 1985) and an additional 438,000 were in the immigration pipeline to the U.S. as of 1980 (Maingot, 1985). Although virtually all Caribbean island nations have been significant contributors to this flow, a few countries have been clearly dominant (See, Table 1:1) and routinely account for between 90 and 95 percent of all Caribbean immigration to the United States from the Caribbean islands.

While regular permanent immigration from the Caribbean islands to the U.S. has been significant (See, Table 1:2), nonimmigrant admissions from that area have far outpaced immigrant admissions. Among the nonimmigrants one finds visitors for pleasure, who routinely account for between two-thirds and four-fifths of all nonimmigrant visas issued annually (69% in 1983); businessmen, who in 1983 accounted for nearly 18 percent of all nonimmigrant visas; students (3% of total in 1983); and diplomatic personnel and other official and quasi-official representatives of foreign governments and multinational corporations and their dependents. Of the nearly 10,000,000 nonimmigrants admitted to the U.S. in 1983, nearly nine percent came from the Caribbean islands; an additional 10 percent came from Central American and Caribbean Littoral countries, nearly two-thirds of them coming from Mexico [626,000] - making Mexico the third largest source country for nonimmigrant admissions after Japan [1.4 million] and the United Kingdom [1.2 million]; and an additional 300,000 came from Colombia (85%) and Ecuador - two countries of particular interest to this report (See, INS, Annual Report, 1983:111-134). What is also of particular significance to this report is that among these nonimmigrants one often finds many of the individuals who are one of the specific concerns to this study: those who seek and obtain employment in the U.S. in violation of the terms of their visas.

Another significant group of entrants from the Caribbean region to the U.S. involves those entering under a number of nonimmigrant labor programs. In spite of recurring attempts to control them, such programs have existed at varying levels of strength throughout much of the twentieth century. As early as the 1880s for instance, the Alien Contract Labor Law prohibited employers from assisting or encouraging the immigration of aliens under terms of a contract or agreement (Higham, 1969; Briggs 1984a). Yet, this

TABLE 1:1

CARIBBEAN IMMIGRATION TO THE UNITED STATES, 1965-1983

Year	Barbados	Cuba	Dominican Republic	Haiti	Jamaica	Trinidad/ Tobago
1965	406	19,760	9,504	3,609	1,837	485
1966	520	17,355	16,503	3,801	2,743	756
1967	1,037	33,321	11,514	3,567	10,483	2,160
1968	2,024	99,312	9,250	6,806	17,470	5,266
1969	1,957	13,751	10,670	6,542	16,947	6,835
1970	1,774	16,334	10,807	6,932	15,033	7,350
1971	1,731	21,611	12,624	7,444	14,571	7,130
1972	1,620	20,045	10,760	5,809	13,217	6,615
1973	1,448	24,127	13,921	4,786	9,963	7,035
1974	1,461	18,929	15,680	3,946	12,408	6,516
1975	1,618	25,955	11,055	5,145	11,076	5,981
1976[1]	2,210	35,996	15,088	6,691	11,100	6,040
1977	2,763	69,708	11,655	5,441	11,501	6,106
1978	2,969	29,754	19,458	6,470	19,265	5,973
1979	2,461	15,585	15,519	6,433	19,714	5,225
1980	2,667	15,054	17,245	6,540	18,970	5,154
1981	2,394	10,858	18,220	6,683	23,569	4,599
1982	1,961	8,209	17,451	8,779	18,711	3,532
1983	1,849	8,978	22,058	8,424	19,535	3,156

Source: For data up to 1977, *Annual Report:* Immigration and Naturalization Service; for 1978 to 1983, *Statistical Yearbook:* Immigration and Naturalization Service.

[1] The figures for 1976 are for a 15-month period—from July 1, 1975 through September 30, 1976. The change was necessitated when the U.S. Government changed its fiscal year to run from October 1 through September 30th.

TABLE 1:2

IMMIGRANTS TO THE U.S., BY COUNTRIES OF BIRTH: 1965, 1979, 1983

Country of Birth	Number			Percent Change
	1965	1979	1983	1965 - 1979
All countries	296,697	460,348	559,763	+ 55.2
Europe	113,424	60,845	58,867	- 46.4
France	4,039	1,705	2,061	- 57.8
Germany	24,045	6,314	6,725	- 73.7
Greece	3,002	5,090	2,997	+ 69.6
Italy	10,821	6,174	3,225	- 42.9
Poland	8,465	4,413	6,427	- 47.9
Portugal	2,005	7,085	3,231	+ 253.4
Romania	1,644	1,554	2,543	- 5.5
Spain	2,200	1,933	1,507	- 12.1
United Kingdom	27,358	13,907	14,830	- 49.2
Yugoslavia	2,818	2,171	1,382	- 23.0
Asia	20,683	189,293	277,701	+ 815.2
China and Taiwan	4,057	24,264	25,777	+ 498.1
Hong Kong	712	4,119	5,948	+ 478.5
India	582	19,708	25,451	+3,286.3
Iran	804	8,476	11,163	+ 954.2
Korea	2,165	29,248	33,339	+1,250.9
Pakistan	187	3,967	4,808	+2,021.4
Philippines	3,130	41,300	41,546	+1,219.5
Thailand	214	3,194	5,875	+1,392.5
Vietnam	226	22,546	37,560	+9,876.1
North America	126,729	157,579	168,487	+ 24.3
Canada	38,327	13,772	11,390	- 64.1
Mexico	37,969	52,096	59,079	+ 37.2
West Indies	37,583	74,074	8,424	+ 97.1
Cuba	19,760	15,585	8,978	+ 21.1
Dom. Republic	9,504	17,519	22,058	+ 84.3
Haiti	3,609	6,433	8,424	+ 78.2
Jamaica	1,837	19,714	19,535	+ 973.2
Trinidad and Tobago	485	5,225	3,156	+ 977.3
Other West Indies	2,388	9,598	—	+ 301.9
Other North America[1]	12,850	17,637	24,601	+ 37.3
South America	30,962	35,344	36,087	+ 14.2
Argentina	6,124	2,856	2,029	- 53.4
Brazil	2,869	1,450	1,503	- 49.5

TABLE 1:2 (continued)
IMMIGRANTS TO THE U.S., BY COUNTRIES OF BIRTH: 1965, 1979, 1983

Country of Birth	Number			Percent Change
	1965	1979	1983	1965 - 1979
South America				
Colombia	10,885	10,637	9,658	- 2.3
Other South America[2]	11,084	20,401	—	+ 84.1

Source: For the 1965 and 1979 figures and the percent column, INS, *Annual Report*, 1979; for the 1983 figures, INS, *Statistical Yearbook*, 1983.

[1] Includes the remaining Caribbean Islands and Central America; for 1983, it includes only Central America.

[2] Includes the countries in the Northern and North Western rim which contribute substantial numbers of immigrants to the United States.

nation has experimented repeatedly with temporary labor programs under the guise of responding to "extraordinary" circumstances. As a result, numerous such programs have dotted the legislative landscape of the twentieth century--in 1917-22 with Mexico,[7] in 1942-1964 (the "Bracero" program)[8] again with Mexico, and a number of lesser-known programs. In addition, one must recognize such **de jure** labor programs as the "labor commuters", the special programs for the British

––––––––

7.   Nearly 77,000 Mexican workers were admitted to the U.S. during that program but less than half returned to Mexico (Briggs, 1984).

8.   As many as half-a-million Mexicans a year were working in the U.S. during the height of the Bracero Program. Unknown proportions of them remained in the U.S. Both programs with Mexico proved to be controversial and the U.S. resorted to mass roundups and deportations both times (Briggs, 1983).

West Indies (BWI) and the U.S. Virgin Islands[9], and the "H" provisions of the Immigration and Nationality Act (INA) of 1952. The significance of these programs lies in the fact that, together with illegal immigration, they rival or may even exceed the impact of regular (legal and presumably permanent) immigration to the United States.

Border commuters live in Mexico but work in the United States. Although treated as nonimmigrants until 1927, they have been since classified as immigrants on the basis of the 1929 Karnuth v. Albro Supreme Court decision (279 U.S. 231) which equated employment with residence (Briggs, 1983). In spite of language in the 1965 INA which seems actually to prohibit such practice, the Supreme Court recently reaffirmed this classification (Saxbe v. Bustos, 419 U.S. 65, [1974]; see Briggs, 1983).

The BWI program has existed since 1943. Its authorization stems from the temporary worker provisions of the 1917 INA. Its purpose has been to facilitate the entry of citizens of the British West Indies and the Bahamas to work in agricultural occupations in 11 East Coast states. The program works on the basis of tripartite agreements among U.S. employers, the governments of sending Caribbean states, and the workers themselves (See, North, 1980; McCoy, 1984).

Finally, the 1952 INA (the McCarren-Walter Act) expanded substantially the classes of nonimmigrant visas and introduced the "H" program for temporary workers "...if unemployed persons capable of performing such service or labor cannot be found in this country...." This program includes

─────────

9.   The BWI program has existed since 1943 and seeks to facilitate the entry of citizens of the British West Indies and the Bahamas to work in agricultural occupations in eleven East Coast states. The authorized industries include the sugar cane industry in Florida, the apple industry in the Northeast, the woodcutting industry in Maine, and the sheepherding industry in the West. With regard to the Virgin Islands' programs, the reference is to the easing of the restrictions in converting the status of the many Caribbean workers who had lived and worked there since early in World War II from "nonimmigrants" to "immigrants." See Briggs, 1983.

both an agricultural group (H) (ii) or H-2, which comprises between one-third and one-half of the annual admissions, and another group composed of workers, entertainers, athletes and white-collar and skilled workers (INA, 1980, Section 101H). The professional standing of this latter group is lesser than the standing of those of "distinguished merit and ability" categories of (H) (i). The terms of employment, wages, impacts on the U.S. labor market, and the public debate surrounding (H) (ii) and (H) (i) admittees vary enormously - in spite of the small size of the program. The H-2 component of the program in the 1977 to 1983 period for instance, averaged less than 20,000 persons per year with a high of over 29,000 for 1983 and a low of slightly over 10,000 for 1982. Virtually all of the agricultural workers in the program (about 12,000 per year) come from Caribbean islands (INS, Annual Report, 1977-1983).

Although these programs may not be very significant in size, they have been extremely important in some of the messages they have conveyed: that the U.S. is not serious about its willingness either to control its borders or to reform its labor market, and that certain groups - especially the agricultural interests - have a virtual veto power on immigration legislation.

One final nonimmigrant "program" is of paramount interest to this study and is of great significance for both source and destination countries: the institution of undocumented (illegal) immigration. Although undocumented immigrants are in this country in violation of U.S. immigration statutes, one may argue that they are part not only of a massive **de facto** quasi-nonimmigrant program but, considering the propensity of these persons to remain in the U.S. indefinitely, also of a **de facto** immigration program. This line of argument can be supported on the grounds that the often deliberate failure on the part of U.S. immigration authorities to enforce the law, and the equivocal legislation with regard to such matters as the hiring of undocumented workers tolerates, and in fact encourages, further undocumented immigration. The existence of active ethnic networks with their well-established pathways to the U.S. - and the ability of these networks to provide a number of essential services to newcomers - further serves to reduce the many risks attendant to the decision to emigrate without appropriate documents and facilitates the cultural economic insertion of the newcomers into the receiving society. Such services range from providing newcomers with short-term accommodations and assistance with labor market placement to the erecting of informal but critical buffers against socio-cultural alienation, temporary socioeconomic displacement, and a number of other similar "safety nets" (See, especially Pessar, 1982a, b; Kritz and Gurak, 1984; and Wood, 1982).

RECENT CARIBBEAN REGION IMMIGRATION TO THE UNITED STATES

The 1970s experienced the largest inflow of legal immigrants into the U.S. since the 1910-1920 decade, and the fourth largest inflow in U.S. history by decade.[10] This ranking, however, includes neither undocumented aliens nor the actual number of refugees accepted into the country in the 1970s.[11] If one adds the mid-point estimate of the recent "official" figures of 2,000,000 to 4,000,000 undocumented aliens for 1980 (3,000,000; See, Levine et al., 1985) and the figures for actual entries under our refugee program,[12] the 1970s have probably experienced the largest infusion of foreign nationals in the history of the Republic.

The contribution of immigrants originating in the Caribbean region to this swelling in immigration is extraordinary. Table 2 offers a distillation of immigration flows to the U.S. for 1965, 1979, and 1983 - disaggregated by key countries of immigrant origin. Of particular interest is the dramatic change in the relative weight of the various

----

10.   Following 1901-1910, 1911-1920, and 1891-1900.

11.   Refugees are not shown on U.S. immigration statistics as "admitted immigrants" until they become eligible for permanent resident status. This usually involves a two-year lag before they appear in the "Exempt from Numerical Limitations" columns of INS data.

12.   Beginning with the Refugee Act of 1980, refugees no longer enter under the preference categories of the 1952 INA (See Papademetriou and Miller, 1983a).

immigration source regions. These changes are not only the result of the 1965 legislation (**See,** Papademetriou and Miller, 1983b), which became effective in 1968 and abolished discriminatory quotas based on national origin in favor of hemispheric numerical limits. Rather, they reflect a process of realignment in the share of different regions and countries in the total U.S. immigration picture which was becoming evident even before the changes in the nation's Immigration and Nationality Act. The largest beneficiaries of these changes have been immigrants coming from Asian countries. They saw their representation rise by almost 1,400 percent between 1965 and 1983 - from seven percent of total immigration to almost 50 percent (down from nearly 53% in 1982; **See,** INS, Annual Report, Table 2, appropriate years).

At the same time, immigration from the Americas was able to maintain and augment its already privileged position under the 1965 INA in spite of the fact that the Act instituted numerical limits for the Western Hemisphere. In fact, the share of the Americas (except Canada) in total immigration increased from about one-quarter for the decade of the 1950s, to about 39 percent in the 1960s and over 40 percent in the 1970s. That proportion has been rather erratic since 1980 with 40 percent, 31 percent, and 35 percent for 1981, 1982, and 1983, respectively (INS, Annual Reports, 1965-1983). Within this context, additional long-term changes are also evident. In the 1960s Canada relinquished its position as the key regional source of immigration to the U.S. to Mexico - which now provides between 30 and 40 percent of the total immigration from the Americas to the United States. While Mexico's ascendance has paced that of the region as a whole, the most substantial gains have been registered by the grouping of countries appearing under the heading of "West Indies". Their numbers during the past 20 years have doubled and the share of certain countries has increased at almost geometric rates.

As can be seen from Table 1:3 (Data Categories 1 and 2), Caribbean immigrants are not distributed equally across the United States. Such factors as the existence of significant concentrations of each ethnic group, expectations about employment and other opportunities, distance, and ease of access and entry all influence the choice of initial residence. In most instances, and with the expected exception of

TABLE 1:3
DEMOGRAPHIC AND ECONOMIC CHARACTERISTICS OF
SELECTED FOREIGN BORN IMMIGRANTS COUNTED IN THE 1980 CENSUS

Data Category	Dominican Republic No.	%	Haiti No.	%	Jamaica No.	%	Ecuador[1] No.	%	El Salvador[2] No.	%	Colombia[3] No.	%
1. Size												
1a. Total Immigrants	169,147	—	92,395	—	196,811	—	86,128	—	94,447	—	143,508	—
1b. Of whom, those entering since 1965	138,077	81.6	83,342	88.0	162,924	82.8	68,293	79.3	83,342	88.2	113,503	79.1
2. State of Residence												
2a. New Jersey	14,269	8.4	5,172	5.6	11,016	5.6	10,333	11.6	2,260	2.4	19,870	13.8
2b. New York	131,313	77.6	55,363	59.9	107,130	54.3	42,426	49.2	9,293	9.8	48,486	33.8
2c. Florida	7,139	4.2	17,280	18.7	25,387	12.9	5,116[1]	5.9[1]	2,103[2]	2.2[2]	23,577[3]	16.4[3]
3. Sex												
3a. Male	—	44.6	—	48.6	—	44.3	—	47.0	—	43.8	—	46.3
4. Naturalized Citizens	—	25.5	—	26.1	—	36.3	—	24.7	—	14.3	—	24.9
5. Age												
5a. Ages 0-19	—	27.8	—	25.0	—	32.0	—	19.8	—	20.1	—	19.8
5b. Ages 20-44	—	58.0	—	61.1	—	48.9	—	58.5	—	66.0	—	59.5
6. Marital Status												
6a. Male (Married)	—	58.2	—	57.8	—	55.9	—	60.6	—	49.6	—	59.1
6b. Female (Married)	—	46.5	—	47.8	—	42.9	—	55.2	—	47.8	—	55.4

TABLE 1:3 (continued)
DEMOGRAPHIC AND ECONOMIC CHARACTERISTICS OF
SELECTED FOREIGN BORN IMMIGRANTS COUNTED IN THE 1980 CENSUS

Data Category	Dominican Republic		Haiti		Jamaica		Ecuador		El Salvador		Colombia	
	No.	%	No.	%	No.	%	No.	%	No.	%	No.	%
7. Labor Force Participation												
7a. Male, 16 years and older	—	77.3	—	80.9	—	77.8	—	82.1	—	85.1	—	83.6
7b. Female, 16 years and older	—	50.0	—	64.0	—	68.9	—	56.8	—	63.8	—	58.1
8. Employment Status												
8a. Unemployed, both sexes	—	11.2	—	11.3	—	7.2	—	8.1	—	8.0	—	7.4
8b. Average duration of unemployment period 1979	—	15.6 weeks	—	18.0 weeks	—	16.2 weeks	—	14.6 weeks	—	13.7 weeks	—	13.7 weeks
9. Employed in:												
9a. Construction	—	2.0	—	2.8	—	3.9	—	2.2	—	3.9	—	2.7
9b. Total manufacturing	—	47.2	—	27.3	—	16.3	—	43.0	—	33.4	—	36.5
9c. Transportation, communication, public utilities	—	3.8	—	6.5	—	6.6	—	6.1	—	3.3	—	6.2
9d. Wholesale and retail trade	—	19.6	—	12.8	—	12.3	—	16.9	—	17.9	—	17.8
9e. Finance, real estate and insurance	—	5.7	—	6.9	—	9.7	—	7.3	—	4.4	—	6.7

TABLE 1:3 (continued)
DEMOGRAPHIC AND ECONOMIC CHARACTERISTICS OF
SELECTED FOREIGN BORN IMMIGRANTS COUNTED IN THE 1980 CENSUS

Data Category	Dominican Republic		Haiti		Jamaica		Ecuador		El Salvador		Colombia	
	No.	%	No.	%	No.	%	No.	%	No.	%	No.	%
9. Employed in:												
9f. Business and repair services	—	4.9	—	5.8	—	5.6	—	5.8	—	6.4	—	6.0
9g. Personal services	—	5.0	—	9.1	—	8.4	—	5.3	—	17.8	—	6.4
9h. Professional and related services	—	9.3	—	23.9	—	32.9	—	10.5	—	9.3	—	14.2
9i. Other	—	2.5	—	4.9	—	4.6	—	2.9	—	3.6	—	3.5
9j. Total	—	100.0	—	100.0	—	100.0	—	100.0	—	100.0	—	100.0
10. Education of Immigrants 20 years and over												
10a. 0-4 years	—	16.1	—	7.3	—	2.8	—	3.8	—	12.4	—	4.9
10b. 5-8 years	—	33.2	—	11.5	—	16.7	—	20.1	—	28.6	—	14.7
10c. 9-12 years	—	36.5	—	46.1	—	50.6	—	48.6	—	39.5	—	46.0
10d. 13-15 years	—	10.4	—	22.8	—	19.3	—	18.9	—	13.9	—	20.9
10e. Over 15 years	—	3.9	—	12.3	—	10.6	—	8.7	—	5.7	—	13.5
10f. Total	—	100.1	—	100.0	—	100.0	—	100.1	—	100.1	—	100.0

TABLE 1:3 (continued)
DEMOGRAPHIC AND ECONOMIC CHARACTERISTICS OF
SELECTED FOREIGN BORN IMMIGRANTS COUNTED IN THE 1980 CENSUS

Data Category	Dominican Republic No.	%	Haiti No.	%	Jamaica No.	%	Ecuador No.	%	El Salvador No.	%	Colombia No.	%
11. Income												
11a. Median full-time worker	$7,281		$8,956		$10,869		$8,689		$7,078		$9,127	
11b. Per capita income in households with head or spouse foreign born	$3,736		$4,470		$ 5,750		$5,114		$4,527		$5,974	
11c. Percent of households below poverty level	31.0		19.5		12.4		15.7		18.8		12.5	

Source: U.S. Bureau of the Census, *Foreign Born Immigrants: Tabulations from the 1980 Census of Population and Housing*, countries as indicated, 1985.

[1] California was the residence of 13,130 Ecuadorians (15.1 percent of total).
[2] California was the residence of 67,656 Salvadorans (71.6 percent of total).
[3] California was the residence of 16,256 Colombians (11.3 percent of total).

Mexicans and the understandable exception of Salvadorans, the New York Metropolitan Area[13] has been the principal destination of immigrants from the Caribbean region.

In fact, the New York Metropolitan Area in general, and New York City in particular, have been the initial destination point of tens of millions of immigrants during the history of the United States. Even a cursory look at the countries of origin and the demographic composition of these immigrants documents each historical period's configuration of major regional and global political and economic events, the role of the U.S. in them, and the relative power of U.S. domestic political coalitions.

The Caribbean region is a case in point. It is a region in which the U.S. has long played a dominant role both in economic and political/military matters. This involvement has led to frequent criticisms that the U.S. is taking the area, and Latin America in general, for granted and either neglects it or treats it shabbily (Pastor, 1984). This pattern is particularly obvious in the matter of immigration. In typical fashion, U.S. immigration policy, in spite of its significance for a number of the region's "sending" countries, is fashioned in a manner in which the concerns of the countries of origin are either remote to or completely absent from the debate. As Lowenthal (1983) has observed with a number of other decisions, the U.S. seems to be either insensitive to or unaware of the possible impact of its policies on Latin America. In certain areas, this thoughtlessness appears to be ignorant of history and tradition, as in the case of immigration in the U.S. Southwest which exists in a complex and deep historical symbiosis with Mexico and forms an almost binational cultural, social and economic community with it. In other cases, the deep roots of this relationship may not be as obvious but are equally strong. The New York Area is an example of the latter relationship. Immigration to New York takes place along well-established pathways to the point where it takes a life of its own and, in a complex but predictable manner, responds to forces which are at times only marginally

---

13.   Roughly similar to the New York Standard Metropolitan Statistical Area (SMSA) which also includes parts of Northern New Jersey.

related to such "objective" factors as the economic and employment climate there - and even less so to decisions about immigration policy in Washington.

One need not be more than a casual observer of life in the New York Metropolitan Area to notice the continuing pervasiveness and vitality of the presence of new immigrants. The area is teeming with newcomers with increasingly more exotic costumes, new sounds, and novel customs. In this constantly evolving mosaic, all but the most persistent and methodical observers are quickly lost as the character of entire ñeighborhoods changes, often in a matter of a few years. These changes, obvious as they might be to those who continue to live there, are extremely resistant to empirical analysis by outsiders. When one adds to this the frequent unreliability of official statistics, it is not surprising that valid general statements about the parameters of the changing character of the area can be extremely difficult to make (**See**, Papademetriou, 1983c).

The reasons for the paucity of reliable statistics on the new immigrants are many. First and foremost, one must mention the invisibility of those who are in the U.S. in violation of the immigration law. As a result, efforts to speak authoritatively about these individuals are stymied by the nature of the research problem: undocumented migrants are in the U.S. clandestinely and are extremely difficult to locate and interview. A second problem compounds the first one and stems from the inherent unreliability of those data which are available. Until 1981, when budget considerations led to the discontinuance of the practice, intercensal data on new immigrants used to be obtained principally from the Annual Alien Registration of the Immigration and Naturalization Service (INS). Although these data were never accurate (illegal aliens did not file, ethnic groups had differing and difficult-to-gauge rates of noncompliance, and compliance itself had become essentially voluntary because noncompliance carried not-discernible risks), they at least provided a barometer of shifts and trends in the movement of new immigrants. In the absence of such data, official statistics can no longer give one a feel for the dynamism and changing composition of ethnic communities. Yet, a combination of the Decennial Census, the periodic Current Population Surveys, and the better collection, tabulation, and analysis of INS data could yield more useful information in a number of areas.

Among them are the initial destinations and subsequent moves by immigrants, longitudinal data on patterns of naturalization and the socioeconomic incorporation of immigrants, patterns of visa abuse by nonimmigrants, and, with new initiatives, patterns of emigration by recent immigrants. It must be obvious, however, that in the absence of fundamental reforms in the data collection and analysis system of the INS, the most detailed record of these trends will remain the decennial Census and, to a much lesser degree, the various Current Population Surveys. The analysis herein has benefited as much as possible for the 1980 Census (**See,** Table 1:3).

THE POLICY PROBLEM

The data problems become more acute when the topic of inquiry becomes undocumented immigrants. It is generally accepted that such immigrants have variable impacts on different geographic regions, labor markets and specific industries and communities. Yet, our knowledge base about them often relies on anecdotal and merely suggestive data and assumptions about their impacts on host communities are frequently difficult to test. Hence, the formulation and implementation of policies aimed at addressing the problem in a thorough and integrated manner is severely handicapped.

The policy consequences of this inability to produce authoritative research results have been serious and have contributed to a public debate which has been often aimless with too much room for advocacy, equivocation and demagoguery. In the absence of unassailable conclusions, advocates have felt free to attach their own interpretation to tentative research results and wildly contrasting views have been portrayed as carrying equal scientific validity. Otherwise capable analysts have not been immune to this confusion and public officials have received, and are acting on, advice which makes them subject to manipulation by special interests. Such groups as growers of perishable agricultural crops and the increasingly powerful restrictionist Federation for American Immigration Reform (FAIR) seem to have thrived in this interpretative morass - as have labor unions, church groups and ethnic group activists.

In reality, however, most areas of contention are not nearly as open to diametrically opposed interpretations as we are often led to believe - in spite of the inherent methodological weaknesses of most studies. It will be one of the main goals of this research report to dispel some myths and bring some analytical order in the confusion surrounding the issue of undocumented immigration. Among the areas to be examined will be the labor market impacts of undocumented aliens, the relationship between legal immigration, nonimmigrant and temporary worker programs, and undocumented immigration, the extent of unauthorized utilization of services and social programs by undocumented aliens, the relationship of undocumented immigration to such issues as competition with and displacement of indigenous workers, and the socioeconomic incorporation and the long-term plans of such aliens.

CHAPTER TWO

RESEARCH DESIGNS

A central impetus for this study has been the conviction that regardless of the final shape of the immigration reform legislation, neither will the need for reliable information on undocumented immigration abate nor the pressure for emigration from key areas of origin be relieved. The former conviction stems from the thorough analysis of all major legislative proposals offered in Congress since 1977 (See, U.S. Congress, 1985a, b; 1983a, b; U.S. House of Representatives, 1980, 1977; U.S. Senate, 1983, 1979; Papademetriou, 1984c, 1985b; Papademetriou and Miller, 1983b; Papademetriou et al., 1983; and DiMarzio, 1985). These proposals are neither likely to make the issue of past undocumented immigration moot by offering a legalization plan intended to attract a substantial majority of out-of-status aliens, nor put in place sanctions which take into account the labor market contributions of undocumented aliens, nor contribute to an understanding of the process of undocumented immigration. Without such an understanding, policy initiatives will at best be likely to address only the proximate, rather than the root, causes of the phenomenon.

At the same time, and with regard to relieving the pressures for emigration, it is neither reasonable to expect dramatic shifts in U.S. involvement in the Caribbean region nor to expect that present policies might substantially alter the shape and direction of the emigration flow from that region. Neither is there reason to believe that the Caribbean Basin Plan, in its present configuration and size, and with its present exclusion of such labor intensive products as textiles and leather, might generate enough new employment to affect significantly emigration from and return migration to the region (Hakim and Weintraub, 1985). Most preliminary studies of the Plan urge extreme caution in postulating any relationship between this and other development initiatives and migration, and expect that pressures for emigration are likely to be fueled in the short-to-medium-term as a result of development (Pastor, 1985; Diaz-Briquets, 1985). Although the uncertainty about the relationship between development and emigration does not deny the possibility of a noticeable drying-up of emigration for some countries, in terms of formulating immigration policy, this relationship might not be very relevant.

Furthermore, the long standing "culture of emigration" of many Caribbean states - a culture shared by both individuals and governments (See, Maingot, 1985; Marshall, 1985) - makes it reasonable for the U.S. to expect to witness increasing, rather than diminishing, pressures for legal and undocumented immigration. The probability of this trend increases significantly when one considers the presence of the following forces: the region's continuing economic predicament; continuously high - though decreasing - population growth rates; the subsequent failure by most of the region's governments to generate sufficient new employment (the 1979 unemployment rates for the Caribbean Community Member States, for instance, were 24.4 % - 13.9 % for men and 36.6% for women; See IBRD, 1983); the inability/unwillingness of the political elite to help bring about the social and economic changes which might enable these economies to meet substantial proportions of the growth in their labor force in the near-to-medium term; and the unabating political instability in the region. The sharp increases in the apprehension figures of the Border Patrol, even as they partly reflect increased vigilance and commitment of resources by the INS and refer only to a single entry area (Mexico-U.S. Border), attest to this reality (See, INS, Annual Report, 1980-83, and preliminary figures for 1984 and 1985 which indicate that the figures might exceed the previous high of 1.3 million).

ESTIMATING THE SIZE OF UNDOCUMENTED IMMIGRATION IN THE UNITED STATES

Robert Pastor recently (1982) observed that the proximity of the Caribbean region to the U.S. has been both boon and bane to the Caribbean states. For Pastor, the U.S. is "...both solution and problem, source of capital and competition, destination for emigrants and magnet for the region's talent" (1984:8). The tension to which Pastor alludes is nowhere more obvious than in the appraisal of the migration process. That process has seen over two-and-one-half million legal immigrants arrive from the region between 1965 to 1983 (INS, various years). Although Mexico has accounted for about one-third of that, the six countries profiled in Table 1:3 have contributed nearly 650,000 persons. In addition, the region has also contributed substantial amounts of undocumented immigrants.

Estimates of this latter population for 1980 have fluctuated wildly. The more reasonable among them have ranged from as low as one million (Morris and Mayio, 1980, excluding Mexican undocumented immigrants), to between three-and-one-half and five million (SCIRP, 1981, based on a Census Bureau review of such estimates in the literature). Although more recent estimates may have a higher degree of reliability - the most recent such estimates place the number of undocumented aliens in the two to four million range (Levine et al. 1985) - they all make assumptions which cannot be adequately supported.

For instance, one series of studies offers estimates on undocumented aliens based on three data sets: the 1979 Current Population Survey (CPS), the 1980 Decennial Census and the 1983 CPS. Although these studies utilize innovative methodologies, and as a result may lay claim to better accuracy, they are still inadequate. One might pause briefly and consider their probable effect on Congressional policy and the shaping of public opinion. Because of the institutional affiliation of their authors (usually the Census Bureau), they may acquire a mantle of respectability and may as a result be relied on for policy decisions which can prove to have far-reaching consequences for the U.S. and its allies in the Caribbean region.[14]

----

14.   The most important among these consequences would depend on the decision about the effective legalization date. If that date is unduly ungenerous (such as January 1, 1980), the entire legalization program may become a vast enforcement program which, because of the ineligibility of many undocumented aliens, may a. disrupt U.S. regional labor markets; b. lead to enforcement excesses; c. strain relations with the countries of these workers because of the treatment afforded them; and d. fail to accomplish that program's foremost goal, i.e., together with employer sanctions, to give the U.S. a handle in controlling undocumented immigration. Hence, since the effective legalization date and federal cost

The best known among these estimates have used a "residual method" and compared a 1980 Census-based estimate of all aliens in the U.S. with estimates of the legal resident alien population from data collected by the INS in the same year. The difference (residual) is hypothesized to represent the number of undocumented aliens. The INS data were collected from that Agency's I-53 (Alien Registration) forms adjusted by a number of assumptions about underregistration (based on 1970 census information for each ethnic group), emigration (assumed to be at 100,000 annually in the 1970s) and mortality. The underregistration was estimated to average 11.1 percent across all ethnic groups, with a range of 5 to 17 percent, and added 648,000 to the alien population reported to the INS in January of 1980. In juxtaposing these adjusted data with previous estimates on how many undocumented aliens were counted in the decennial census, the size of the total undocumented population counted in the decennial U.S. census in 1980 is estimated to be about 2.1 million people (Warren and Passel, 1983, revised; Passel and Woodrow, 1985).

Because of the intricacy and softness of the assumptions made, and of what Hill (1985:243) calls the lack of "compelling upper or lower limits" to these estimates, it might be more reasonable to assume that the number of undocumented aliens counted in the 1980 census were between 1.5 and 2.5 million people. Obviously, there is little policy benefit that can be derived from such an estimate unless additional efforts would succeed in fine-tuning the range for all undocumented aliens in the country at that time. The upper limit of another of Hill's estimates (1.5 to 3.5 million people) might be a reasonable figure for total undocumented aliens (Passel suggests a figure between 2.5 and 3.5 million [1985]). It, however, like previous estimates (See, SCIRP, 1981), simply refers to a figure which is merely consistent with the findings of a number of other studies - each one of which has its own methodological shortcomings and many of which neither make their methodological details nor their assumptions explicit.

----

reimbursements to localities agreed to by Congress are sensitive to estimates of the undocumented population in the U.S. at different times, Census estimates can be extraordinarily influential.

While the nature of these estimates is problematic, however, they can be useful in allowing certain generalizations and identifying trends. For instance, the 1979 CPS - a monthly survey of over 60,000 U.S. households - can be used to corroborate the 1980 census estimates. When used as a base, and when compared to the 1983 CPS, the 1979 CPS can give one a general sense of the changes in the undocumented population. All three data sets, finally, can be used to provide a glimpse into the likely ethnic composition of this population. For instance, the 1980 Census estimates suggest that Mexicans are still the predominant group among undocumented aliens, that about half of the undocumented population is in California, that the majority is composed of males, and that about half of the total population entered in the second half of the decade of the seventies. Although one can take issue with any one of these generalizations, they do provide a frame of reference from which the necessary fine tuning can proceed.

Likewise, the CPS estimates for 1979 and 1983 - although even more troublesome than those for the 1980 Census - can also point to certain useful trends. And, depending on the assumptions one makes, it might be reasonable to argue that the number of undocumented aliens has not increased sharply since 1980 and that Mexico has continued to provide the dominant group among the undocumented. Where one must be extremely cautious, however, is in the specific figures - rather than ranges - and in the estimates for undocumented aliens coming from areas other than Mexico.

Using the adjusted figures for the total legal alien population counted in the 1980 census (2.1 million), the figure for the estimate of undocumented aliens from the 1979 CPS (1,168,000 persons), and estimating emigration in the 1980 to 1983 period to have averaged 133,000 persons per year, Warren and Passel (1985) have analyzed the 1983 CPS and have arrived at a minimum estimate of 1,233,000 undocumented aliens aged 14 and older and a final estimate of about 2 million. Of those, the share of Mexicans is reported to be about 70 percent, while an additional 20 percent originates in other Latin American countries. In addition, the annual increase in the undocumented population since 1980 is estimated to be between 117,000 and 291,000 people and the increase in the total size of the Mexican undocumented community about one-half million. Finally, 50 percent of the total undocumented population is estimated to have arrived in the U.S. in the 1970s, with the rest split evenly between before 1970 and after 1980 (See, Passel and Woodrow, 1985).

Although the authors of that last report acknowledge that their figures are only "...indicative of overall levels" (Passel and Woodrow, 1985:21), and that their methodology misses "...certain key pieces of vital information in key data systems" (ibid.), the folly of attaching too much significance to these findings can be best demonstrated in some of the figures from these reports. For instance, the size of the undocumented population from North and Central America other than Mexico and Canada (but including the Caribbean islands) is reported to have decreased between 1980 and 1983, while the decrease for Asian undocumented aliens is supposed to have been even more pronounced. Furthermore, the increase in the number of undocumented aliens originating in the rest of South America is estimated to be 9,000 persons (Passel and Woodrow, 1985). In addition, these estimates suggest that there has been virtually no movement of undocumented aliens from Europe for the past decade and that the size of the undocumented population entering New Jersey between 1975 and 1980 was 2,000 persons (Passel and Woodrow, 1984, Table 2). Although anyone with even a casual interest in this topic can see the problems with these figures, it is important to point out the degree of their unreliability: accepting them, for instance, would mean that the Northern New Jersey Catholic Community Service organizations from where the project reported on here obtained its data would have had to have assisted virtually all of these individuals in its four Northern New Jersey locations between 1980 and 1983.

STUDIES ON UNDOCUMENTED ALIENS

One cannot overestimate the importance of reliable figures on undocumented immigrants. In view of the passions which the issue arouses, and its eventual potential to reverse this nation's tradition of generosity with the admissions both of legal immigrants and refugees, it is essential that public policy should proceed from an educated perception of the magnitude and profile of this population. The Panel on Immigration Statistics of the National Research Council of the National Academy of Sciences recently spoke of the policy significance of the issue in no uncertain terms. The policy questions on which the Panel focused went beyond the labor market effects of undocumented aliens and the degree to which this population utilizes services legally available only to U.S. citizens and permanent residents. Although these questions have routinely defined the parameters of the public debate on the issue, the Panel also expressed its concern about whether the undocumented "...hold down wage rates for menial jobs and slow productive investments..., increase crime rates either as perpetrators or as victims..., [and] come to work temporarily or to settle permanently" (Levine et al., 1985:132). Yet, surprisingly, the Panel failed to identify a number of other issues on which U.S. et al., policy on undocumented immigration will have an impact: regional economic and political/military initiatives and internal questions of social policy vis à vis the increasing Hispanic and Asiatic populations in such areas as bilingualism, regional political cohesion, and the shaping of the allocative mechanism for the distribution of future political and economic resources.

It is with all of these questions in mind that one must develop a typology and evaluate the importance of studies of undocumented communities - for without understanding the forces which shape these communities and guide the actions of their members no policy can be effective. The types of studies to be catalogued here have been chosen for their representativeness of an entire genre and for their influence on policymakers. Most of these studies have taken place in the southwest, and especially California and, as a result, an entire generation of policymakers has been taught to think of the immigration dilemma in terms of the experience of that region. Hence, although there is wide recognition that undocumented immigration is a national issue (See, Table 2:1), knowledge about it has often involved extrapolating from studies based largely on the behavior of undocumented Mexican labor in the Southwest.

The first type of study often focuses on the sending community. On the basis of information about the sons and daughters of the community working without authorization in the U.S. (obtained from their families at home), researchers have been able to locate some of the aliens in the U.S. and use them as key informants to create a snowball sample of

TABLE 2:1

Distribution of Immigration in the United States by Immigration Type, Economic Sector, Region of Destination, and Country or Region of Origin[a]

Immigration Type	Legal			Undocumented			Refugee		Temporary[b]
Economic Sector	Agriculture	Manufacturing	Services	Agriculture	Manufacturing	Services	Manufacturing	Services	Agriculture
Region[c]									
Southwest[d]	Mexico	Mexico, Asia, Central Am.	Mexico, Asia, Central Am.	Mexico, Central Am.	Mexico, Asia, Near East[e]	Mexico, Asia, Near East	Asia, Caribbean	Asia, Caribbean	Mexico, Caribbean
Pacific Northwest[f]	Mexico, Central Am.	Other[g], Asia	Other, Asia	Mexico	Mexico, Asia	Mexico, Asia	Asia	Asia	Mexico
Central[h]	i	Mexico, Asia, Other	Mexico, Asia, Other	i	Mexico	Mexico, Asia	Asia, Caribbean, East Europe	Asia, Caribbean, East Europe	i

Source: Adapted with changes from a table initially developed by the first author for the GAO (1985a: Table 2). The figures for legal immigrants, temporary immigrants and refugees are from INS annual yearbook; illegal immigrants estimated from field studies.

[a] Ethnic representation generally in rank order in each cell.
[b] Includes H-1 and H-2 categories.
[c] In the past 25 years, the principal destination of legal immigrants, in rank order, were CA, NY, TX, FL, IL, NJ, MA, MI, PA, CT, CH, and WA. The six top states usually account for over two-thirds of all legal immigrants.
[d] CA, TX, and AZ in rank order.
[e] Includes Middle East Arabs, Palestinians, and Iranians.
[f] WA and OR in rank order.
[g] Principally Europeans and Canadians.
[h] IL and OH in rank order.
[i] Substantial numbers of immigrants were not evident.

TABLE 2:1 (continued)

DISTRIBUTION OF IMMIGRATION IN THE UNITED STATES BY IMMIGRATION TYPE, ECONOMIC SECTOR, REGION OF DESTINATION, AND COUNTRY OR REGION OF ORIGIN

Immigration Type	Legal			Undocumented			Refugee		Temporary[b]
Economic Sector	Agriculture	Manufacturing	Services	Agriculture	Manufacturing	Services	Manufacturing	Services	Agriculture
Northeast[j]	i	Other Caribbean[k] Asia	Other Asia Caribbean	Caribbean	Caribbean Other Asia	Caribbean Other Asia	USSR East Europe Asia Near East	USSR East Europe Asia Near East	Caribbean
Southeast[m]	Caribbean	Caribbean Other	Caribbean Other	Caribbean	Caribbean	Caribbean	Caribbean (Cuba) Asia	Caribbean (Cuba) Asia	Caribbean

j NY, NJ, MA, PA and CT in rank order.
k Excludes Mexico; includes Caribbean islands and states in the Caribbean littoral and the upper rim of South America.
m FL.

respondents. The research conducted has been often by necessity ethnographic, i.e., it has used the anthropological method to study a few subjects intensively. Many of these studies took place in the late 1970s and have been frequently associated with the work of Wayne Cornelius and his many associates over the years (Cornelius, 1977a, b; Cornelius, et al. 1982, 1984; See also, Reichert and Massey, 1979, 1980; Grasmuck, 1984; Massey, 1985; Massey, et al., 1983; Mines and Massey, 1982; and Mines and De Janvry, 1982).

A second type of study is much more recent and still lacks full and systematic dissemination. This genre of studies investigates the behavior of specific immigrant groups in a specific urban setting. Some of this work can be extremely comprehensive in that it too investigates the behavior of a group both at home and destination, such as the work of Pessar and her associates with the Dominicans in New York (Pessar, 1982a, b; 1984; Grasmuck, 1984) and the work of Dawn Marshall on immigrants from the Eastern Caribbean to New York and Toronto (1982). The usual pattern, however, is one of investigating one or more groups at destination (See, Arias, 1981; Keely et al., 1977; Browning and Rodriguez, 1982; Foner, 1982; Garcia, 1982; and Glaessel-Brown, 1984). Gurak's ongoing work on (legal and illegal) Dominicans and Colombians in New York is a most competent example of this type of research (1982; Gurak and Kritz, 1983; Kritz and Gurak, 1984).

A third type of research design focuses on a specific industry usually in a local labor market. The best examples of this research often go beyond reporting the mere characteristics of the undocumented aliens employed by that industry to an examination of the structural features of the industry/firm and an analysis of its entire lifeline and operational process, including its product demand structure, labor market operations and investment decisions. As a result, these studies can shed light on such often obscure and overlooked processes as the recruitment, training, advancement, and retaining practices of the organization, the position of the industry/firm in the economic life of the area, the alternatives to employing undocumented labor, and the role that this labor plays in the industry's overall labor pool. These studies may also use secondary data and ethnographic research techniques to give depth and contextual richness to their work. Recent works by Mines and Martin on perishable crop agriculture in California (1984; See also, Martin, 1984); Mines on the janitorial services industry in California (1985); Morales on the automotive parts industry in Los Angeles (1983); Maram and his associates on the garment industry in Los Angeles (1981; Maram and Long, 1981); Waldinger on the same industry in New York (1981; 1983); Glaessel-Brown on New England's light manufacturing industry (1984); and the work by Bailey and his associates on the New York restaurant industry (Bailey and Freeman, 1981, 1983; Bailey, 1983, 1984) are useful examples of this type of study (See, Balmori, 1983; Fogel, 1983; and Gallo, 1983). Although the impact of these studies covaries with the quality of the research design, the ability of the investigators to obtain unhampered access to the firm under investigation, and the overall qualifications and experience of the research team, the strongest predictor of the usefulness of the research seems to be the predispositions of the main investigator. Researchers with an identifiable point of view seem to produce predictable results which makes it necessary to exercise extreme caution in the evaluation of the results of these studies - and particularly of the methodologies employed (See, Huddle, 1982 and Huddle et al., 1985).

A fourth type of study retains the focus on the labor market and involves the investigation of the regional, and, at times, national impacts of a particular profile of worker. These studies often utilize Census Bureau and Labor Department data on the characteristics of domestic workers and specific job categories and juxtapose these characteristics with those of (legal and illegal) immigrants. The work of Muller in southern California (1984) exemplifies this genre but the weaknesses of the design in extrapolating the impacts of undocumented workers from those aggregate data are many and serious (See, Morales, 1983; Bailey, 1984, 1985; Waldinger, 1983; Tienda and Neidert, 1980; Baca and Bryan, 1981; Stolzenberg, 1982; Bean, et al., 1984; Borjas, 1984; Chiswick, 1984; and Community Research Associates, 1980). Yet, the possibility of obtaining a better knowledge about impacts of recent immigrants on the regional labor markets, disaggregated by ethnicity and race, and the opportunity to test hypotheses about the role of these workers on the key issues of displacement and wage depression, makes replications of the Muller design in other regions of substantial immigrant concentrations a potentially useful analytical tool. When integrated with a thorough study of the region's economy, an avenue explored more by Muller than most of the other authors, the yield can be further enhanced.

The promise with many of the four types of studies discussed so far is that the researchers usually set for themselves ambitious but attainable goals and have thus made important contributions to our understanding of many aspects of the migration process. When problems arise, they are usually the results of the injudicious interpretation of these findings and often by the consumers of the research results - rather than the investigators themselves. For instance, the works by Cornelius and many of the ethnographic studies cited earlier have frequently been misused to make claims which the data simply do not support. This problem seems to be more common with research on Mexican undocumented aliens. Hence, it is necessary for researchers to guard against such misinterpretations by designing studies carefully and by repeatedly cautioning the reader that some of these studies have inherently low generalizability levels as they tell only some things, about some undocumented aliens, in certain types of occupations, on one (or from one) particular region. For instance, studies on Mexican undocumented aliens in the Southwest might not tell us much about the Mexican population in Illinois or undocumented Mexican workers in the Eastern United States. Irresponsible extrapolating from such studies is always dangerous and fails to generate wide confidence in most findings among members of either the research or policy communities.

Adding to this problem is the more general, and pernicious, problem of unconsciously attributing the characteristics from the study of a non-random sample of one ethnic group to other ethnic groups in other regions and labor markets. One demonstration should suffice to identify the degree of the damage which results from such carelessness. A lot of the work on undocumented Mexicans undertaken during the late 1970s and early 1980s drew a profile of largely single young males who were repeat temporary immigrants to the United States. The modal Mexican undocumented alien was said to be a hard-working agricultural and service worker who earned low wages, saved at extraordinary rates, and had little interest in settling permanently in the United States (Cornelius, 1977). This profile was reinforced repeatedly with the findings from equally unrepresentative studies of deported Mexican aliens by Mexican scholars, often revolving around a much publicized massive study of returning Mexican undocumented aliens and of over 60,000 Mexican households with a member working in the United States (Zazueta, 1980; Ranney and Kossoudji, 1984; Belsasso, 1981; See also, Bustamante, 1977, 1978, 1979). Finally, that profile was further reinforced by the findings of the first large-scale study of apprehended undocumented aliens conducted in the mid-seventies and discussed below (See, North and Houstoun, 1976). Although the methodological shortcomings and uniqueness of these studies are now well known, and large numbers of subsequent studies have refined and redefined the profile of undocumented aliens originating from points south of the United States, an entire generation of policymakers and policy influencers still defines the issue by the terms of reference outlined in these studies.

North and Houstoun's study (1976) represents a fifth type of design on the study of undocumented aliens. The sample was drawn from illegal aliens who were, at the time of the interview, in the custody of the immigration authorities. The sample was skewed toward Mexicans (481 out of 793 interviews) and Western Hemisphere aliens (an additional 273 respondents). Only 75 respondents came from other regions. Among those interviewed, 457 subjects were in custody in the states of Texas, Arizona and California, while the remaining 40 percent were interviewed in seven other Eastern, Midwestern and Northwestern locations. Besides playing the role discussed in the preceding paragraph, it also reinforced assumptions that undocumented migration might be principally a regional problem (Southwest) and is composed largely of Mexicans. Its finding that undocumented aliens impose few strains on this nation's social service network and overall infrastructure continues to be a source of contention in policy and scientific circles. Research undertaken since then shows that the first two assumptions might be of somewhat limited usefulness while the last one (about social services) appears to be much more complex than the North/Houstoun analysis might indicate at first.

The North/Houstoun study has opened the way for other attempts to learn from the results of INS enforcement actions. In this sixth type of research design, researchers both from within and outside of the agency have frequently drawn profiles of apprehended undocumented aliens utilizing both in-person interviews and the analysis of INS "record of deportable alien" (I-213) forms. While some internal INS studies do not reach wide circulation frequently (See, Davidson, 1981), it is not unusual for investigators outside of the agency to juxtapose the results of their study on an undocumented population with a profile of the agency's apprehended aliens obtained through interviews or a review of a sample of I-213 forms. Keely et al. (1977) and the present study are two examples of studies which have utilized this tool. Another researcher recently undertook the reanalysis of the original North/Houstoun study and concluded that the occupational attainment and earnings of the undocumented aliens studied by North/Houstoun responded systematically to the same variables as those for the entire 1970 cohort of immigrants - principally to education and labor market experience in the U.S. (Chiswick, 1984).

In a variation of this sixth type of study design, several researchers have taken advantage of a recent INS enforcement initiative deliberately designed to create additional employment opportunities in the more desirable wage categories for unemployed U.S. workers by targeting and raiding suspected large-scale users of undocumented aliens and removing such aliens from these jobs - an initiative labeled "Operation Jobs". Although these studies could have provided an invaluable service to the research community by a thorough study of both the profile of the firms targeted for enforcement action by the INS and of the apprehended undocumented aliens, they focused principally on the latter. Furthermore, most of these studies were conducted by the INS and have never been put to the test of independent outside review. As a result, the results have been received with considerable skepticism. Some researchers, however, have visited a number of the 560 firms in the nine cities which were the targets of the INS "Operation Jobs" and have tried to see who had taken the place of the deported aliens - with results which have not been very enlightening (Huddle, 1982, 1984).

The often conflicting nature of the findings of many of the studies under all six research designs, and the interpretative morass which has resulted from them, has led a number of methodological purists to react with pessimism to the prospects of obtaining reliable information about undocumented aliens. Some among these purists have responded to this seemingly insurmountable problem of reliability by resigning themselves to the argument that since the universe under investigation cannot be specified with accuracy, and the available data cannot meet the requirements of stringent scientific rigor - particularly the tests of randomness and replication - all efforts at profiling undocumented foreign workers are an exercise in futility. As discussed by Lawrence Fuchs, the Executive Director of the Select Commission on Immigration and Refugee Policy (SCIRP), this was the conclusion of the Commission staff at least with regard to funding surveys on the undocumented population (1981; See also Cornelius, 1982; and Briggs, 1984b). While one can appreciate decisions resulting from a strong interest in scientific validity, however, one can become weary of overreactions to the validity problem. Randomness would obviously be preferred. In the absence of randomness, however, research should not be abandoned. It is important, however, that analysts and other consumers of non-random research should be alerted to resist the urge to confuse detail with social structure and overgeneralize from these research findings. Careful, explicit, and responsible claims about the applicability and limitations of one's findings can go a long way toward allaying the fears of all who are interested in the accurate interpretation of research results.

In other words, in spite of the so far insurmountable validity problems, and in view of the continuing need for information on undocumented immigration, it is necessary to remain flexible and not make a basic accord on "preferred method" the prerequisite for research in this area. Together with George (1979), we might wish to consider a number of alternatives in research design developed precisely for cases where generalizable quantitative evidence is extremely hard to obtain. The most promising among the alternatives discussed by George involves the initiating and fostering of a catalogue of systematic case studies which would then allow one to move "iteratively" from quantitative to case-study designs and back. In other words, what may ultimately hold the most promise in learning more about the impacts of undocumented immigration on the U.S., and about the migration process itself, is the methodical building of a reservoir of case studies which sheds light on specific migration flows or on a specific part of the migration process while specifying, and thus making more accurate, extant theoretical models. The studies on Mexican workers in the Southwest (especially in California) and on Caribbean-region immigrants in the New York Metropolitan Area hold enormous promise in setting the parameters and foundation of such knowledge. What is still needed, is similar painstaking and imaginative research to establish a similar base of knowledge about other groups (especially the Asiatics) in a variety of geographical settings and work contexts, and the utilization of unique study designs and unexplored data sets.

It is in this light and for their exceptional, yet largely unmined, potential that one must return to and discuss briefly an additional four study design types and data sets. This seventh type utilizes the paired cities design (GAO, 1985b). This design would be similar to that of a recent study on wage depression in a number of Texas cities with varying concentrations of immigrant flows (Smith and Newman, 1979). In replicating the basic methodology, one could study the impacts of undocumented aliens in two matching cities (in terms of type of industries, profile of the labor force, unemployment and other general economic characteristics), only one of which would have a large concentration of undocumented aliens. The data to be relied on could be both official (Labor Department, Census, and INS) and quasi-and un-official (such as data from city planning, education, and employment services divisions, as well as those from chambers of commerce and other private agencies). The appeal of this design lies in its ability to be infinitely flexible both with regard to what to study and what data to utilize. For instance an entire industry, such as restaurants, can be the subject of the study across two or more cities as could firms with subsidiary operations in two dissimilar cities.

The eighth study design is grossly underutilized and involves the collection and analysis of data obtained from social service agencies. The National Research Council (Levine et al., 1985:107) took note of this relatively "unexplored" avenue of immigrant studies and pointed out that the case records collected by private voluntary organizations might offer many of the "...advantages of a longitudinal survey at a fraction of the cost". Yet, in spite of the obvious advantages of such studies, outside of the study reported on here, there is only one other large-scale study of this genre (Van Arsdol **et al.**, 1979). In that study, the authors examined the social, labor force, and earning patterns of a sample of unapprehended, undocumented migrants in Los Angeles who had sought the assistance of the One Stop Immigration Center in regularizing their immigration status. The sample was drawn from the Center's records for the period from 1972 to 1975. The limitations of these data, of course, were that those seeking status regularization assistance had an obvious interest in long-term residence - thus biasing the results in the opposite direction of that for most other studies about Mexican undocumented aliens. As a result, the data showed a significantly stronger female component than other studies of Mexican undocumented aliens, a lower labor force participation rate (due to the larger overall household component of the sample), and the existence of a substantial kinship network.

Although the Van Arsdol findings are indeed significant, their usefulness is limited by the age of the data (over 10 years old) and by the fact that the questionnaire (agency intake form) was geared toward the needs of the agency in question. As a result, the research group was unable to find direct answers to such pressing questions as the nature, manner and role of family networks in the migration process and the motivations and long-term goals of the immigrants. Yet, its large n sheds some welcome light in the confirming/disconfirming process of the many hypotheses and mere assumptions of previous studies.

The final two types of research designs have no clear representatives among studies on undocumented aliens. The ninth design would involve looking at how different types of industries obtain their labor in different settings. Industries can be disaggregated according to the level of organization of their work force, economic vitality, and wage structure. For instance, one might choose steel as an example of a highly organized, high wage, but declining industry; footwear, as a moderately organized, moderate wage but declining industry; and electronics as a poorly organized, moderate wage, vibrant industry. Other candidates for the cells of this matrix would be restaurants, janitorial services, automotive parts manufacturers, garments, messenger and delivery services, and the construction industry - particularly the small-scale repair and remodeling arm of that industry.

The idea here would be for teams of researchers in localities with both similar and dissimilar labor markets to study the degree of penetration by undocumented and other disadvantaged and low-wage labor in different types of work environments. For instance, taking janitorial services as an example, how does the organization of work and wage structure of that industry affect the type of worker that it attracts? In view of the bullish demand for such services, who does the work, and under what wage and working conditions, in cities with such sharply different labor force profiles as New York, Pittsburgh, Nashville, or Buffalo? One can see the as-yet untapped potential of such studies for understanding several of the key questions often asked in the discussion about undocumented migration - including the question of the place of such aliens in sectors other than agriculture and certain services, their impact on wages and working conditions, and the key matter of their competition with and/or displacement of U.S. workers.

The tenth and final study design would focus again on a diachronic look at specific industries, or firms within a single industry, which are presently known to be heavy users of undocumented workers. Labor-intensive agriculture, garments, the fast-food industry, or janitorial services would again be excellent examples. The questions to be asked, however, would be whether and how demand, output, and employment trends may have changed over time; how these changes might compare with changes in other labor-intense industries in the same area over the same period of time; whether these changes have paced or followed population shifts in that area over the same period of time; whether similar industries have followed similar paths in responding to product demand upsurges/employment increases in other regional settings; and whether and how the racial and ethnic profile of the labor force employed in such industries may have changed over time. Although this study design may have several "chicken-or-the-egg" components to it, the careful choice of an industry and the thorough investigation of local demographic and labor market changes during the period of investigation can minimize them.

The knowledge gained from such studies can be invaluable. It will document the process of change in certain industries - and the probable role of undocumented labor in that change. More significantly, however, it will allow us to understand the social and economic conditions which make the continuing "recruitment" of illegal aliens - through immigrant networks, the offering of certain wages and working conditions, and the unofficial but unmistakable "signaling" that one may have ample opportunity for work in the U.S. regardless of legal status - a fact of economic life.

While there might be some component overlap in some of the 10 study designs outlined here, and some of the required data for a number of the cases may be the same, the core concerns and the specific methodology of each study make them distinct. It must also be obvious that the research priorities of people working in the area of immigration may need to be reordered to respond to the knowledge gaps identified in this chapter. For instance, it might be necessary to allocate more resources to designs four, seven, eight, nine, and ten. While resource allocations need not be zero-sum-games, and the preferences recommended here neither pass a value judgment on the quality and richness of the remaining designs nor suggest that the non-chosen designs should be abandoned, it is obvious from the review of the field conducted by the authors of this report that the best possible knowledge yield would come from more theoretically informed designs. These designs, while relying on the results of continuing studies under designs one, two, three, five and six, can move toward a better understanding of the more structural conditions which shape communities, social realities, and labor markets. A marriage, then, rather than mutually exclusive hierarchical choices in research designs, is the course of action recommended in the future study of undocumented migration.

STUDY DESIGN FOR THE PRESENT RESEARCH PROJECT

This study is a variation of design number eight and shows the advantages which one can reap from obtaining the full and active cooperation of one particular type of social service agency with a frequently large clientele of undocumented immigrants: denominational, and specifically Catholic, social service agencies. The superiority of this approach over that of either simply looking at a sample of the records of such agencies, or merely utilizing the setting of a social agency or the good offices of a person working for such an agency, are substantial. Even the perusal of active and "dead" files of social agencies can yield sparse but interesting information about a number of sociodemographic characteristics. It is on forging a partnership with such organizations, however, especially with regard to contacting potential subjects and obtaining their cooperation with the project, that the success of such projects hinges.

There is, however, one way when even agency records can become an invaluable resource in the study of undocumented migration. That is when agency intake forms are well-designed and efficiently and conscientiously filled-out, when these files are utilized primarily as background and as a means of defining the universe of the clients whom the agency assists, and when the active files are used as a means of drawing a sample of subjects who will then be interviewed in order to understand better the entire undocumented immigration process. None of these opportunities would be possible, of course, without the commitment by both agency management and personnel to the goals of the research project. Finally, the success of such research rests to an enormous degree on the quality of the relationship between agency personnel and clients. Close relationships and the impression that counselors care about their clients, as well as the effectiveness of each case worker, influence the ability of project personnel to obtain interview subjects and insure their cooperation.

THE SAMPLES

The social service agency whose clients became the subjects of this study are the Migration Offices of the Catholic Community Service (CCS) organizations of the Archdiocese of Newark, the Diocese of Brooklyn and Queens, and the Regional Office of the United States Catholic Conference located also in New York. Four of these offices were located in Northern New Jersey - Newark, Jersey City, Elizabeth, and Union City - and four in New York City. Two of the latter were located in Brooklyn (Ridgewood and Prospect Park), and one each in Queens (Astoria) and lower Manhattan.

Sample I reports on data culled from the case files of the CCS Migration Offices of the Archdiocese of Newark. These data will be referred to as the "Newark" or "New Jersey" sample. The files of this organization were reviewed and 856 CCS clients who received assistance by the organization between January 1, 1980 and the end of 1981 were found to be undocumented aliens (Sample I, n=856). These clients were frequently referrals by other clients and Catholic organizations and had come voluntarily to CCS for assistance with a full complement of services - including legal assistance, immigration-related assistance, and assistance with job placement.

For the reasons already mentioned, the yield from this research step was modest - although we were able to obtain an initial profile of the agency's undocumented clientele along a number of sociodemographic and labor market characteristics.

To enhance the yield from the agency's intake forms, and prepare the ground for future tappings of the agency's records, a new intake instrument was developed to enrich the information base of the research project and ensure the continuity of the management and informational needs of the organization. This new form has been used continuously by CCS Migration Offices in the Newark Archdiocese since January 1, 1982 and was used intermittently by the Migration Counselors of the Brooklyn Diocese. An attempt to institute that system for the Migration Offices of the Archdiocese of Manhattan was never successful and was abandoned. Users of the 1982 instrument were trained in three separate formal sessions, a User's Manual was developed, and individual counselors were assisted as the need arose. Between the beginning of 1982 and the fall of 1983, 778 valid cases of undocumented aliens were processed, nearly four-fifths of whom came from the Newark CCS offices. This new sample (Sample II, n=778) became a basis for comparisons with Sample I. Whenever the categories permit, the values for key variables for the two samples are reported next to each other. Because of the differences between the two intake forms, however, we have far more information about Sample II subjects than Sample I subjects. Most significantly, however, Sample II affords us the opportunity to have a diachronic look in such important categories as sex, age, education, length of stay, and several labor market characteristics.

CONSTRUCTING THE QUESTIONNAIRE

At the same time that the new intake form was becoming established, the preparation of an extensive questionnaire to serve as the study's survey instrument had commenced. At the outset, the objective was to develop an instrument which would be comprehensive. We sought to examine the entire migration process and develop data to test a number of the key concerns of all disciplines in the social sciences concerned with the study of international migration.

The result was a thorough and comprehensive instrument essentially free of disciplinary parochialism and addressing what seemed to have been the critical controversies on legal and clandestine international migration research. The price paid for such a holistic view was one of length and, consequently, of the time and cost required to administer the questionnaire.

In constructing this questionnaire, we were eclectic in our reliance on some other available instruments. Extensive consultations were conducted individually with a group of researchers in the Northeast who have had first hand experience with projects similar to our own.[15] These actors played major roles in assisting our research team with conceiving and fleshing out the various components of the instrument and reacting extensively to questionnaire drafts.

The resulting instrument has been successful in approaching international migration research from the perspectives of both sending and receiving communities. The questionnaire affords one a microscopic view of the migration process while allowing the investigation of many of the

----

15. Among them were economists David North (New Transcentury Foundation, Washington, D.C.), Edwin Reubens (City College of the City University of New York), and Vernon Briggs (Cornell); sociologists Maurice Van Arsdol (University of Southern California) and Douglas Gurak (Fordham); and anthropologist Patricia Pessar (New York University). The disciplines of the two authors of this report are Political Science (Papademetriou) and social work (DiMarzio).

structural causes and consequences of international migration without losing sight of the goals and motivations of the family unit and the individual. Consequently, relevant social, economic, and political conditions at home and destination were given equal opportunities to be highlighted. As a result, the instrument sheds light on the most complex relationship between emigration, remittances, return, and development, while obtaining hard evidence on many of the principal componentts of the arguments made both by opponents and proponents of a liberal immigration policy.

In all, the questionnaire (**See,** Appendix I) collects extensive data on the following areas:

- demographic characteristics of respondents and their households;

- internal and international migration patterns;

- social and economic status of the household in the country of origin and reasons for emigrating;

- the process of settlement in the U.S.;

- the subjects' evaluation of the U.S. migration experience;

- English-speaking ability;

- remittances/income transfers to home country and their utilization;

- social service program utilization by undocumented respondents and their families;

- work experience in the U.S. involving up to three experiences in the labor market;

- detailed household composition of the undocumented population in the U.S.; and

- home ownership and internal U.S. mobility of the undocumented respondents (**See,** Appendix II for additional design and methodology discussion.)

In addition, an effort was made to draw a profile of the clientele of each office involved in the research in an attempt to specify the universe from which the respondents were drawn. As is noted in the text, this effort was quite successful in the Newark locations, where records were fairly centralized, but rather unsuccessful in other locations.

To compare this sample with that of undocumented aliens detained by the INS authorities, the cooperation of the regional offices of the agency in Newark and New York was enlisted. Random sample of "sanitized" (i.e., without any identifying information) I-213 Record of Apprehension Forms were provided which spanned the same period of time as the research in each area. As will become obvious in the last chapter, the Newark comparisons were more complete and useful than those from New York.

Finally, the sample was further specified by comparing CCS undocumented service providers. This phase of the research proved futile as it appeared that none of the agencies we contacted (See, Appendix III) serviced substantial numbers of undocumented aliens, or at least acknowledged doing so. Consequently, and since we were not interested in agencies which provided assistance to undocumented aliens for profit, and could not gain access to the various storefront ethnic associations who might provide most of this assistance, we abandoned the effort.

CONCLUSION

Unlike the first two samples, Sample III (n=192) is made up of the respondents who answered the survey instrument. That sample is composed of 99 New York cases and 93 Newark cases. The subjects were present and recent clients of the Migration Offices of Catholic Community Service organizations in four Northern New Jersey cities situated on the west side of the Hudson River directly across from New York City and in three of that city's five boroughs. The field phase of the study was completed in April of 1985.

Whenever possible, these data will be compared and contrasted with data reported by a number of other studies in this research area. Of particular relevance will be research results which focus on Caribbean-origin immigrants in the New York area - regardless of legal status. At the same time, comparisons will be made with the results of studies which attempt to paint national pictures of illegal immigration to the U.S. from the Western Hemisphere and pictures of illegal aliens from Mexico. Before the presentation of the empirical evidence commences, however, certain caveats about the data must be made clear: with the qualified exception of the CENIET Mexican study (Zazueta, 1980; Belsasso, 1981; Ranney and Kossoudji, 1983) and the Gurak study in New York (1982, 1983), virtually all other studies, including the one reported on here, have studied samples which are neither replicable nor representative in a statistically valid sense. Many of them rely on "snowball" techniques while samples I and II used here are self-selected samples of persons who voluntarily seek the assistance of New York-area Catholic Community service organizations.

Even the two studies which on their face are more statistically rigorous than those used here, however, are not representative in the strictest sense. The Gurak survey concentrated only in areas known to be dominated by Colombians (Queens County) and Dominicans (Northern New York County [Manhattan]), and CENIET concentrated on a sample of return migrants to Mexico who were over 15 years of age and had worked or had looked for work in the U.S. during the previous five years. Consequently, the results of that survey will not convey any insights about those undocumented Mexican aliens who did not happen to return to Mexico during the time of the survey in 1978/1979. Furthermore, this latter study is most useful only when one seeks to compare the characteristics of those who are regular commuters to the U.S. (almost half of whom have legal residence and/or legal work status in the U.S.) with those of non-commuters (almost all of whom are undocumented and are defined in the study as those who entered the U.S. fewer than six times during 1978). Hence, and as a result of the different timing - ranging from the mid-seventies for some of the Mexican studies and the North/Houstoun study to 1984/1985 for the New York CCS study - and the different objectives, priorities, and methodologies of these studies, the comparability of the data sets is diminished. It is with these caveats in mind that the discussion of our data proceeds.

CHAPTER THREE

SOCIODEMOGRAPHIC BACKGROUND

The three samples show remarkable similarities in their composition. In each sample, at least three-quarters and up to 96 percent of the subjects originated in the Western Hemisphere (See, Table 3:1) and virtually all respondents from South America came from the countries in the northern rim of the region. Altogether, the following six countries accounted for the largest numbers of respondents in all three samples: Colombia, the Dominican Republic, Ecuador, El Salvador, Haiti, and Jamaica.

Table 1:3 offers a panoramic view of some key characteristics of these same six legal immigrant communities in the United States. With the exception of the Salvadorans, the largest concentrations of each legal immigrant community are found in New York - ranging from a high of nearly 78 percent for the Dominicans to a low of nearly 34 percent for the Colombians. When adding the proportions from each community who live in Northern New Jersey, the range changes to 86 percent for the Dominicans and 48 percent for the Colombians (Table 1:3, Data Category 2). Significantly, and in line with the discussion on Caribbean region migration in Chapter 2, the overwhelming majority of these immigrants came to the U.S. since 1965, ranging from 79 percent for Colombians to 80 percent for Salvadorans (Table 1:3, Data Category 1).

A number of key demographic characteristics are remarkably close for most of the six legal immigrant communities. The majority in all six communities are females. Male representation ranges from 43.8 percent for the Salvadorans to 48.6 percent for the Haitians (Table 1:3, Data Category 3). This confirms a trend which is strongly evident in much recent legal immigration to the U.S. (See, Houstoun et al., 1985) and also appears to be the case with many undocumented immigrant communities - including the New York City component of the present study. As one might expect from the recency of these immigrant flows, the age structure is skewed dramatically toward the economically dynamic 20-to-44 year age group. With the exception of Jamaicans, whose representation in that age group dips below 50 percent (48.9%), all other groups have three out of five

UNDOCUMENTED ALIENS

TABLE 3:1
PRINCIPAL COUNTRIES AND REGIONS OF ORIGIN[1]

Country of Origin	Sample I No.	Sample I %	Sample II No.	Sample II %	Sample III No.	Sample III %
Argentina	8	1.0	13	1.7	4	2.1
Bolivia	3	0.4	6	0.8	–	–
Chile	15	1.9	6	1.2	1	–
Colombia	101	13.1	105	13.5	37	19.4
Costa Rica	11	1.4	6	0.8	–	–
Dominican Republic	24	3.1	33	4.2	16	8.4
Ecuador	42	5.5	37	4.8	10	5.2
Egypt	54	7.0	18	2.3	–	–
El Salvador	96	12.5	210	27.0	29	15.2
Grenada	–	–	–	–	2	1.0
Guatemala	18	2.3	12	1.5	4	2.1
Guyana	–	–	–	–	4	2.1
Haiti	110	14.3	85	10.9	33	17.3
Honduras	14	1.8	12	1.5	4	2.1
Italy	3	0.4	7	0.9	–	–
Jamaica	6	0.8	10	1.3	14	7.3
Mexico	15	1.9	32	4.1	6	3.1
Nicaragua	10	1.3	15	1.9	4	2.1
Panama	–	–	–	–	4	2.1
Peru	35	4.5	30	3.9	4	2.1
Poland	39	5.2	57	7.3	–	–
Portugal	35	4.5	6	0.8	–	–
Trinidad / Tobago	3	0.4	7	0.9	4	2.1
Uruguay	7	0.9	10	1.3	–	–
Other	121	15.8	58	7.5	12	6.3
Caribbean Isl.	–	27.0	–	20.0	–	37.0
Central America	–	22.0	–	37.0	–	27.0
South America	–	29.0	–	28.0	–	32.0
Subtotal (Western Hemisphere)	–	(78.0)	–	(85.0)	–	(96.0)
Total	770	100.0	778	100.0	192	100.0

[1] An arbitrary cutoff of 3 subjects per country for Sample I, 5 subjects per country for Sample II, and 2 subjects per country for Sample III has been employed. The countries with one subject per country in Sample III are as follow: Antiqua, Belize, Costa Rica, Dominica, Ethiopia, Ghana, Kenya, Nigeria, Portugal, Spain, Uruguay and Zaire.

persons in this age category. There are significant variations, however, in the size of the age group with the next highest representation: the group under 20 years of age. The size of this group ranges from a high of 32 percent for Jamaicans and around 25 percent for Dominicans and Haitians to only about 20 percent for the other groups (Table 1:3, Data Category 4). Although the distribution in the age data may appear unusual at first, it reflects expected trends when considering the strong bias in U.S. immigration law in favor of the reunification of nuclear families by exempting spouses and minor children of U.S. citizens from numerical limits and giving priority (although within numerical limits) to the unification of spouses, parents, and minor children for permanent resident aliens (**See,** Papademetriou, 1983b).

Information on marital status also shows remarkable homogeneity among at least five of the legal immigrant groups. With the exception of Salvadorans, between 55 and 60 percent of the men were married. Among women, Ecuadorian and Colombian women are married at rates similar to those of men while the range for the remaining groups is between 43 percent for Jamaican women and 48 percent for Salvadoran and Haitian women (Table 1:3, Data Category 6).

Finally, education tends to differentiate the various groups in significant, if predictable, ways (Table 1:3, Data Category 10). Among immigrants 20 years old or older, the majority for each of the six legal immigrant groups has completed at least eight years of formal education. When looking at the component of those who have higher than high school education, however, the variations become substantial. These rates range from a low of 14.3 percent for Dominicans to a high of over one-third of the total group for Haitians and Colombians. The rates for the remaining groups are 30 percent for Jamaicans, 28 percent for Ecuadorians, and 20 percent for Salvadorans. As one might expect, the rates for the proportion of the largest group of the least educated show the Dominicans and Salvadorans leading this category, the Haitians falling in the middle, and the remaining groups recording insignificant proportions (between 3% and 5% of the total).

The explanations for these data values lay with a tradition of emphasis on education in some of these countries; a tradition of emigration by certain classes; the social, economic, and political conditions in sending countries; and the "culture of education" adopted by virtually all immigrant groups after immigration to the United States. For example, much of the emigration from the Caribbean region fits under the rubric of "brain drain" as it is not only the most talented and risk averse, but also the better educated who emigrate. Specific conditions at some of the countries of origin reinforce this trend (See, Bach, 1985; Chaney, 1985). Colombia's inability to absorb its educated class, both economically and politically, partly accounts for the high educational profile of that group. Similarly, the systematic terror campaigns and emasculation of most middle and professional class opposition by the two Duvalier regimes, and the long-standing practice of emigration for those who lose in the incessant political conspiracies of that country (most of whom are from the middle and professional classes), accounts for the immigration of much of that country's educated elite to the United States.

The lower figures for the highly educated among Dominicans and Salvadorans probably also reflect political and economic conditions endemic to these countries. In neither of these countries did the middle class consider themselves generally under siege prior to early 1980 (the date of the collection of data), although economic decisions by the political and economic elites of these countries in the past 20 years have resulted in severe losses in economic status for many members of the middle classes (Bach, 1985; Diaz-Briquets, 1985; Chaney, 1985; Grasmuck, 1984). Furthermore, the tradition of education - or emigration - does not appear to be so deep in these countries as it is in the other four countries. In addition, the persistence of the U.S. authorities to opt not to recognize Salvadoran claims for asylum probably distorts that sample in unpredictable ways and makes assumptions about the overall Salvadoran population in the U.S. subject to large, and unsystematic, biases. Finally, the post-immigration "culture of education" places an enormous premium on education for all these ethnic groups. In fashion typical of most other immigrant groups, second generation immigrants tend to attain significantly higher levels of education vis à vis their parents and native Americans than other variables might predict (See, Chiswick, 1984a, 1979). Ethnographic research among some of the groups included in Table 1:3 (Pessar, 1982a, b,   Gurak, 1984) supports both the trend and the explanation.

REGION OF ORIGIN CHARACTERISTICS

The profile of Sample III respondents prior to their emigration to the U.S. discloses a wealth of information (Table 3:2). Over 77 percent of them had lived in an urban area during the first 15 years of their lives and 80 percent of the entire sample reported no internal migration during that period. Over 45 percent of the respondents, however, had moved at least once prior to their first trip to the U.S. and over 88 percent of the total sample reported an urban residence prior to that first trip. These findings support recent speculation and some tentative research findings that undocumented immigrants from many Caribbean region locations (Chaney, 1985; Diaz-Briquets, 1983) originate largely from urban locations. It seems to suggest further that the degree to which urban areas are supposed to serve as staging areas for international migration by rural internal migrants may have been overestimated - suggesting an important distinction with the Mexican undocumented aliens studies in the Southwest (See, various studies by Reichert, Massey, Mines and Cornelius). Finally, it gives tentative support to arguments that large Third World cities tend to be frequent platforms of international migration due to large informal sectors (Portes and Walton, 1981) and the frequent release of secondary sector workers (and especially female workers) by the unpredictability in the behavior of international capital (Sassen-Koob, 1984). Nearly 60 percent of our respondents reported a city larger than 100,000 people as their last residence before coming to the United States.

Information on the social and economic status of the respondents' households in the country of origin points to some further important findings. The different than often expected economic profile of these households becomes immediately obvious from the occupational structure of the respondent's father. Over 30 percent of these individuals have occupations which fall outside the categories of the International Standard Classification of Occupations of the International Labor Office, probably suggesting a large number of not easily classifiable informal activities (See, Portes and Walton, 1981).

TABLE 3:2
SELECTED LABOR MARKET AND BACKGROUND CHARACTERISTICS OF SAMPLE III RESPONDENTS AND THEIR FAMILIES PRIOR TO EMIGRATION TO THE U.S./*

Labor Market Characteristics	Respondents (n=192)	Fathers of the Respondents
Had work experience prior to emigration	77.1	—
Employed prior to emigration[1]	82.4	—
Average number of months employed during the 12 months prior to emigration	11 months	—
Employed in manufacturing	15.0	7.6
Employed in construction	4.7	8.1
Employed in services[2]	21.6	19.5
Finance and real estate	19.4	3.2
Self- employment[5]	6.7	28.0
Other	22.23	30.34
Background Characteristics		
Home ownership by respondent's family at home country	53.1	
Parents' household size in home country	5.0 persons	
Average number of persons employed in that household	2.1 persons	
Moved at least once before coming to the U.S.	45.3	
Lived in an urban area during the first 15 years of life	77.5	
Lived in an urban area immediately prior to emigration to the U.S.	88.4	

* In percentages, unless otherwise indicated.

[1] As a percent of those with labor market experience prior to emigration.

[2] Including utilities, retail services, transportation, communication and personal services.

[3] Of whom, 9.4 percent were in professional, technical, administrative and managerial occupations.

[4] Of whom, 10.8 percent were in the categories above (fn. 3).

[5] Only a small proportion of those self- employed reported activities of a professional, technical, administrative or managerial nature.

An additional 28 percent are self-employed, often in managerial and professional positions. We did not detect anything approaching an intergenerational tradition of emigration to the United States - although 9 percent of the fathers and 11 percent of the mothers of the study's subjects had some previous work experience in the United States (data not shown).

These household employment data must be viewed together with other data reporting over 50 percent home ownership by the families of Sample III respondents and moderate size households - averaging under five persons per household, of whom 2.1 persons are gainfully employed and contribute toward the payment of household expenses. The picture that emerges from these data argues for the reconsideration of some profiles of undocumented aliens as frequently rural immigrants ejected into the U.S. undocumented immigration stream by rural poverty and urban unemployment. Instead, and in line with much recent research on non-Mexican immigrant groups, our respondents are often members of lower middle-class and even middle-class households who, faced with economic uncertainty, have made a rational decision to pursue long-term strategies for economic advancement by throwing in their lot with a U.S. labor market which has increasingly international, rather than national, boundaries. The economic uncertainty and dislocations which often accompanied choices by the elite of these countries for certain industrialization initiatives during the past two decades, and the dependent economic relationships which these initiatives have fostered **vis a vis** the U.S. and the world economy, help explain why individuals and households have responded to the structural forces which are dominant in this region by emigrating (**See,** Portes and Walton, 1981; Bach, 1985; Papademetriou, 1983c, 1984a, 1985a; Diaz-Briquets, 1985).

These relationships take on additional significance when viewed in the light of both the behavior of other members of these households and the work experience of this project's respondents prior to their emigration to the United States. These respondents are members of households which, in increasingly typical fashion among survival strategies employed by Third World families, seek to "diversify the family portfolio" through emigration (**See,** Findley, 1977; Arizpe, 1982a; Pessar, 1982a; Wood, 1982). Specifically, 25

percent of Sample III respondents reported that other members
of the households in their country of origin lived in countries
other than either their own or the United States.

Furthermore, and with regard to the economic situation
of respondents prior to emigration, 14 percent reported owning
land in their own country but only two respondents claimed to
have an ongoing interest in any business activity at home --
suggesting a fundamental absence of an economic incentive to
return. In addition, 77.1 percent of the study's subjects
reported work experience prior to coming to the U.S., spread
among all major categories of economic activity. Specifically,
15 percent were in manufacturing, 21.6 percent in services,
4.7 percent in construction, 19.4 percent in financial and real
estate services, 6.7 percent were self-employed and 22.2
percent were in "other" (See Table 3.2). Unlike their parents,
however, of those in the "other" category, only 9.4 percent
were in professional, technical, administrative and managerial
occupations - indicating a substantial intergenerational loss in
economic (and presumably social) status vis à vis that of their
parents. Finally, two-thirds of Sample III respondents (and
82.4% of those with work experience prior to coming to the
U.S.) were employed for an average of 11 of the 12 months
prior to migration. Without anticipating the discussion on the
labor market characteristics of Sample III respondents, it must
be obvious that these undocumented aliens carry with them an
enormous human capital potential from which the U.S. as a
whole can only benefit - although population components
within the country may in fact be negatively affected.

THE UNDOCUMENTED HOUSEHOLD IN THE
UNITED STATES I: BACKGROUND CHARACTERISTICS

The majority of Sample III respondents of this study are
married and nearly 94 percent of those who are married live
with their spouses in the United States. In only five cases is
migration identified as the cause for a temporary physical
separation. Of those with spouses in the U.S. (n=121), nearly
two-thirds are married to a mix of legal U.S. residents (41%),
naturalized citizens (9%), and Puerto Rican migrants (15%).
Only 39 percent reported having a spouse out of immigration
status.

These spouses have educational levels which approximate those of the project's subjects (See, Table 3:2). The mean value for years of education is 9.4 and the median 9.6 years. The proportion of those spouses with better than high school education is a significant 22.2 percent - slightly higher than that for the study's subjects. Finally, 73.4 percent of the spouses of our subjects were reported to be employed and only 7 percent were reported to be unemployed and looking for a job.

The characteristics of the children of the undocumented respondents in Samples II and III reveal some interesting information for the policy debate about the use of U.S. infrastructure by undocumented aliens. Sample II indicates that 45.9 percent of its subjects had children while 62 percent of Sample III respondents did so (See, Table 3:3). The average numbers of children per respondent who had children in the two samples were similar - 2.7 for Sample II and 2.6 (318 total children) for Sample III. The child's average age for Sample III is 9.6 years. Significantly, however, only 58.9 percent for Sample II respondents and 61.5 percent for Sample III respondents had their children living with them and/or their spouses or relatives in the United States. Of the children who lived in the United States, over three-quarters for each of the two samples are under 18 years of age and 26.0 percent of the total number of children of respondents from Sample II and 43.0 percent of the same universe for Sample III are attending U.S. schools (n=222 and n=84, respectively). Finally, 33.4 percent of the children of Sample III undocumented aliens who live in the U.S. are U.S. citizens (n=65).

It is obvious from these data that undocumented aliens are members of households of mixed legal status - both in terms of their spouses and children. This fact makes many of the questions about making demands on U.S. services and infrastructure extremely complicated to address and, in a sense, even moot. Further analysis of the data will identify with more precision the immigration status of each alien receiving benefits ranging from education and unemployment to Aid to Families with Dependent Children (AFDC). As it stands now, it appears that a substantial proportion of children of undocumented aliens attending public schools have a right to this service by reason of their citizenship - in addition to the recognition of that same right to a public school education for all children of undocumented aliens by the Supreme Court decision of Plyler vs. Doe (**See,** Hull, 1985; Flores, 1984).

DEMOGRAPHIC RESULTS

The age profile (Table 3:4) of the study's three samples shows considerable similarities. Sample I shows a mean age of 33.6 years compared with 31.4 years for Sample II and 32.6 years for Sample III. Median age values hover close to 30 years of age, while the mode seems to be lowest for Sample II. As with the age structure of the legal immigrant groups (**See,** Table 1:3), the age distribution of our samples exhibits a significant bias toward two groups - the economically active who are in the prime of their participation in the labor force and minors. In fact, the age pyramid structures for the six groups highlighted in Table 1:3 would be remarkably similar to those for all three of our samples, with Sample I scoring slightly lower and Sample III slightly higher than the range for the six legal immigrant groups. There is, however, a significant difference between the two subsamples which comprise Sample III. The New Jersey group is somewhat older than the New York group and shows a more clear "aging" progression when compared to Samples I and II. It is important to recall that Sample I came entirely from 1980-1981 Newark CCS files and that over four-fifths of the files for Sample II (1982-1983) also came from the same migration offices. Newark subsample III includes a large number (about 60%) of respondents whose records were included in Sample II. Hence the relative continuity and progression in a number of sociodemographic characteristics between these two samples.

Information on sex distribution and marital status for our samples sharpens and reinforces many of the observations made so far. As shown on Table 3:5, Samples I and II are predominantly male but Sample III shows a slight majority of females. Disaggregating Sample III explains this apparent anomaly. The Newark subsample remains primarily male (56%) hence showing again its lineage from Sample II. The New York subsample, however, is 57 percent female - a figure which fits in with the data from Table 1:3 and other studies of key immigrant communities in New York City (**See,** Houstoun

TABLE 3:3

CHARACTERISTICS OF CHILDREN OF UNDOCUMENTED ALIENS

	Sample II (n=798)	Sample III (n=192)
Proportion of total number of children of undocumented aliens who live in the U.S.	58.9%	52.0%
Respondents with children in the U.S.	45.9%	62.0%
Average number of children per respondent with children in the U.S.	2.7 children	2.6
Child's average age	—	9.6 years
Proportion of children in U.S. under 18 years of age	80.0%	77.0%
Proportion of children of undocumented aliens who are U.S. citizens	—	33.4%
Proportion of minor children attending U.S. schools	26.0%	43.0%

TABLE 3:4

AGE

Age Group	Sample I		Sample II		Sample III[1]	
	No.	%	No.	%	No.	%
> 21	88	10.3	103	13.2	14	7.3
22-30	316	30.9	330	42.4	75	39.3
31-44	265	36.9	247	31.8	80	41.9
< 45	136	15.9	95	12.2	22	11.0
Unascertained	51	6.0	3	4.0	1	0.5
Total	856	100.0	778	100.0	192	100.0
Mean	33.6		33.4		32.6	
Median	30.9		29.3		31.15	

[1] Of the two groups comprising Sample III, the New Jersey group (n=93) was somewhat older than the New York group (n=99). The mean values of the former were 34.0 (mean) and 32.5 (median). The differing sampling methodologies probably account for the difference.

et al., 1984). The male predominance in the New Jersey samples I and II and subsample III probably reflects the influence in the composition of these groups of Salvadoran and Haitian undocumented aliens, who tend to be predominantly male (Table 3:1), as well as the significance of non-Western Hemisphere aliens (in Samples I and II) who are also predominantly male (data not shown).

One must be careful, however, about generalizations on the sex discrimination of undocumented aliens. Many of the existing surveys, as well as INS apprehension statistics and estimates based on recent CPS and Census data, show an overwhelming predominance of males (Warren and Passel, 1985; INS, Statistical Yearbook, 1979). Yet, it is a fact that much of post-WW II legal immigration to the U.S. has been female dominated. This domination is reflected by the New York subsample but not by the New Jersey one (See also, Mann and Salvo, 1984). Possible (if tenuous) support for the applicability of this trend toward a male domination of undocumented alien flows comes from the 1979 and 1983 CPS, which estimate that the female/male distribution of undocumented aliens might be along the 40/60 percent lines, and from the estimates derived from the 1980 Census which concluded that there was a 53 percent male advantage among the undocumented (See, Passel and Woodrow, 1984; Warren and Passel, 1983). Although these Census estimates suggest that the representation of women among undocumented populations is still in the minority, it is considerably closer to the mid-point than such surveys as North/Houstoun and INS apprehension and detention data suggest. Smaller samples from other studies also report indications of female majorities among undocumented communities in New York (See, Pessar 1982a; Grasmuck, 1984; see also the NACLA study of 1979 [Badillo-Veiga et al.]).

The information on marital status (Table 3:6) indicates that with each sample, a progressively larger majority of undocumented aliens was married. Sample III shows a large increase in that proportion which becomes even larger than adding the numbers for "consensual unions" (i.e. common law families) to the total for "married". The explanation for this increase may again be found in the disaggregated subsamples. While the New Jersey group of respondents follows suit with Sample II and reports that 54 percent of the subjects were married, the figure for the New York City subsample is 7

TABLE 3:5
SEX OF UNDOCUMENTED ALIENS BY SURVEY SAMPLES

Sex	Sample I		Sample II		Sample III	
	No.	%	No.	%	No.	%
Male	519	60.6	461	59.3	95	49.5
Female	325	38.0	316	40.6	97	50.5
Unascertained	12	1.4	2	—	—	—
Total	856	100.0	778	99.9	192[1]	100.0

[1] The New York component of the sample was almost 57 percent female, while the New Jersey one was 56 percent male.

TABLE 3:6
MARITAL STATUS[1]

Status	Sample I		Sample II		Sample III	
	No.	%	No.	%	No.	%
Never married	297	34.7	295	37.9	47	24.5
Married	422	49.3	416	53.5	121	63.0
Widow(er)	21	2.5	18	2.3	4	2.1
Divorced	26	3.0	23	3.0	7	3.6
Separated	28	3.3	17	2.2	7	3.6
Consensual Union	—	—	—	—	4	2.1
Unascertained	62	7.2	9	1.2	2	1.0
Total	856	100.0	778	100.0	192	99.9

[1] Seventy-two percent of the New York component of the sample was married (54 percent for New Jersey); 18.4 and 31.5 percent of each sample were single, respectively. Of those married, only 70 percent of the New York component, but 95 percent of the New Jersey one, had their spouse living with them at the time of the interview (data not shown).

percent. It should be noted, however, that the figures for married respondents probably carry within them a bias of unknown quantity. Since one of the principal activities in which the Migration Offices in question engage is immigration services, a higher proportion of married clients are likely to contact them because marriages convey a number of immigration law privileges to the spouse both in terms of the possibility of regularizatión of status (if married to U.S. citizen or U.S. legal residents), and of enabling them to bring their dependents.

In all, the demographic categories examined so far place our samples within the range for most other studies on undocumented aliens. The age characteristics of this sample are a little on the high side of the norm when compared to such national or Southwest studies as North/Houstoun (under 29 years mean value), Bustamante (1977), who found a mean age of 28 years, van Arsdol et al. (1979), with a figure of 31 years of age, and CENIET (1983), with a figure of 31 years old for "noncommuters" (and 39 years old for "commuters"). At the same time, however, our figures are within range for all of the New York area studies. The sex characteristics, finally, place our samples within the range for studies on undocumented aliens in the New York region, although our marital status data should not be casually compared with those of most other studies - except with that of van Arsdol with which it shares certain biases - and, interestingly, with the Weintraub and Cardenas group of Mexican undetained aliens in Texas (1984). This comparison places the van Arsdol sample higher than, but close to, our own samples in terms of marital status while the figures for the Weintraub and Cardenas group are identical to those for Sample III.

It is in their educational profile, however, that respondents here differ most decidedly from Mexican undocumented aliens. The three samples in this work (Table 3:7) show a steady upward progression in terms of the proportion of respondents reporting educational levels between nine and twelve years of schooling. Furthermore, 15.2 percent (Sample II) and 21.3 percent (Sample III) of the two sets of respondents had post-secondary school education. These figures put the subjects of this study within the range for the six legal immigrant populations profiled earlier in Table 3. Sample III respondents, especially, are near the middle of that range. In other words, the CCS undocumented clients studied here report substantial human capital characteristics which would lead one to expect considerable success in the labor market - if immigration status or ethnic racial prejudice could be rendered moot.

The education findings of this project (mean and median values slightly over 10 years of formal schooling) also offer general support to the information obtained in several other studies of Caribbean immigrants - although they are somewhat higher than those reported by any of these studies. Among them are Pessar's sample of Dominicans in New York (1984a), Mann and Salvo's 1980 Census-based comparisons among Puerto Ricans, Dominicans and Colombians in New York (1984), Gurak's 1981 New York City survey of Colombians and Dominicans (1983), and Grasmuck's sample of documented and undocumented Dominicans in New York (1984). They also compare favorably with the findings of an earlier National Survey of Emigration from the Dominican Republic (Ugalde et al., 1979), two samples of Costa Ricans and Salvadorans (Poitras, 1980a,b), and a sample of Haitians drawn in 1977 (Keely et al.). The average distribution of the educational levels of our samples also coincides with that of legal immigrants from the region reported annually by the Immigration and Naturalization Service (INS, Annual Report, 1978-83).

TABLE 3:7

EDUCATION[1]

Years of Education	Sample I		Sample II		Sample III	
	No.	%	No.	%	No.	%
0- 8	250	29.2	268	34.4	59	30.7
9- 12	313	36.5	335	43.1	87	45.3
13- 16	121	14.1	100	12.9	35	18.2
over 16	25	2.9	18	2.3	6	3.1
Unascertained	147	17.2	57	7.3	5	2.6
Total	856	99.9	778	100.0	192	99.9
Mean	8.04		10.00		10.21	
Median	7.69		10.33		10.56	

[1] Data collection procedures for years of education were different in Sample I where information was collected in group form. Although both New York and New Jersey samples reported similar educational levels, New Jersey respondents were slightly better educated in terms of holding "Associate or Technical" degrees while New York respondents held higher proportions of university degrees.

These same data, however, are in sharp contrast with most of the data reported for Mexican undocumented aliens. For instance, while 58.3 and 66.6 percent of the respondents respectively, in Samples II and III had over nine years of formal education, the comparable figures for the North/Houstoun sample (1976) were under 30 percent; for Maram's Hispanic legal and illegal garment and restaurant workers in Los Angeles, 10 and 32.7 percent, respectively (1981); for van Arsdol's sample of illegals in Los Angeles slightly under 21 percent (1979); and for the Weintraub and Cardenas Texas study, 12.7 and 8.3 percent for the unapprehended and apprehended samples, respectively (1984). Finally, while the reporting method is different, findings here also contrast sharply with those for the illegal noncommuter respondents to the CENIET survey who reported an average education of 4.2 years (1981).

CONCLUSION

The review of the background and key demographic characteristics of the respondents in all three samples, and the comparisons with the profiles both of Mexican undocumented aliens in the Southwest and legal and undocumented aliens originating in the Caribbean region in general, indicate that: respondents here often come from a lower middle-class to middle-class background and from households with substantial labor market skills and a mixture of informal sector and self-employment characteristics; they are somewhat mobile in their own country; they are of basically urban background; and they are members of households which exhibit substantial amounts of international mobility in search of improving the lot of family members. The modal demographic characteristics of our groups of respondents indicate that the distribution among men and women is about even, that the majority of both men and women were married and with children, that only a proportion (about two-thirds) of these children are in the U.S. and only about half of them attend U.S. schools. Among the latter, many are U.S. citizens. The families of the respondents are composed of both legal and undocumented members, and both the respondents and their spouses have formidable human capital characteristics - including a high overall educational average with substantial amounts of secondary education and an age structure strongly skewed toward the prime years of economic activity.

CHAPTER FOUR

GOING NORTH

In terms of policy formulation, it is important to know what motivates undocumented aliens to emigrate. Many of the early assumptions of absolute indigence or extended unemployment are not borne out by recent research (Ugalde et al., 1979; Grasmuck, 1984; Pessar, 1982; Badillo-Veiga et al., 1979; Waldinger, 1981). In fact, these recent findings, as well as the data reported in the previous chapter and the monetary resources necessary to undertake the trip to the U.S., effectively establish that households of undocumented immigrants must have the ability to commit the necessary funds to finance the trip north. Neither are these aliens "target" workers (i.e., usually male migrants who come to the U.S. to earn enough money to be able to meet a specific goal at home), or of the type who seek to supplement their annual income from an economic activity in which they engage regularly in their home country. In other words, the respondents here do not fit the image of the Mexican undocumented aliens as portrayed in the literature by such researchers as Reichert, Mines, Cornelius and Massey but also largely by Poitras for Costa Ricans and Salvadorans. The respondents in this survey seem to have more in common with the Weintraub/Cardenas group of Mexican undocumented aliens than the geographic location of that sample might lead one to expect.

Furthermore, with the increasing incidence of political instability in many countries in the region, one must anticipate that motives for emigration will begin to be increasingly colored by political events and that assumptions that emigration is a purely economic decision will have to become more conditional. This is certainly the direction toward which data used here point. Information on those who have taken more than one trip to the U.S. (n=57) on Table 4:1 confirms that interest in improving one's economic opportunities is the largest single factor responsible for the immigration of our sample of undocumented aliens (35.8 percent). The opportunities referred to by respondents include both better and more stable income and the availability of jobs.

TABLE 4:1
REASONS FOR COMING/STAYING IN THE U.S.

	First Trip		Present Trip		Reasons for Staying in the U.S. Longer than Initially Intended	
	%		%		%	
	Main Reason	Second Reason[2]	Main Reason	Second Reason	Main Reason	Second Reason
Better economic opportunities in the U.S.[1]	35.8	(29.8)	19.0	(38.4)	33.9	(26.1)
Family situation[3]	13.2	(6.2)	26.1	(-)	16.9	(19.2)
Political reasons	12.1	(7.7)	9.5	(19.0)	9.8	(10.3)
Studies	10	(18.3)	4.8	(9.5)	—	(—)
Better quality of life in the U.S.	—	—	—	—	9.3	(21.2)

[1] Including better income and availability of jobs.

[2] These proportions become further augmented when considering that respondents also selected them as a secondary reason for coming to the U.S.

[3] Including maintaining the family unit and aspirations for the future of the children.

A number of other motivations also became obvious from the answers of our respondents. Among them, family matters (and especially aspirations for the future of their children), political reasons (understandable, in view of the country composition of the sample and the discussion in Chapters 2 and 3), and the pursuit of studies seem to be most important. Interestingly, the values of some of these answers, especiallly "economic opportunities" and "studies", increase significantly when one includes the answers of those respondents who also have checked these categories off as the "second most important reason" for emigration. Data on the present trip, however, which includes the entire sample (n=192), show a somewhat different picture - partly as a result of the shifting priorities of those who have come to the U.S. more than once.

Although economic opportunities remain important, they seem to have moved more in the background (they are the dominant "second reason" for emigration). Their previous place as the main reason for emigration is now occupied by family reasons, and political reasons seem to have a much higher background importance than they did for those who reported coming to the U.S. more than once. Studies, finally, seem to diminish in importance as a priority among undocumented aliens.

The increased concern of our subjects with family-related matters, as well as the increased importance of political reasons as a background issue, is probably related to and reflects concern for the integrity and safety of the family unit as a result of deteriorating economic and political conditions at home. Furthermore, it may also point to an actual reordering of the priorities of repeat immigrants who, having found a way to satisfy minimum economic needs, are placing the family - and especially the well-being of the children - as the modal reason for reemigrating. Pessar's research on Dominican women immigrants in New York would seem to support this latter interpretation (1984b), as do the Gurak (1983) and Badillo-Veiga **et al.** (1979) studies.

THE QUESTION OF PERMANENCE

One of the continuing controversies in this policy area is whether undocumented aliens constitute a temporary or permanent addition to the population of the country of destination. The contending assumptions are captured rather appealingly in the metaphors used in the titles of two important publications in this field: Piore's **Birds of Passage** and Pessar's **When the Birds of Passage Want to Roost** (1979 and 1984a, respectively). That each assumption argues for potentially different policy responses to undocumented migration is evident. The appropriate policy initiatives, hence, must proceed from decisions about the interests and priorities of this nation based on sound empirical answers to the question of permanence.

However, permanence in immigration is itself an elusive concept. Legal immigrants are presumed to be permanent additions to the country of destination. Yet, as one can see from the assumptions about emigration from the U.S.

discussed in Chapter 2, about one-third of recent immigrants, and even larger proportions of some groups of European immigrants in previous immigration periods, are presumed to re-emigrate (See, Keely, 1979; Keely and Kraly, 1978). The numbers are probably even higher for immigrants to other advanced industrial societies, such as Canada and Western Europe (Papademetriou, 1983b). If only two-thirds of legal immigrants stay permanently in the U.S., what assumptions can one make about the long-term behavior of undocumented aliens? Numerous studies on Mexican undocumented aliens show them to be by and large only temporary U.S. residents. Can, however, policymakers assume that this behavior is typical of all, or most, undocumented aliens? The answer appears to be that they should not. Evidence supporting this latter position comes both from the methodological flaws of the studies on Mexicans (since many were studied in Mexico, only those involved in a circular flow would be interviewed), and from a number of other studies which point to the much more mixed character of the data. For instance, Poitras (1980a) found a shifting pattern of quasi-circular movement among his Salvadoran and Costa Rican subjects, as did North/Houstoun (1976) and Weintraub and Cardenas (1984). Furthermore, a number of researchers are discovering behavior among recent immigrants which indicates that many of them had lived in the U.S. as undocumented aliens before their last (legal) entry (Waldinger, 1981; Portes and Bach, 1984; Portes, 1979; Hirshman, 1978). Finally, research in the New York area indicates that undocumented aliens report substantial periods of stay in the U.S. (Foner, 1982; Pessar, 1982a; Gurak, 1983). Data here support this tendency and suggest that it might be largely futile to develop immigration policy on the assumption that undocumented aliens are interested in, and in fact intend to stay in the U.S. for a savings-goal oriented, brief, or at least finite, period of time.

In other words, in spite of the commonly held (and generally accurate) belief that most immigrants long to return to their homelands (Maingot, 1985; Palmer 1979; Chaney, 1985; Marshall, 1985), for undocumented aliens as well as for legal immigrants this is more in the nature of a dream than a reality. What is interesting, however, is that subjects in this study continue to cling on to this myth even after they have missed various self-imposed deadlines for their return. For

TABLE 4:2
Settlement Plans for Sample III

Original Intentions About Length of Stay in the U.S. (n=189)	%
Less than 1 year	25.9
1-2 years	14.8
3-5 years	9.0
More than 5 years	23.8
Not sure	26.5
Total	100.0

Changes in Intentions [1] (n=101)	
Decided to stay longer	98.0
Decided to stay less	2.0
Total	100.0

Reasons for Planning to Stay/Having Stayed Longer	
Adapted better than expected	17.0
Started a family here	19.0
Economic conditions at home not improved[2]	12.0
Political conditions at home not improved	10.0
Just became more involved here	9.0
Joined by family here	6.0
Other	27.0
Total	100.0

Likelihood of Duration of Extended Stay[3]	Probable (%)	Very Probable (%)
1 year from now[4]	8.2	83.3
3 years from now	11.5	80.9
5 years from now	10.4	77.0
10 years from now	12.0	66.7
15 years from now	10.4	63.7

Would You Return Home to Accept a Job With a Similar Salary?	
Yes	18.9
No	81.1

[1] 101 subjects reported change in their intentions about the future (53.4 percent of the sample).

[2] New Jersey respondents showed a strong interest in this category because of the large number of Haitians and Salvadorans in the sample.

[3] The scale ranged from "very unlikely" to "very probable".

[4] Interestingly, 93 percent of the respondents had no plans to leave the U.S. other than to visit abroad. About half of them explained that they "liked the U.S. better than their home country".

instance, Table 4:2 shows the settlement plans for Sample III respondents and points to the large discrepancy between original intentions about duration of stay in the U.S. and the actual picture. About one-quarter of the respondents indicated that they initially expected to stay in the U.S. for less than a year - about the same proportions as for those who were undecided and those who had originally planned to stay more than five years. The next highest category consisted of those planning to stay between one and two years. Only a small minority thought initially of a three-to-five year commitment.

TABLE 4:3
Point of Entry, Year of Entry and Length of Stay in the United States

Point of Entry [1]	Sample III %
Mexican Border	33.3
Canadian Border	4.4
Florida Coast	48.9
California Coast	13.3
Total	99.9
	(n=90)

Year of Entry into the U.S.	Sample II (n=778)	Sample III (n=192)
Before 1978	10.9	12.3
1978	5.4	8.0
1979	13.0	14.2
1980	21.9	17.2
1981	27.9	17.7
1982	16.5	8.2
1983	4.4	10.5
1984	—	10.9
1985	—	1.0
Total	100.0	100.0
Length of Stay in the U.S. (Present Trip)	37.9 months	56.1 months [2]

[1] For those entering without a visa.

[2] The length of stay was higher for N.J. (62.1 months) than for New York (50.5 months).

When asked whether there had now been a change in their intentions to stay (average length of stay for Sample III respondents is over 56 months-See, Table 4:3), 53.4 percent of the study's subjects admitted to such a change and 98 percent of them had now decided to stay longer than they had planned to initially. When queried why they had continued to stay in the U.S. past their original projections, six conditions seemed to be of particular relevance (although none of them attracted more than one-fifth of the sample). Two responses revolved around family matters - the starting of a family here and the ability of the family to reunite in the United States. These answers account for 25 percent of all responses and, when taken together with the data from Table 4:1, clearly establish the importance of the family as a key variable in immigration. Two other responses revolved around the continuing economic and political uncertainty at home, accounting for an additional 22 percent of the explanation. The fifth answer was chosen by 17 percent of the respondents and probably alludes partly to an economic reason - their "success in adapting to the United States". Finally, 9 percent reported that they "simply became more involved here".

The continuing importance of economic considerations - perhaps not so clear in the above answers - becomes evident again when those respondents who indicated that it was probable that they would be in the U.S. 10 years from now (two-thirds of the total) were asked why they now planned on such lengthy stays (Table 4:1). Nearly 34 percent identified "economic opportunities in the U.S.", followed by "plans for their children" (17%), "restrictive political conditions at home" (10%), and "the superior quality of life" in the U.S. (9%). All of these answers are further reinforced with strong support among choices as "second reasons" for staying in the U.S. longer than intended. Finally, more than 93 percent of all respondents had no plans to leave the U.S. in the near future, other than to visit their home country, and more than half volunteered that they simply "liked life in the U.S. better than in their home country".

This apparent strength of the resolve among respondents to remain in the United States, and the depth of their adjustment in their adopted community, seems to offer some support to one controversial view about the nature of work among immigrants. The reference is to Piore's (1979) often cited hypothesis that (temporary) immigrant workers tend to view their stay in advanced industrial societies in functional economic terms, i.e. with little regard to the social status of the job. While our evidence is rather indirect and would benefit from additional in-depth interviewing, it appears that respondents might have been quite concerned about the noneconomic rewards/liabilities of transposing their current job to their home country. Finally, data here also seem to support Pessar's findings about the reluctance of immigrant households to return to their home country although the analysis cannot test at this time her assertion that it is those women performing wage labor outside of the household who are most reluctant to return (1985).

Table 4:3 helps explain some of the findings reported on Tables 4:1 and 4:2. The average length of stay for Sample II respondents is about 38 months which makes the origin of that sample relatively recent. In fact, nearly 90 percent of these respondents came to the U.S. after 1978 and more than 70 percent since the beginning of 1980. The figures for Sample III are somewhat different but the basic difference can be attributed to the timing of the two surveys and the relationship of part of Sample III to Sample II. The average length of stay of Sample III subjects was more than 56 months and it was even higher for the Newark subsample (more than 62 months). Since Sample II was collected in 1982-83, while Sample III in 1984-85, the latter sample can be expected to be more mature - especially since the Newark subsample drew almost 60 percent of its cases from Sample II.

That aside, however, Sample III offers strong support to the finding that the vast majority of respondents came since the beginning of 1978 (nearly 88%). The significance of this result for the policy debate is critical. First, it seems to give some independent, though indirect, support to the estimates of several studies utilizing official CPS and Census data which argue that most undocumented aliens may be of relatively recent (post-1975) origin (Warren and Passel, 1985; Hill, 1985). Second, Muller's assumptions (1984) about the recency of the undocumented population in Southern California also receive some support. We separate paths from these findings, however, on assumptions about the vitality of these flows since the beginning of 1980. Well over 70 percent of both samples have entered the U.S. since then. This is significant for S.1200, the Immigration Reform and Control Act recently passed by the U.S. Senate (1985), which sets a January 1, 1980 cut-off date for legalization. Under this plan, most of the respondents of this study would not qualify for this program, while the House version of this Bill (H.R. 3080, 1985), with its January, 1982, deadline, would allow over 70 percent of our Sample III to regularize their status.

To recapitulate, it is obvious that the question of intended length of stay is a difficult one to address because it is often inextricably intertwined with one of the most enduring and elusive of concepts: the almost universal expression by immigrants of their intention to return. When probed, however, respondents expressed rather clear intentions, which, to a large degree, expose the often mythical nature of this concept. While a plurality of respondents were "not sure" about how long they expected to stay in the U.S. when they first came to the New York metropolitan area, only a little more than one-fifth said that they expected to stay for as long as five years. Five years later (the average length of stay of the respondents in Sample III, from which these data have been culled, was 56.1 months), almost all subjects admit to a change in plans in favor of a longer stay. In fact, over three-quarters of them now expect to stay in the U.S. for a minimum of an additional five years (Table 4:2). In other words, if an assumption needs to be made about the permanence versus the temporariness of stay of our sample of undocumented aliens, it must be that they are likely to remain here in proportions which are probably similar to those for legal immigrants.

MODE OF ENTRY INTO THE UNITED STATES

Although the entire set of questions on the physical process of entry is also policy relevant, its relevance is in the policy enforcement and execution realm - rather than the formulation one. Table 4:3 identifies the points of entry for those who enter without inspection (E.W.I., in immigration parlance). Among them (n=90 for the present trip of the study's subjects), one-third crossed the Mexican border, 48.9 percent came through the Florida coast, 13.3 through the California coast, and only 4.4 percent crossed the Canadian border.

Table 4:4 offers more detailed information on this broad question. The modal means of entry for all Sample III respondents (n=192) is by air, followed by those who came in by sea, and, at some distance, by those who crossed land

TABLE 4:4
MODE OF ENTRY INTO THE UNITED STATES (IN %)

Mode of Entry	Sample II	Sample III	
		First Trip to the U.S.[1]	Present Trip to the U.S.
Air	—	—	57.8
Land	—	—	15.6
Sea	—	—	25.5
Total	—	—	99.9
			(n=192)
Type of Visa Held at Entry			
Visitors for pleasure (B- 2)	45.8	20.3	42.7
Visitors for business (B- 1)	1.7	1.0	3.6
Students (F- 1)	1.1	0.5	4.2
Entered without documents	33.6	6.8	41.1
Other visas	2.0	1.0	2.6
No answer	15.8	70.4	5.7
Total	100.0	100.0	99.9
	(n=778)	(n=192)	(n=192)
Of Those Not Having Documents		(n=13)	(n=79)
		EWI=61.5%	EWI=87.3%
E. ⌈ Crossed border illicitly	—	23.1 ⌉	39.2 ⌉
W. | Were smuggled in[2]	—	38.4 |	8.9 |
I. ⌊ Coastal entry	—	— ⌋	39.2 ⌋
Used false documents	—	15.4	3.8
False statement to a border guard	—	—	1.3
Other	—	23.1	7.6
Total	—	100.0	100.0

[1] Sample III had an average of 1.3 entries in the U.S. The average stay during the first trip for those who had been to the U.S. more than once (29.6%) was 27.9 months.

[2] Of those smuggled in, the fee for the New Jersey (more mature) sample was $743.00, while for the New York one was $1,202.00.

borders. The composition of this sample helps explain the distribution in the mode of entry of this group. The high representation of Haitians explains the much higher than expected incidence of entries through the Florida coast. Distance from the Mexican border, and the expense of reaching Canada first to take advantage of the more porous Northern land borders, explain the lower than expected incidence of land border crossings. Finally, the distribution of the sample between those who entered with documents (regardless of type or authenticity) and the E.W.I. entrants explains the high incidence of entries by air.

Table 4:4 also identifies the types of visas used by this project's undocumented respondents to gain entry into the United States. Sample II shows that slightly more than 50 percent of the respondents had entered the U.S. with a visa and an additional one-third were E.W.I. - with nearly 16 percent of the sample of 778 respondents not answering. The more carefully controlled Sample III has a much lower proportion of "no answers" (5.7%), but basically the same proportion of those who entered the U.S. with a visa and then overstayed or otherwise violated the terms of these visas (53.1%). These values are for the subjects' last entry into the United States. The nearly 30 percent of that group who had entered the U.S. before, however, reported much higher rates of visa abuse (about three-quarters of all first trips to the U.S.) which, if valid, would seem to suggest that somehow the visa route to undocumented immigration to the U.S. may be either more difficult or generally less preferable for entries subsequent to the first one. In terms of enforcement, finally, one has to point to one category which dominates all others in terms of its contribution to undocumented migration in our sample: the B-2 visas issued to visitors for pleasure.

The closer examination of those who entered without initially valid documents also shows some other interesting patterns. Of the 57 persons who had been in the U.S. more than once (Sample III averaged 1.3 entries per person, and the average duration of the first trip to the U.S. by that group was nearly 28 months), 13 persons had entered without proper documents and of them 61.5 percent were E.W.I. cases. The proportions are sharper for Sample III respondents - nearly nine out of ten of them were E.W.I. cases (sample size n=79). In all, it is instructive to note that E.W.I. entries are higher than one might expect from the representation of Haitians and Mexicans in the sample (combined n=39) which may indicate that there may be a wider than expected dispersion across the U.S. by undocumented aliens who cross the U.S.-Mexican border. That this pattern of dispersion would follow the distribution of legal immigrants across the key states identified in Tables 1:3 and 2:1 is certainly a warranted assumption.

CONCLUSION

It is evident that the New York undocumented aliens in this sample are particularly resourceful individuals motivated by a mixture of complex personal and structural forces which effectively make them permanent additions to the economic and sociocultural life of the New York area. The average respondent had been in the U.S. since June of 1979 and one-third of the sample had been in the U.S. for more than 10 years. Two-fifths of the sample had been in the U.S. for less than two years. Between the two subsamples comprising Sample III, the New Jersey one is more mature (average entry date of June, 1978). In addition, since that sample was interviewed between six and nine months before the New York sample, its length of stay at the writing of this report is at least one year longer than the data indicate.

Our subjects also help support many of the assumptions about the process of illegal entry into the United States. Although visa overstayers are the majority of subjects, E.W.I. entrants are also heavily represented. These latter entrants came predominantly via the Florida coast and the Mexican border. Among the entire sample of respondents, 35 subjects (18.2%) utilized a smuggler to enter the U.S. - 20 of whom were found in the New York subsample. Smuggling fees averaged $1,000.00, but there was a wide discrepancy between the Newark subsample ($743.00) and the New York one ($1,202.00). A possible explanation might reflect the point of origin and entry differences between the two groups and the inflation in smugglers' charges as a result of increased U.S. Border Patrol and Coast Guard enforcement activities. The slight differences in the composition and length of stay of the two subsamples also suggest that the New York City respondents may have been "penalized" more by these higher fees.

The subjects have also experienced considerable success in evading the immigration authorities. Only 16 percent of Sample III had even been apprehended by INS - all but five only once. Interestingly, New Jersey proved to be more than twice as dangerous as New York in terms of the probability of being apprehended, and among those who had been apprehended equal proportions had been apprehended at the workplace and the street.

TABLE 4:5

THE DECISION TO EMIGRATE AND ASSISTANCE WITH EMIGRATION FOR
SAMPLE III RESPONDENTS

Who Influenced You in Your[1] Decision to Emigrate?	%	
The person emigrating	58.6	
Spouses	6.8	⎤
Parents	12.6	⎥ 26.7
Siblings	7.3	⎦
Others	14.7	
Total	100.0	
With Whom Did You Travel To the U.S.?		
Alone	68.6	
With spouse	4.7	
With children	5.2	
With friends	6.8	
Other	14.7	
Total	100.0	
Who Financed the Cost of the Trip?[2]		
The Emigrant (savings)	42.7	
The Emigrant (borrowed funds)	13.8	
Parents	13.8	
Siblings	4.2	
Spouse	3.1	
Other relatives	4.2	
Other	17.4	
Total	100.0	

[1] In 54.2 percent of the cases, the person most responsible for the trip to the U.S. was already in the U.S. at that time (nearly 70% for the New York subsample).

[2] In 45 percent of the cases not involving personal funds or borrowing, the funds came from a person who was already in the United States.

Finally, Sample III respondents also offered valuable insights on two other components of the emigration process: the questions of who influences one's decision to emigrate and how the trip is financed. Both questions offer unequivocal support to what are becoming the dominant paradigms on migration decision-making, that is that the decision is made jointly by the migrant and his/her family and that the migrant travels along well-developed, and smoothly functioning, ethnic pathways to the destination location. As can be seen in Table 4:5, among the potential influencers in the making of the decision to emigrate, spouses, parents, and siblings account for 26.7 of the main influencers and an additional 46.5 percent of the second most-important influencers (data not shown), while in over half of the cases (and even higher for the New York subsample) the person most responsible for the trip was already in the United States. In nearly 83 percent of the cases, the trip was financed by the emigrant's savings (42.7%), assistance from other family members (26.7%), and borrowing of funds by the emigrant (13.8%). In almost half of the cases where the emigrant did not finance his/her own trip, the funds came from the United States.

The importance of the ethnic networks in the migration process is further reinforced by the number of relatives and friends of the prospective immigrants who are already established in the United States. Two-thirds of the respondents had an average of 5.8 relatives in the U.S. with brothers and sisters leading the way (data not shown). Of them, nearly 80 percent offered assistance to the newcomer, which ranged from financial assistance (28.8% of the cases) and food and clothes (15.4%), to employment assistance (12.5%) and housing (10%). In addition, however, nearly two-thirds of the subjects of this study also had close friends in the United States who had come from their region. Forty-four percent of these respondents received assistance from those friends, mostly in finding employment.

CHAPTER FIVE

THE NEW YORK LABOR MARKET

One of the most divisive components of the debate about immigration in every country focuses on the impact of "immigrants" on the receiver's labor market. The present U.S. debate is no exception. Some recent analyses have studied the economic behavior of different groups of immigrants and have found them to be not only significant contributors to this country's socioeconomic well-being but also capable of substantial economic achievements. Some of these analyses argue that even during the early years of the twentieth century, the open nature of the U.S. labor market allowed immigrants who possessed only a modicum of appropriate human capital characteristics (but could adapt their skills to U.S. labor market needs), to advance economically after gaining some experience (See, Sowell, 1981; for an opposite view see Higham 1969; see also Bach, 1985). In more recent years, in fact, legal immigrants have been shown to be able to surpass the economic achievements of natives within about 15 years after immigration, and their offsprings have been shown to advance economically further than the offsprings of native citizens (Chiswick, 1979, 1984a; Simon, 1984).

The closer examination of some of these analyses, however, suggests that this issue is much more complex than it appears at first. For instance, the cohort of immigrants from the 1970 Decennial Census analyzed by Chiswick included mostly European immigrants who in fact brought with them many of the characteristics and skills necessary for economic success. Since the 1965 Act did not become effective until 1968, however, most of the Third World immigrants who dominated the 1980 Census immigrant categories were not in the U.S. (See, Table 1:3 Data Category 1) - and those who were here were often middle class and professional people. As a result, and unlike more recent immigrants, the 1970 cohort had the human capital profile which is necessary for substantial economic advancement without being hampered by ethnicity or race-based discrimination. Hence, simply transposing the finding from the economic advancement of the 1970 cohort of immigrants to the 1980 cohort, and using these assumptions as the basis for immigration legislation, may be whimsical at best.

In other words, while Chiswick's and other, essentially classical, economic analyses point to the economic mobility attained by immigrants from Europe in recent years, they ignore the structural conditions which often inhibit the advancement of certain immigrant groups especially when gender, ethnicity, and race - but also immigration status - enter into the picture. In this latter view, immigrants, and especially undocumented immigrants, play a specific labor market role which is often at the interstices of local labor markets. Although their presence in Southwestern agriculture or the service and certain manufacturing sectors of large cities is anything but vestigial, one of the most interesting - and least understood - aspects of the economic behavior of undocumented aliens is that they have penetrated virtually all layers and components of the labor market (**See**, Portes, 1979; Bach, 1985; Papademetriou, 1985a, 1983d, Piore, 1979; Berger and Piore, 1980). The debate heats up again, however, when one advances explanations for this penetration. The preferred explanation discussed at some length below is based on the modified concept of the segmentation of labor markets elaborated upon by many economists and sociologists. We should point out that although its founding assumption is heatedly contested by many mainstream economists and sociologists, its value in understanding and explaining migration is beyond dispute.

To the adherents to this concept, immigration is seen in the context of a dual (segmented) labor market whose lower (secondary) segment thrives on the "type" of labor offered by immigrant groups - especially regulated "contract" or "guestworker" labor and undocumented flows. By "type" of labor, the reference is to a workforce which will occupy low level jobs in such secondary labor market occupations as waste removal, simple sales and clerical jobs, cleaning, and simple processing and assembling; jobs in declining industries and in industrial plants with variable demand patterns (such as textiles, garments, dyeing, etc.); and, finally, in occupations with seasonal or erratic labor demands, such as agri-business, restaurants, hotels, and other tourist-catering activities. The characteristics of such jobs include low wages, poor working conditions, high instability (including high voluntary turnover by such workers as students, women, and undocumented immigrants), inferior social standing, low skill requirements, few opportunities for advancement, and an often highly personal relationship between worker and supervisor with only a token procedural due process for review of authority (Piore, 1979; Berger and Piore, 1980; Papademetriou, 1983d).

The segmentation arguments are anchored on a particular understanding of the internal structure and dynamics of labor markets and of the economic and political forces which shape the contour of specific markets. The upper (primary) tier of this dual labor market is comprised of firms which have considerable opportunities to influence the market place substantially. As a rule, they utilize high capital intensity to enhance productivity and are able to pass wage increases on to consumers. Firms in the lower tier, however, face an uncertain economic environment while participating primarily in only local markets. They rely on labor-intense production processes and are unable to pass on increases in their wage bill to consumers[16] (Piore, 1979; Edwards, 1979; Morales, 1983; Papademetriou, 1983d).

Similarly, the social relationships of production which prevail in each market are conditioned by each market's respective internal structural determinants. Accordingly, the primary market emphasizes stability and tenure in social relationships and reinforces it with the bureaucratization of management and production processes and the creation of internal markets. Work is stratified into finely graded job

---

16. This interpretation of the dualist argument on immigration is considerably more conditional than the one Piore makes in his 1979 work. For instance, where we refer to the ability of primary sector firms to "influence" the market place dualist argue that these firms could "control" the market place. Likewise, while we adopt the dualists analytical framework, we reject a number of unfortunate ideas, such as the question of inter-sectoral mobility discussed later in the text. For a complete analysis of the application of the dualist argument on immigration, see Papademetriou, 1983c.

ladders which provide for institutionalized promotion and advancement. The secondary market, on the other hand, if unstable, enforces work discipline in a more direct and arbitrary manner, cannot generate an internal market, and offers no incentive for either employer or worker to stabilize employment. It is precisely this market that some authors suggest often suffers from relative labor scarcity as the disadvantaged indigenous groups - as well as the second generation external and internal immigrants - may, during good economic times, reject secondary market jobs.

Many of the reasons for this rejection are said to center on the social component of secondary labor market jobs. These jobs usually carry negative social implications in addition to low wages, sub-standard working conditions and irregular tenure. Thus, most indigenous workers find them unappealing. But with economic uncertainty and demand unpredictability on the rise, not only is the secondary labor market constantly expanding and thirsting for more labor, but many previously primary labor markets are beginning to erode as a number of basic industries are going through phases of rapid industrial transformation. The need in these firms for what Morales (1983) calls "transitional" labor (i.e. principally, but not exclusively, undocumented workers) is anything but casual and often becomes a key element in corporate strategy for survival.

In the absence of immigrant labor, a locality's supply of marginal groups, such as women, students, and farmers may become quickly exhausted. Employers, then, would be confronted with the alternative of either investing in labor-saving machinery or increasing wages and benefits to attract and retain workers. Neither alternative is viable for many of the firms undergoing such a transformation. Hence, and in view of the abundance of undocumented workers, legal immigrant and native workers, fearful of redundancy and concerned about management threats to mechanize or go overseas, may allow firms to restructure wages and working conditions permanently downward. The latter course also involves a substantial qualitative change in the relationship between labor and management in formerly robust but currently fringe industries. The other threatening alternatives (from the perspective of the workers), such as relocation to areas of abundant supplies of inexpensive labor in the U.S. or abroad, must also be considered although their viability is shaped by such forces as market considerations, expense of relocation, and whether or not the operation is transferable (Piore, 1979; Edwards, 1979; Papademetriou, 1983d).

Under these circumstances, there is enormous pressure for workers to become more docile and become parts of an expendable, and thus flexible, labor pool. Undocumented aliens are the archetypical examples of such workers because they seem to satisfy most requirements of lower segment employment in that they form an elastic labor supply, regardless of the mode of their "recruitment" and their legal status. They are more expendable than indigenous labor because of a system which formally and informally gives them few procedural rights to contest changes in the terms of employment or dismissals. In some parts of the country, they are themselves only interested in temporary (i.e. flexible) commitments and will accept relatively modest wages. They are often suspicious of or afraid to organize, hard working, honest, and quite exploitable. Finally, certain types among undocumented workers, especially those who are repeat sojourners with viable family and economic interests in their home countries, may retain their home social identity for extended periods of time. By remaining rooted in the social structure of their point of origin, they view and treat work abroad in largely instrumental terms, in almost a social vacuum, with little regard to the social component of their job. While most undocumented immigrant workers, however, at least initially may view work abroad as only a temporary adjunct to their primary identity as members of a different social system, this is only a temporary and transitional attitude.

This most intriguing scenario has important implications for policy formulation. The most important one, we believe, is hinted at by the social context of the identity of foreign workers. As long as the social identities of undocumented migrants are anchored in their home community, these workers might indeed be the conjunctural and convenient target workers needed by marginal, traditional, and transitional industries. Once they begin to develop roots in the community of destination, and become more conscious of the social component of their jobs, a shift in their job aspirations is likely to occur and they may begin to avoid the jobs they initially coveted. At this point, these undocumented aliens become **de facto** permanent additions to the native labor force and host society and begin to behave like and compete with, but not necessarily displace, natives from better secondary segment jobs and, eventually, from jobs in the primary labor market. While this transition is taking place, the need for low skilled and flexible labor by marginal firms does not abate and additional numbers of foreign workers become engaged. In the process, entire categories of jobs may become labeled "undocumented or alien worker jobs", thus adding to their already negative social connotation; wages may fail to keep up with rising living costs because of the dampening effect of an abundant labor supply; working conditions may undergo only marginal improvements (if any at all); and, finally, one might observe the coexistence of high levels of unemployment among indigenous marginal groups with a constantly increasing demand for foreign workers (Papademetriou, 1983d).

While this scenario, and its underlying theoretical formulations, are clearly applicable in the majority of firms which employ large numbers of undocumented aliens, it appears to falter in an increasing number of cases where the profile of the industry or firm in question is one of robustness, rather than decline. Janitorial services (**See,** Mines, 1985) and a number of food services (Bailey and Freeman, 1981, 1983) would be examples of expanding industries which, however, rely heavily on undocumented labor. To see whether there might indeed be a fit between the theory and these cases, it might be necessary to look at variables other than demand-cycles and predictability. Instead, one could look at the organization of production, internal structure, social organization and prestige, wages, and the recruitment practices of these industries. When this is done, it becomes quite obvious that the theory's explanatory power encompasses such industries. The theory also holds when considering that in major international centers like New York, Miami, or Los Angeles, legal and undocumented workers play a role essential to the smooth functioning and continuing profitability of capital - a role which depends on a reciprocal process involving both the export of capital and the import of labor (Sassen-Koob, 1981; A. Marshall, 1982). Such labor importation, however, is heaviest in markets which already have large surpluses of workers. While this may appear paradoxical at first, it becomes much less so when one of the major assumptions of the segmentation thesis is kept in mind: that undocumented workers are particularly useful in labor markets which are undergoing significant transformations and assist marginal industries (such as garments) remain competitive. Whether in doing so they may also induce such industries to ignore many opportunities for the structural reorganization necessary to their long-term survival, as some have argued (A. Marshall, 1982), would require another analysis utilizing another of the designs discussed in Chapter 1.

As has already been alluded, labor market segmentation is not the only possible theoretical scenario. Classical, individualistic, and what may be called "assimilationist" (Bach, 1985) scenarios would view the entire migration process as part of a necessary spatial reallocation of labor to guarantee the optimum utilization of capital (Papademetriou, 1983d, 1985a; Wood, 1982). Although reductionist and static (See, Papademetriou and Hopple, 1982), such theories do provide a clear alternative both to the segmentation thesis and to structural explanations. The latter view all migration through the lens of disparities between economically advanced sectors (such as cities or "core" countries) and less developed ones (such as rural areas or "peripheral" countries). These two sectors exist in a system of cumulatively unequal interdependence characteristic of a single integral totality - the world capitalist economy (Portes and Walton, 1981; Wallestein, 1979; for an orthodox Marxist argument see Bonacich, 1981).

To recapitulate, the segmentation model is anchored on certain assumptions about the internal labor markets of advanced industrial societies and on a certain understanding of the economic and political forces which shape the contours and the composition of these labor markets (See, Berger and Piore, 1980). These forces influence not only the regional and sectoral concentration of foreign workers, but to a degree, also their skill and occupational profile. In view of the political and ecnomic conditions in the Caribbean region, and the finely tuned - although independent - networks among immigrant groups, neither the supply nor the destination of new undocumented workers is left to chance.

One of the segmentation school's most provocative theses is that the segmentation between the two markets is dichotomous and stable (Piore, 1979). Although Piore allows for some internal disaggregation, and he does insert craftsmen (artisans) between the primary and secondary sectors, both efforts are unconvincing. Allowing for a blue collar/white collar division within the secondary sector, and for an upper tier/lower tier distinction within the primary one are, at best, only afterthoughts and yield insignificant analytical gains. Likewise, positioning craftsmen in the void between the two sectors is little more than an expedient move to find a place for a group which defies the theoretical order.

Additional reflection might have shown that the boundaries of the two labor markets are in fact permeable, i.e., they allow for some inter-segment mobility (See, the discussion of the "human capital" model which follows), and that intra-sector mobility can also be significant. Furthermore, although upward inter-segment mobility may be indeed infrequent, inter-segment downward mobility can be substantial because of increasing instances of peripheralization of previously robust and/or technologically advanced industries. Morales' study is one recent example of this process (1983). In both cases, such devolution can be attributed to precipitous demand declines. In the former case, labor costs have given comparable industries abroad a marked competitive advantage (the New England shoe industry and most of the textile industry would fall under this category); in the latter case, failure to invest in new technology has robbed some heavy industries of international and, increasingly, internal markets (the United States steel industry is a good example).

Finally, and with regard to intra-market disaggregations, one must take into account their multiple segmentation. For instance, foreign-educated doctors occupy a similar position vis à vis graduates of U.S. medical schools as legal and undocumented foreign workers do vis à vis indigenous workers in the competitive (secondary) sector. A variation of the same theme might hold for technically and other highly qualified foreign personnel in Canada or the Middle East: in both cases, the demand for such personnel is finite. It will end with each society's ability to educate and train indigenous personnel for these jobs. Of course, Canada's response at that juncture will probably differ from that of the Middle East states by virtue of a permanent immigration policy which is skewed in favor of labor market considerations when compared to the revocable nature of immigration to the Arab region.

In contrast with the segmentation school adherents, the proponents of the "human capital" (classical) model begin with two different assumptions: that individuals can act as rational economic beings and "purchase" enhanced skills as they would any other commodity, and that wages reflect an individual's marginal productivity, i.e., his value to the employer (Sjaastad, 1962; Todaro, 1976). Education or technical training, and presumably, migration, would be seen as investment decisions involving time and money which give the investor a rate of return analogous to the slope of regression line. Similarly, income differences, as well as unemployment and poverty, might be considered as largely voluntary. That is, since long-term unemployment reflects the absence of relevant skills which would make one desirable to prospective employers, poverty and unemployment form a mutually reinforcing vicious circle.

While the analytical focus of the human capital model is predictably the individual, the "structuralist" model focuses on jobs and gradates them according to such criteria as prestige, access to power, unionization, race, sex, and ethnicity. It is particularly interested on inequalities in labor markets resulting from the confluence of both supply and demand-side reasons, i.e., individual and structural determinants. For structuralists, mobility between the two sectors is insignificant not because of the worker's own lack of human capital but because of institutional restraints, most notably discrimination. Thus, the distinction between the two sectors is not so much between skilled and unskilled workers as between "good" and "bad jobs" (Wachter, 1974; Tienda and Neidert, 1980; Beck et al., 1978).

The question of barriers to socioeconomic advancement has received a great deal of research attention, particularly as it pertains to ethnicity and race. The tentative direction of this research indicates that while ethnicity may have begun to dissipate as a major attribute of differentiation, it has again become extremely relevant with race intruding again as an important variable. Steinberg (1981) has assaulted the dominant U.S. paradigm on ethnicity, that of pluralism, and its presumed compatibility with equality. For him, the integrative mosaic of groups who share a fundamental commitment and loyalty to the U.S., while maintaining distinct cultural identities (Fuchs, 1984) may in fact reinforce existing class inequalities. If indeed the value of culture and other ethnic characteristics in explaining the success (or failure) of members of ethnic groups are secondary, such other variables as a group's race, place on the economy, and time of immigration might gain in significance in predicting that group's status in the socioeconomic ladder. Recent research on Hispanics points to these much more complex explanations for the lower economic achievement of that group (See, Borjas, 1982; Ford Foundation, 1984; Tienda and Neidert, 1982; Tienda, 1983a, b; Papademetriou, 1983c; Mann and Salvo, 1984).

EMPLOYMENT CHARACTERISTICS

Before discussing the employment characteristics of our samples of undocumented aliens, it is important to emphasize again certain rather unique aspects of our survey which allow us to obtain longitudinal labor market information about our respondents. We have asked, and are reporting here, information on up to three different labor market experiences of the study's subjects. Their present job, previous job (i.e., job held immediately prior to their present one), and first job (i.e., the job held when the subject first came to the United States). Altogether, information was obtained on 323 distinct labor market experiences - 138 presently held jobs, 71 previous jobs, and 114 first jobs.

The process of obtaining employment in the New York area by respondents can be anticipated somewhat by the data from Chapters 3 and 4. Direct questioning of the study's subjects yielded some very consistent results. Table 5:1 indicates that in each of the jobs held by respondents, friends and relatives were responsible for finding about two-thirds of them. In an additional one case in five, our respondents found their own jobs either by asking the employer directly or by going through newspaper ads and employment agencies.

The significance of this finding must not be lost. Not only are ethnic networks quite adept in assisting new

TABLE 5:1
METHOD OF FINDING A JOB AND IDENTIFICATION REQUIREMENTS*

	Present (n=138) %	Previous (n=71) %	First[1] (n=114) %
Friends/relatives in the U.S.	66.2	60.6	63.2
Asked employer directly	14.4	12.7	15.8
Newspaper ad	3.6	7.0	2.6
Employment agency	5.0	5.6	6.1
Friends/ relatives in home country	2.2	1.4	3.5
Recruited by employer	1.4	5.6	2.6
Other	7.2	7.0	6.2
Total	100.0	99.9	100.0

Were You Asked to Give Your Social Security Number?

Yes	n=106	79.9 (69.8)	n = 33	67.6 (60.00)	n=70 61.9 (51.0)
No		22.1		32.4	38.1

Were You Asked to Show Any Identification?

Yes	n=78	56.5	n=33	46.5 (28.6)	n=61 53.1 (43.1)
No		43.5		54.9	46.9

If "Yes", What Type of Identification?

INS papers	21.8	18.2	15.3
Social Security card	74.4	78.8	79.7
Driver's license	2.6	3.0	3.3
Other	1.2	—	1.7
Total	100.0	100.0	100.0

* Numbers in parentheses reflect values for the N.Y. sample. The convention will be that these values will appear only when there is more than a 6 percent difference between the value for the entire sample and that for either of the subsamples.

[1] Those who had only two jobs in the U.S. used the categories of "present" and "first" job.

undocumented aliens in all stages of the migration process but, more importantly, it seems that the recruitment and placement process for most of the three jobs held by our Sample III respondents consisted of an informal, "word of mouth" mechanism - much in the same manner observed by Martin (1984) in his study of the recruitment process by California labor-intensive perishable-crop agricultural growers.

This finding is not totally unexpected. Obtaining jobs through informal means is certainly widespread in many industries regardless of whether they employ undocumented aliens or not. Yet, its confirmation at this scale does provide ammunition to those who might argue that undocumented aliens deprive indigenous workers with similar labor market characteristics from many jobs in industries where the former are dominant. In other words, if informal recruitment dynamics dominate labor markets where there are substantial concentrations of undocumented aliens, many job openings which might have otherwise become available to the registered unemployed may never do so. The major counterargument to this position is only the theoretical one that the presence of large supplies of low wage workers, by making one key production factor (labor) cheap, may encourage other similar industries to remain labor-intense. In extreme cases, such industries may even opt to revert to more labor intensive production methods. Such "investment decisions", in turn, would multipy the number of jobs available in low wage labor markets and absorb more disadvantaged indigenous and immigrant workers - as well as additional undocumented aliens (Simon, 1984; Reubens, 1978; Chiswick, 1979).

But which are the industries employing our respondents? Table 5:2 offers information on the occupational structure of Sample III subjects which enables us to have a clearer idea of where they are employed. The modal economic activity of the respondents is employment in unskilled manufacturing jobs. For all three jobs, between 25 and 30 percent of the sample reported employment of that type, followed by employment as semi-skilled industrial workers. In all, between 42.5 and 48 percent of respondents in each job held positions in the manufacturing sector. A second important occupation for subjects was the hotel, restaurant, and retail services industry which occupied a declining proportion of respondents between the first and present jobs. This may suggest that employment in that industry may be viewed as transitional, i.e., as a stop-gap while one is looking for a better job. Among other services, financial, community and real estate services seem also to be important, followed by transportation and construction. It is obvious from Table 5:2, and from data indicating that only a small proportion of subjects are in the professional, technical, and managerial components of their

TABLE 5:2

OCCUPATIONAL STRUCTURE FOR SAMPLE III (IN %)

Economic Activity[1]	Present Job		Previous Job		First Job	
	Total Sample	New York Sample	Total Sample	New York Sample	Total Sample	New York Sample
Primary Sector Activities[2]	—	—	—	—	—	—
Manufacturing — Unskilled	26.9	22.7	29.0	35.3	25.7	21.6
Manufacturing — Semi- Skilled	18.2	12.2	11.6	5.9	15.9	9.8
Manufacturing — Skilled (technician)	2.9	3.0	5.8	5.9	0.9	—
Construction	1.4	1.5	1.5	2.9	0.9	—
Hotel/Restaurants/ Retail Services	5.0	7.6	8.7	5.9	14.2	5.9
Transportation	2.9	3.0	4.3	5.9	1.8	2.0
Financial Services	4.3	7.6	7.2	11.7	2.7	5.9
Social/Community/ Personnel Services	7.2	4.5	5.8	—	4.4	2.0
Other	30.9	37.8	16.1	26.5	33.6	52.9
Total	99.9	99.9	100.0	100.1	100.1	100.0

[1] In accordance with the International Labour Office's International Sandard Classification of Occupations.

[2] Agriculture, mining and quarrying.

occupations (data not shown), that many among these undocumented aliens undergo at least an initial substantial drop in occupational status as a result of emigration (See, discussion in Chapter 3). It is also obvious from Table 5:2 that there are substantial differences between the New Jersey and the New York subsamples. The latter exhibits lower concentration in the manufacturing sectors and higher concentration in financial and other services, as well as a greater dispersion among jobs outside of those specifically identified here. A large share of this variation can be attributed both to the differences in tenure between the two groups and differences in the labor markets between New York City and northern New Jersey - the former more oriented toward services, the latter more industrial.

These tendencies receive additional confirmation when considering certain relevant workplace characteristics for the firms employing our subjects. Large majorities of these undocumented aliens are employed in rather small firms employing between six and 100 workers, followed by firms employing between one and five workers and firms employing between 101 and 250 workers (Table 5:3). There are differences again between the two subsamples. New York undocumented aliens have a tendency toward the smaller size firms which have been the mainstay of successive waves of new immigrants (Badillo-Veiga et al., 1979).

Further investigation of the job characteristics of Sample III respondents suggests that substantial majorities of those currently holding a job believe that they enjoy job security and among those who have changed jobs about two-thirds reported that the change occurred at their own initiative. Among those who had changed jobs, about 45 percent did so because they "found a better job", another 15 percent because their previous job was "disagreeable", and another 10 percent because of health matters and especially pregnancy (data not shown). In other words, the profile which emerges from these data is that our respondents can be mobile although they feel secure in their jobs.

LABOR MARKET STATUS AND WAGES

Table 5:4 reports the employment rates of the three samples. It shows employment rates ranging from a little over 40 percent for Sample I to nearly 72 percent for Sample III.

TABLE 5:3
Selected Workplace Characteristics Disaggregated for N.Y. Sample (in %)

	Present		Previous		First	
	Total	N.Y.	Total	N.Y.	Total	N.Y.
Employee Benefits						
Medical	47.5	36.4	31.7	27.8	19.8	16.0
Life insurance	20.9	21.2	9.9	8.3	10.8	12.0
Retirement	12.9	9.1	9.9	8.3	7.2	6.0
Sick time	34.5	36.4	22.6	19.4	14.4	14.0
Vacation days [1]	62.6	54.5	34.9	22.2	32.4	26.0
Maternity leave	14.1	10.9	6.0	2.8	3.7	2.0
Terms of Employment						
Hired explicitly for a specific contract of a limited duration	6.6	6.3	7.0	5.5	10.1	12.2
Laid-off according to seniority	67.6	68.6	49.2	48.4	42.0	34.7
Expect to be called back according to seniority	68.2	68.4	44.9	50.0	35.8	41.4
Reasons for Leaving Job						
Own accord	—	—	61.1	69.4	67.6	68.0
Employer initiative (fired/laid-off)	—	—	33.3	30.6	28.7	28.0
Workplace Size						
1-5	17.6	21.4	16.4	11.8	18.4	21.4
6-25	27.2	30.4	37.3	41.2	36.9	35.7
26-100	35.2	30.4	37.3	29.4	24.3	28.6
101-250	14.4	14.3	9.0	14.7	15.5	11.9
Over 251	5.6	4.4	—	9.9	4.9	2.4
Total	100.0	100.0	100.0	100.0	99.9	100.0
Taxes Were Withheld	76.1	68.2	75.0	75.0	61.3	54.0

[1] The average number of paid vacation days was 8.6, 8.7 and 7.7 respectively for each of the three jobs.

[2] When probed, those who left their jobs voluntarily mentioned as the key reasons "found a better job" (about 45%), "something disagreeable about the job" (about 15% of the total), and health matters (including pregnancy) (about 10 percent).

[3] Nearly 60 percent among them noted that they were laid-off because "business was bad".

UNDOCUMENTED ALIENS

TABLE 5:4
LABOR MARKET STATUS

Status	Sample I N	Sample I %	Sample II N	Sample II %	Sample III * N	Sample III * %
Sample size	836	100.0	778	100.0	192(99)	100.0
Employed	355	41.4	447	57.4	138(67)	71.9(67.6)
Unemployed and currently looking for work	—	—	—	—	15(3)	7.8(3.0)
Subtotal	355	41.4	447	57.4	153(70)	79.7(70.6)
Of those looking for work, average search time (months)	—	—	—	—	4.7 (8.7)	
Not looking for work	—	—	—	—	32(25)	16.7(25.3)
No information	48.1	58.6	33.1	42.6	7(4)	3.6(4.1)
Of those not looking for work:						
Pregnant	—	—	—	—	1(1)	—
Stays home to care for family	—	—	—	—	6(4)	—
Going to school	—	—	—	—	4(3)	—
Health reasons	—	—	—	—	3(2)	—
Does not need the money	—	—	—	—	3(3)	—
Other	—	—	—	—	15(12)	—
Effective unemployment rates[3]	—	—	—	—	153(73)	9.8(4.1)

* Numbers in parentheses are for the New York sample.

[1] The average figure reported here is extremely skewed because one subject reported a 24 month search for work.

[2] Of those employed, 9 subjects (3 in New York) had been self-employed. The average length of this employment was 32 months, and it earned an average income of $11,739 per year. Five of these subjects see this employment as permanent.

[3] These are the "effective unemployment rates" for the samples. They have been figured out by using as the sample size the total of those employed and those looking for a job, i.e. the total size of the sample's labor force.

One should be careful, however, not to assume here that undocumented aliens have high rates of unemployment. Instead, the rates here are uneven because the person interviewed in every instance was the person who approached the agency for a service. At times, that service was job placement - hence the rate of "unemployment" may be artificially high. Furthermore, because of the time-consuming nature of obtaining a service, the spouse without employment was more likely to undertake this task. Finally, Samples I and II also include a small number of minors (16-to-18 year olds) while Sample III questionnaires were administered only to those over 18 years of age and, hence, employable.

Looking further at the data reported on Table 5:4, one notes that only 7.8 percent of the total Sample III can be said to be unemployed according to the standard definition of unemployment as those who are without a job and are looking for work. An additional 16.7 percent are not considered to be in the labor market because they are not looking for a job. For those who were unemployed and were actively looking for a job during the 12 months prior to the interview, the average length of successful search time was 4.7 months - a figure which appears higher than that for the six legal immigrant groups profiled in Table 1:3 (Data Category 8) but which is skewed upward because of a single case of one long-term unemployed person (See, Table 5:4, footnote 1). Overall, the effective unemployment rate for the Sample III economically active respondents (i.e., those available to work) is 9.8 percent. Information was also obtained on those who were not available to the labor market at the time of the interview. Responses varied widely but caring for the family and going to school were the categories which attracted the largest numbers of responses.

One notes again some substantial differences between the two subsamples which comprise Sample III. The New York subsample seems to be more thoroughly incorporated in the area's labor market with an effective unemployment rate of only 4.1 percent, well under half that for the City as a whole (8.6% for 1982 and 1983) and several times smaller than the unemployment rate for blacks (13.8 and 14.5% for the same two years) or Hispanics (13.2 and 12.2%, see, U.S. Department of Labor 1985). One tentative explanation for this finding might lie with the opportunities for employment in the large ethnic service sector available in New York City (A. Marshall, 1982). The Northern New Jersey respondents, on the other hand, have to rely on more formal manufacturing sector jobs. Also of interest is the figure for self-employment. Nine of our employed subjects (three for New York) are long-term self-employed (average length of self-employment of 32 months) earning a much higher income than the mean for our group – almost $12,000 per year.

Of those employed, only small percentages earned less than the minimum wage – a finding confirmed by virtually all field studies on undocumented aliens outside of the agriculture or apparel industries. Only 16.2 percent of Sample I respondents profiled in Table 5:5 earned $3.35 or under per hour, the U.S. minimum wage since 1980. The figures for Sample II were 22.5 percent for their present job and 41.8 percent for their last job. One should be careful, however, not to draw unwarranted conclusions from these figures. First, the data for the last job of Sample II subjects include large numbers of jobs held before 1980, when the minimum wage was less than $3.35 per hour. Second, the data did not allow us to disaggregate this wage category into those who earned $3.35 per hour and those earning less than that amount. At the same time, however, one should not attach much significance to the figure of $3.35 per hour. Minimum wage has not gone up for the past five years and many employers in the manufacturing sector in the Northeast offer entry wages which are 30 to 65 cents per hour higher than the federally mandated minimum.

Sample III data do allow for the necessary disaggregation of wages and indicate a more positive wage profile for the respondents. Only 3.6 percent earned less than the minimum wage in their present position, compared with 9.9 percent for their previous jobs and 34.2 percent for their first job. Although these latter two figures may appear troubling at first, one must bear in mind that one-third of this sample has been in the U.S. for over 10 years. As one would expect, the modal wage category for present and previous jobs had by Sample III workers was the $3.36 to $4.99 per hour although nearly one-third of the current jobs held by the respondents were paid between $5.00 and $7.00 per hour and an additional 17.3 percent were paid over that figure.

TABLE 5:5
HOURLY WAGES

Hourly Wage	Sample I		Sample II				Sample III[1]					
			Present		Last		Present		Previous		First	
	No.	%	No.	%	No.	%	No.	%	No.	%	No.	%
Under 3.35	–	–	–	–	–	–	5	3.6	7	9.9	38	34.2
3.35*	68	16.2	100	22.5	94	41.8	17	8.7	20	28.1	18	16.3
3.36-4.99	275	65.3	204	45.8	96	42.7	54	39.1	27	38.0	37	33.3
5.00-6.99	51	12.1	96	21.6	26	11.6	43	31.2	10	14.1	17	15.3
7.00-8.99	16	3.8	32	7.2	7	3.1	18	13.0	6	8.5	1	0.9
Over 9.00	11	2.6	13	2.9	2	0.9	6	4.3	1	1.4	–	–
Total	421	100.0	445	100.0	225	100.1	138	99.9	71	100.0	111	100.0
Total Sample Size	856		778		778		192		192		192	
Average	3.65		4.62		4.02		5.16[2]		4.34[3]		3.60[4]	

* For Samples I and II, this category includes all those earning "$3.35 and under" per hour.

[1] The total number of jobs ever held by all subjects for each sample. For Sample III, 62 subjects had held only one job, 39 two jobs, 26 three jobs, and 40 over three jobs, but information was collected only on three of them. In all, 167 subjects had had some work experience in the U.S.

[2] For New York, $5.75/hour.

[3] For New York, $4.50/hour.

[4] For New York, $3.89/hour.

The average wage for those employed from Sample I was $3.65 per hour; for Sample II, it was $4.62 for the present job and $4.02 for the previous job; finally, the average hourly earnings for Sample III respondents for their first job in the U.S. were $3.60 per hour, for the job previous to their current one $4.34, and for their current job $5.16 per hour. The figures for the New York subsample were slightly higher for the previous two jobs but 11 percent higher than those for the total sample for the current job. Although these figures are lower than the 1983 mean hourly wage earnings of production workers for either New Jersey ($8.66) or New York ($8.84), the job mix of our sample accounts for much of this difference (U.S. Department of Labor, 1985, Table 86). In fact, the figures here are comparable with the $4.36 hourly wage reported by Pessar's informants in 1982. The average hourly wage earnings of our Sample III subjects are also similar to those reported by Poitras for his Costa Rican subjects (but not for his Salvadoran ones who earned about 17 percent less).

Again, however, one notices an appreciable gap between earnings by Mexicans and other undocumented immigrants originating in the Caribbean and elsewhere. In spite of the problem with comparability across time, the North/Houstoun study (1976) found that Mexican illegals earned between one-quarter and 43 percent less than other identifiable groupings of apprehended undocumented aliens (such as whites, Eastern Hemisphere aliens, and visa abusers); Muller (1984) found low annual wages for all workers in low-level services and wages of about $5.00 per hour for jobs in low-wage manufacturing; and CENIET subjects who worked in the U.S. illegally in 1978 earned an average wage of $23.00 per day for work which concentrated heavily in agriculture (Ranney and Kossoudji, 1983). Immigration and Naturalization statistics on apprehended undocumented aliens, finally, also show non-agricultural undocumented aliens earning in 1981 and 1982 average wages roughly comparable to Sample II subjects, although of an upper range considerable lower than these (dates comparable to those for the current jobs of our Sample II respondents, see, Houstoun, 1983).

Another way of looking at the economic condition of a group is by obtaining its household income. That income was ascertained for Sample III and registered a mean value of $19,574.00 (Table 6:4). As is usually the case with immigrant households, several members pool their income to the point where the household earns an amount substantial enough not only to allow it to enjoy an economic status dramatically higher than that available to it in its home country but also to build some equity in the U.S. The comparable data reported for Sample II are also of interest. Perhaps as one might expect, subjects from Sample II who originated in the Eastern Hemisphere make a substantially better showing in terms both of annual salary and average hourly wage than those coming from the Western Hemisphere, thus confirming a finding of the North/Houstoun study (1976), as well as of Chiswick's analysis of the same data set (1984) and of INS wage data for the apprehended (Houstoun, 1983).

Table 5:6 disaggregates the hourly wage data by sex and a number of expected differences emerge. Males are much more likely than females to earn wages over $7.00 per hour across all three jobs on which data were collected. By the same token, much larger proportions of women than men earned under $5.00 per hour. This is a universal finding, of course, and applies not only to undocumented aliens and immigrants from the Hemisphere, but also to all other immigrants and natives.

TABLE 5:6

HOURLY WAGES, BY SEX, SAMPLE III (IN %)

Hourly Wages (in $)	Present Job		Previous Job		First Job	
	M	F	M	F	M	F
$3.35 and under	10.6	14.2	27.5	51.6	44.0	57.6
3.36-4.99	29.3	50.8	35.0	41.9	37.4	28.9
5.00-6.99	33.4	28.6	20.0	6.4	16.9	13.4
7.00-8.99	20.0	4.8	15.0	—	1.6	—
Over 9.00	6.6	1.5	2.5	—	—	—
Total	99.9	99.9	100.0	99.9	99.9	99.9

While a number of other labor market characteristics of the study's subjects might be of less significance in establishing the place of these samples of undocumented aliens in the U.S. labor market, they are of substantial significance to the policy debate on immigration reform. For instance, Table 5:1 reports on the type of identification documents which employers typically required of respondents as they tried to obtain their positions. In four out of five cases involving the present jobs of subjects, employers asked for a social security number. Two trends, however, might be equally significant. First, employers of the New York subsample were much less diligent in their asking for a social security number for their job applicants than their counterparts in Northern New Jersey. This variance is much higher than one would expect from the differences in the workplace and occupational structure characteristics of the two subsamples. Second, diligence both in asking job applicants for a social security number and asking to see some identification (mostly a social security card but, in about 20% of the cases, INS work authorization documents) has increased substantially with each new job, with the most notable increase occurring between the previous and present jobs. The most likely explanation for this finding is that it reflects increasing public awareness of the issue stemming both from the publicity surrounding this nation's attempt to change its immigration laws, as well as from highly publicized INS enforcement actions. In other words, both of these events are "bearing fruit" in terms of increasing "self-policing" by employers. Whether this action already has serious consequences for this nation's ethnic minorities by leading to discrimination against foreign-looking applicants with accents (many of whom are legal residents and citizens) - as the civil liberties community and Hispanic groups charge - is an issue which our data cannot address.

Finally, one must also consider the implications of another intriguing datum - the rates of unionization in the places where respondents from Sample III are employed and the rates of trade union membership by these subjects. Table 5:7 indicates that 37.3 percent of the respondents currently worked for places which are unionized.

The substantial increase among each of the three jobs on which information was collected, and the lower data for New York (not shown) reflects again the differences between the two subsamples discussed in the previous paragraph. In addition, about 70 percent of the study's subjects currently employed in places where there is a union are members of such unions (up considerably from prior jobs). Finally, few of the respondents reported having belonged to a labor syndicate in their home countries, a result not totally unexpected in view of both their occupational background discussed in Chapter 3 and the low unionization rates for most Latin American countries (ILO, 1982).

TABLE 5:7
UNIONIZATION*

	Present %	Previous %	First %
Is/ Was Your Employment Plac Unionized?			
Yes	37.3	27.5	22.6
No	62.7	72.5	77.4
Are/ Were You a Member of That Union? (n=52)			
Yes	69.2	52	54.8
No	30.8	48	45.2
Did You Belong to a Trade Union at Your Home Country?			
Yes	14.8	8.3	16.1
No	85.2	91.7	83.9

* This question was asked for the previous and first jobs only if the subject had not had a chance to answer it before (i.e., did not have a job at present and/ or only had two jobs before).

These findings are quite significant in that, when taken together with the data on the occupational structure of the sample reported on Table 5:2, one realizes that the respondents work in both primary and secondary sector places where union membership is available and, when given the option, they become union members at substantial rates. In view of this finding, and if this finding is generalizable to the larger New York area, one might suggest that union membership has not been negatively affected by the presence of undocumented aliens in the New York area. Even more important, however, may be the implications of this finding for the position of the labor movement on the immigration reform debate; the explanation which union membership offers for the relatively high hourly wages among substantial proportions of this study's subjects; and the depth of the incorporation of the sample into the mainstream of the area's labor market.

UTILIZATION OF SERVICES AND PARTICIPATION IN INCOME TRANSFER PROGRAMS

One of the questions which have captured the largest share of U.S. media attention about undocumented immigration is the matter of whether undocumented aliens use more in services than they contribute to the public coffers and whether they receive unauthorized public assistance. This is a particularly difficult set of questions to address because the potential for respondent bias is high (due to the "threatening" nature of the questions - see, Appendix II) and the analysis of the costs and benefits of undocumented aliens on the entire gamut of federal, state, and local services and infrastructure extremely complicated.

One way to put some general analytical order to this complex question might be to utilize the organizing framework developed by Greenwood (1979). Greenwood argues persuasively that the cost of immigrant usage of public goods (services) depends largely on whether such goods are produced under conditions of falling or rising average cost. Since immigrants usually have a low local tax base (because of low rates of property ownership), they contribute less than their share toward the cost of services which they use; this leads to

higher than average contributions on the part of the natives
(principally in infrastructure areas). Furthermore, the "price"
for such infrastructure will also rise (in non-pecuniary terms)
because their quality deteriorates due to overusage, or, in the
case of finite resources (such as police), because they are
spread more thinly. These increasing costs must be
juxtaposed, however, against the declining average cost of
producing certain other public goods (services such as
retirement, unemployment, national defense, agricultural
assistance, etc.). These are areas where the participation of
migrants through tax and withholding contributions makes a
marked difference. Furthermore, one must also consider such
other factors as the substantial subsidies to the U.S. by the
countries of immigrant origin which have absorbed the cost of
upbringing, education and training of the undocumented aliens,
the opportunities migrants afford some of the indigenous
primary labor market-based population for social and
economic advancement, and the often non-quanitifiable
negative consequences of the formation of a permanent
underclass of workers who are suspended at the social fringes
of societies (Papademetriou and Miller, 1983b).

Among Sample II respondents, 36.2 percent of the entire
sample possessed a social security card while an additional 1.0
percent was using someone else's card. The data for Sample
III allow us a much more in-depth analysis. Over 70 percent of
the total number of our Sample III respondents, and a
remarkable 89 percent of those either employed or seeking
employment in the labor market (n=153, see, Table 5:4), had
social security cards. An additional 6.3 percent (or 8% of
those in the labor market) were using someone else's card.
Under further examination, it appears that 47.4 percent of the
total sample (60% of those in the U.S. labor market) had social
security cards issued by the Social Security Administration.
Although an additional 17.6 percent of those in the labor
market (13.9% of the total sample) had "employment
authorizing" cards, the assumption can be made that these
cards were not valid.

Table 5:8 also offers information on the withholding
taxes paid by respondents. Although only 44.9 percent of
Sample II respondents had Federal Insurance Contribution Act

(FICA) and all other payroll taxes withheld, this represented virtually all employed respondents. The data do not demonstrate what part of the entire sample was actually unemployed and looking for employment. Sample III confirms that finding.

TABLE 5:8

TAX PAYMENTS AND SOCIAL SECURITY CARD INFORMATION

	Sample II (n=778)		Sample III (n=192)	
	%	N	%	N
Have social security tax (FICA and other taxes) withheld by employer	44.9	349	68.8	132
Have filed federal tax returns in the past	—	—	53.6	103
Filed federal tax returns this year	—	—	49.0	94
Filings this year (n=94) as a percent of those who had FICA and other taxes withheld (n=132)	—	—	71.2	94
Own a U.S. social security card	36.2	282	70.8	136
Use someone else's card	1.0	4	6.3	12
Own a social security card valid for employment[1]	—	—	61.5	118
Card was issued by the Social Security Administration[2]	—	—	47.4	91

[1] Banks also issue a set of numbers to depositors for IRS reporting purposes, as do universities with student numbers, etc. Eighteen social security numbers were found to belong in these latter categories.

[2] Significantly, 106 cards were issued in the post-1973 period, when presumably the identification requirements for issuing such cards were tightened significantly.

Of those among Sample III subjects who were employed (n=138), 132 or 96 percent had FICA and other taxes withheld by their employer. In a fashion perhaps more widespread than researchers often think, however, only 52.1 percent of the total sample (n=100) had ever filed federal tax returns in the past, and an even lesser number (n=94 or 71.2% of those who had payroll taxes withheld) had filed during their last working year.

These findings are extremely significant for a number of reasons. First of all, they discount speculation that at least those undocumented aliens whom we are studying may be participants in and contributors to an underground economy in which few individuals declare their incomes or have any papers which can be considered by employers as authorized employment. Virtually all respondents have social security cards and participate fully in payroll deduction plans. The former has serious implications for current proposals in the U.S. Congress which would try to stop the unauthorized employment of undocumented aliens by requiring employers simply to verify that job applicants can produce such documents as social security cards and drivers' licenses. Obviously, if the policy objective is to reduce the employment of undocumented aliens, any system relying on existing social security cards would only prevent a tiny minority (11%) of respondents who are in the New York area labor force from "lawfully" obtaining employment. The low filing of tax returns by this sample of undocumented aliens also means something of great significance to the tax coffers of this nation: that almost 90 percent of the subjects subsidize tax-supported federal, state, and city programs without filing returns which, in view of the total income of the average undocumented household (under $20,000 per year), would have led to substantial refunds.

Unlike some recent studies which have tried to model and estimate the net contribution of undocumented aliens both as supporters of such tax-based services and as consumers of these services, we will not undertake such an analysis at this time. Suffice it to refer the reader to the findings of some other studies and suggest the degree of the probable fit of our data with these findings. The comparisons will be made with recent works about the contributions of legal immigrants to the public coffers by Simon (1983, 1985), Weintraub and Cardenas (1984), and Muller (1984).

Simon's frequently provocative and controversial work often relies on formal models to theorize about the effects of immigrants and, indirectly, undocumented aliens on native capital. Yet, much of his policy relevant work relies on government collected data (such as the Surveys of Economic Opportunity) to establish the economic behavior of immigrant families and then tries to extrapolate the net effect of an average immigrant family on social services. He finds that for the first 12 years than "average" family uses substantially less in public services than an "average" native family. Use of public services by immigrant families becomes roughly equal to that of native families after that. Extrapolating these findings to undocumented families who are legally denied participation in many of the programs for which legal immigrants are eligible would only augment the advantage of undocumented aliens to public coffers - and to legal immigrant and U.S. native families.

Weintraub and Cardenas use a different approach to reach basically a similar conclusion. Their purpose was to address the issue of use of public services by undocumented aliens directly by estimating the degree and costs of usage of a wide array of services by this population. Such services included many which are rarely examined by researchers in this area - such as public recreation facilities, legal assistance, and public transportation. They concluded that state revenues from the undocumented exceeded the cost of the services offered to them by the state, although localities probably provided more in services than the amount of their reimbursement by taxes. Interestingly, the authors also found that together, states and localities also come out ahead overall - a result hotly disputed by Huddle and his associates (1985) who would like to include in these estimates the cost of unemployment compensation paid to unemployed legal U.S. workers who are presumed to have been displaced by undocumented aliens.

Finally, Muller's analysis of the Southern California economy (1984) is also relevant in terms of understanding the place of undocumented aliens in this entire area of social service delivery. Although Muller did not study undocumented aliens directly, he shows that undocumetned aliens contribute more than they use in all programs funded by regular payroll deductions, unemployment insurance and sales taxes.

Furthermore, undocumented aliens are likely to use most services at lower rates than those for legal workers, except probably health and education. He concludes that in the aggregate, undocumented alien households, as well as over 50 percent of all Mexican American households, probably use more in services than they pay in taxes. This is largely due to California's progressive state income tax structure which includes generous tax credits for household incomes likely to be earned by most undocumented alien households. This results in two-thirds of California households receiving more in services than they pay in taxes.

Data here corroborate many of these findings. For instance nearly half of Sample III respondents receive medical benefits from their present employer, which relieves some of their potential impact on publicly supported medical services (Table 5:3). And although 40 percent of the sample had used a

TABLE 5:9
INCOME TRANSFER AND MAINTENANCE USAGE BY UNDOCUMENTED ALIENS

Income Transfer and Maintenance Category	Sample II		Sample III	
	(n=776)		(n=190)	
	N	%	N	%
AFDC	2	0.3	1	0.5
Food Stamps	7	0.8	3	1.5
Unemployment Compensation	30	3.9	10	5.4
Workmen's Compensation	2	0.3	—	—
General Assistance	5	0.6	1	0.5
Temporary Disability	1	0.1	1	0.5
Medicaid	4	0.5	1	0.5
Other	2	0.3	2	1.1
Total	53	6.8	19	10.0

hospital or public health clinic during the previous 12 months (data not shown), information on the mode of payment for such services indicates that only in one out of five instances were such services potentially not paid for (i.e., the respondents indicated an "other" form of payment when given the opportunity to choose among "paying by cash/check", "own health insurance coverages", "employer provided insurance", or "the service was free" [4.8 %]). Furthermore, and consistent with virtually all previous findings in this area of study, subjects report insignificant rates of participation in income transfer programs (Table 5:9). Even if the "threatening" nature of the questions about income transfer programs has introduced a substantial and consistent bias (underreporting) to the answers of subjects in this area, and bearing in mind that large numbers in the households of the sample of undocumented aliens include U.S. legal residents and citizens who have a legal claim to these programs, the only areas of possible "abuse" are in unemployment compensation and food stamps. Respectively, 3.9 and 0.8 percent of Sample II respondents, and 5.4 and 1.5 percent of Sample III respondents had made use of these programs.

CONCLUSION

Although a number of issues have received large shares of the attention of policy-makers and the public during the ongoing debate on immigration reform, the issues of the impact of undocumented aliens on the labor market and their use of public infrastructure and services have dominated the debate. Findings here shed considerable light on these areas and test some of the assumptions made by the various theories highlighted in the introduction of this chapter.

For instance, it is clear that subjects do indeed work in a modified secondary labor market - a market which exhibits many but not all of the key characteristics suggested by the segmentation school. At the same time, it is also clear that some of the assumptions of this model need to be modified to include firms which could accommodate the nonconforming findings of Morales (1983), Muller (1984), Pessar (1982a, 1984), Badillo-Veiga et al. (1979), and this study. The model falters in at least three important areas: the internal structure of the firms (especially with regard to worker organization), the

assumption that the jobs that undocumented aliens take are
dead-end jobs (and are therefore shunned by legal immigrants
and native workers), and the matter of inter-segment mobility.

Briefly, the manufacturing firms employing the
respondents have high rates of unionization and our
respondents join these unions at substantial rates.
Furthermore, and as a result, substantial but varying
proportions among respondents enjoyed a full array of benefits
- ranging from medical (47.5%) and sick and vacation time
(34.5 and 62.6% respectively), to life insurance (20.9%),
retirement (12.9%) and maternity leave (14.1%; see Table
5:3). Yet, and although the data do not profile specific firms,
their moderate size and the wages paid to respondents suggest
that although they are not the type of firms which would meet
all of the criteria of primary labor market firms developed by
the dualists, they are also not archetypes of secondary labor
market firms. Furthermore, this sample does not indicate a
flattening of wages at the lowest end of the hourly earning
scale. Instead, there seems to exist a fairly spread-out wage
hierarchy which is not out of line with wages for 1983 for the
entire Northeast reported by the Labor Department in the
occupations where subjects are employed (U.S. Department of
Labor, 1985, Table 96).

This showing probably reflects both the substantial
spread in the language and education skills of the respondents,
as well as their previous labor market experience. About half
of the respondents reported, and the interviewers confirmed,
high levels of English language competence, including the
ability to read, understand, and successfully complete job
applications. In fact, only one in five had no basic competence
in English. Finally, although the data do not directly explore
inter-segment mobility, the evidence is undisputable that
substantial job mobility does occur, that it is usually at the
initiative of the worker, and that it leads to substantial
improvement in one's earnings - especially as the subjects
move from the service to the manufacturing sectors.

Eleven percent of Sample III subjects reported currently
holding supervisory positions, a proportion doubling the rate
for both previous and first jobs (data not shown). There is also
additional evidence of gradual advancement and an increasing
potential for both intra- and inter-segment mobility. Although
the respondents work slightly more than five days per week

and a little more than eight-hour days - both of which findings are common for the industries in which the respondents are employed (U.S. Department of Labor, 1985) - two-thirds of them do receive overtime pay for overtime work. Although this may be interpreted by some as evidence of a substantial routine exploitation of undocumented aliens by unscrupulous employers, many of the positions in which some of the respondents are employed (such as restaurants and small-scale retail services) both often require more than a 40-hour week and do not pay overtime.

More significantly, however, with each subsequent job the respondents seem to move toward a higher-paying manufacturing job with higher proportions of overtime pay and payment by a regular payroll check - to the point where more than two-thirds of the respondents get paid by such checks in their present jobs (data not shown). Again as expected, New York subjects score substantially lower in all these indices of formal employment status. Furthermore, another indirect indicator of the evolution of, and economic progress by the study's subjects is the frequency with which they work in places employing large numbers of workers who share many of the same characteristics with our respondents. In a pattern which holds basically steady for all three job experiences, we found that the smaller the firm size, the more likely the respondents are to work with their own countrymen and with other Hispanics. These proportions drop to between 50 and 60 percent for the combined groups when the firm size changes to six to 25 workers. For firms employing more than 25 workers the pattern dissipates as it becomes impossible to assess the ethnic mix of the place with any degree of certainty.

These data also confirm the existence of fairly widespread but typical wage discrimination according to sex and dovetail with the job categories in which most Caribbean immigrants in the Northeastern U.S. - regardless of legal status - are found: moderate- and lower-wage manufacturing jobs and low- level service occupations. This finding is at significant variance with much evidence in the Southwest where one encounters substantial proportions of undocumented Mexican immigrants in service (Weintraub and Cardenas, 1984) and agricultural occupations. For instance, between 40 and 50 percent of those subjects studied by Cornelius in the mid-seventies were employed in the latter sector (1977), while the figures for the CENIET subjects were nearly 50 percent (Ranney and Kossoudji, 1983) and those for North/Houstoun were 18.8 percent for the entire sample and 24.1 percent for the Mexican subsample (1976).

On balance, when considering the analytical insights of Greenwood (1979) and Simon (1985), and the evidence from both the study and the works of Weintraub and Cardenas (1984) and Muller (1984), it becomes difficult not to conclude that undocumented aliens have a pronounced net positive effect on the social service infrastructure of this nation - especially since the relationship between domestic unemployment and undocumented immigration cannot be accurately gauged. In the absence of such a methodology, the programs which receive the most direct and substantial benefits from the presence of undocumented aliens are federal ones - and especially the Social Security Trust Fund and the Federal Treasury. Since states also profit by collecting payroll taxes and, even more significantly, by the collection of sales taxes - and Pessar's research on the consumer behavior of Dominicans in New York (1984) shows them to spend frequently on big-ticket consumer durables - they are also likely to benefit from the frequent failure by many undocumented households to file tax returns - a variable which Muller (1984) could not and did not take into account. Obviously, and as Greenwood has shown (1979), it is at the level of the localities where the benefit/cost distribution may reverse direction - although these data could not be used to support any claims about that relationship.

CHAPTER SIX

THE SETTLEMENT PROCESS

We already have the profile of households with extremely high labor force participation rates and, in view of their labor market characteristics and experiences, with commensurate expectations of economic achievement in the United States. What remains to be seen is whether data which delve deeper into the socioeconomic behavior of Sample III respondents permit any conclusions about the long-term incorporation of these subjects into the social and economic life of the United States.

THE QUESTION OF PERMANENCE: A PROCESS OF DISENGAGEMENT FROM THE HOME COUNTRY?

One of the primary measures for estimating the depth of the ties of the respondents to their home community and the possible impacts of such ties on the long-term stay of the subjects of this study is the degree to which Sample III undocumented aliens maintain an economic presence in their home country via the vehicle of remittances. In fact, it is hypothesized here that besides the effect that remittances may play on the development of the immigrants' home country (See Papademetriou, 1985a,b), regular, frequent, or high rates of remitting, when considered together with a number of other indicators identified below, reflect a close identification with the home country and a probable propensity to return home to enjoy the fruits of one's labor. Conversely, an irregular, infrequent, or low rate of remitting might be a good predictor of an intention to settle permanently abroad.

Table 6:1 indicates that 73.2 percent of Sample III respondents had remitted some funds to their home country during the previous 12 months. The average annual amount remitted was $1,181.00, while the average amount of each remittance was $156. These are substantial figures when considering the average household's annual income reported earlier. Of those remitting regularly, 73 percent reported

TABLE 6:1
REMITTANCES

	N	%
Remitted During Past Year:		
Yes	139	73.2
No	51	26.8
Total	190	100.0
Remitted To:		
Parents only	44	30.9
Parents and children	17	12.1
Parents, brothers and sisters	12	8.6
Brothers and sisters	9	6.5
Total	82	58.1
Amount of Support Provided:		
Less than half of their needs	79	60.8
About half	24	18.5
More than half	18	13.8
All	9	6.9
Total	130	100.0
Need for Support[1]		
Very necessary	78	56.5
Helpful, not critical	15	10.9
Marginally useful	10	7.2
A gift, not support	35	25.4
Total	138	100.0
Average Annual Remittance	$1,181.00	
Average Amount per Remittance	$ 156.00	
Average Number of Persons Assisted Through Remittances	4.4	
Frequency of Remittances	Monthly	

[1] Interestingly, 33.3 percent of the sample claimed that other family members outside of their own family in the U.S. remit regularly to those remaining behind.

remitting a constant amount, while 70 percent of those reporting a change in the amount remitted showed an increase (data not shown). The method of sending followed both formal and informal channels, with bank and postal money orders accounting for almost 60 percent of all cases.

These figures are within range of the findings from the few studies which report such data. For instance, Poitras (1980) reports $3,173.00 average total remittances over the full length of the trip for Costa Ricans (average length of stay of over 25 months) and $1,622.00 for Salvadorans (average length of stay of a little over 17 months). The amounts reported by those studies dealing with illegal Mexican aliens are considerably lower. North/Houstoun (1976) reported $169.00 per trip for Mexican respondents and CENIET (Ranney and Kossoudji, 1983) $115.00 per month in trips which averaged only a little over four months each. The explanation lies with the frequency and brief duration of trips by the studied Mexicans, the frequency of their apprehension, and their lower earnings-- hence their reduced ability to save more substantial sums.

Our data, however, are not really comparable with these findings in one significant way: Poitras' subjects were involved in a form of semi-circular migration which means that they continued to have substantial economic and family interests in their home countries. The Mexican subjects, furthermore, were archetypical examples of seasonal and temporary migrants. As a result, and after considerable probing, the amounts sent home by subjects should be seen in the following light: they are contributions intended to discharge obligations to one's family and financial backers in the experiment of coming to the U.S., as well as to help support household members left behind. Among them are about one-third of the children of respondents. Finally, the fact that nearly 30 percent of respondents do not remit, and that an additional 9 percent report declining rates of remittances is a sign not only of the inability of some to do so and the probable relative financial independence of a proportion of the households in the home country, but also of disinterest by some in maintaining a financial presence at home. The data do not allow us to assign precise values to these alternatives.

Support for some of these assumptions, however, comes from information on the persons who receive the remittance and their relationship to the remitter (Table 6:1). Parents of the respondents were the largest single beneficiaries (30.9 percent of all cases), while the aggregate nuclear family was the principal receiver of assistance in 58.1 percent of all cases. When considering that most of the respondents in Sample III had their spouses and their children with them, the size and distribution of the remittances are easier to understand. Although an average of 4.4 persons were assisted by each remitter, our respondents estimated that in the majority of cases (60.8%) the amount sent usually provided less than half of each recipient's needs. In line with this finding, 56.5 percent of remitting respondents considered the support as "very necessary" for the well-being of their families in the home country although they could not state precisely how the funds were expended.

Although data on remittances by themselves are not always clear in establishing the relationship between household members at home and destination, they do so much more effectively when seen in the context of other variables, some of which have already been examined previously. For instance, one explanation of the relatively high rate of remittances by respondents may be the closeness of the household as shown both by the seemingly collective nature of the decision for subjects to emigrate and the extensive participation of the household in the financing of the trip. Two other pieces of information, on the other hand, may suggest explanations as to why the remittances are not higher or more intense than they are. As will be recalled, several members of the household were emigrants which, presumably, could mean that contributions to the household could come from several sources. In fact, 33 percent of respondents indicated that that was indeed the case (Table 6:1). Furthermore, respondents have reported high rates of marriage with equally high rates of family formation in the United States. In view of that fact, it is to be expected that priorities would gradually shift toward one's own immediate family (which is in the U.S.), while the household of one's parents would gradually become less important.

Two more sets of data further support the hypothesis that respondents are likely to stay here for long periods of time: data on the subjects' reaction to a legislative offer of amnesty (legalization) and their answers to the question of whether they expected to become naturalized U.S. citizens. These questions were asked only of the sujects of the later of the two phases of the field research -- New York City (n=99). With regard to amnesty, nearly three-quarters of the New York subsample said they would indeed apply for amnesty (14% were not sure). Respondents' interest in a provisional legalization program similar to that offered in the 1983 Senate version of the Immigration Bill, however, drops to only 47.5 percent, while the proportion of respondents who would not accept the temporary status offered by that legislation increases by a factor of three.

With regard to subjects' interest in naturalization, 72.9 percent of respondents expressed such an interest, a figure which confronts us with a serious problem of reliability. The problem stems from evidence that among legal immigrants with national origin profiles similar to those for the sample, few naturalize within the first eight years after immigration (most immigrants must wait at least five years before they become eligible for naturalization). The figure for what we have called in this report the Caribbean region is only about 30 to 35 percent and overall naturalization figures for the six immigrants groups profiled on Table 3 are even lower (See Data Category 4). Specifically, the average for immigrants from the Caribbean islands was about 28 percent and for Central America about 45 percent. For individual key countries, those figures were: Dominicans, 25 percent; Jamaicans, 37 percent; Haitians, 47 percent; Colombians, 48 percent; and Salvadorans, 52 percent (own calculations, based on INS Statistical Yearbook, 1983, Table 5.2). In sharp contrast, the naturalization rates for Asiatics was 64 percent, with countries like Korea reporting rates of nearly 77 percent for the same period of time. This striking difference reflects sharply different routes of, and strategies for, access to the U.S. by these two groups. Caribbean region nationals, perhaps as a result of the relative ease and convenience of illegal entry, and the initial nurturing of the hope of return, do not feel compelled to make the commitment implied in naturalization. Many Asians, on the other hand, view immigration to the U.S. as a permanent commitment and are eager to follow the surest route to family reunification: early naturalization.

THE UNDOCUMENTED HOUSEHOLD IN THE UNITED STATES: II

Table 6:2 offers a panoramic of the undocumented households of which the respondents are members. Respondents were head of household in 44.5 percent of all cases. He/she was the spouse in an additional 24.0 percent of the cases. These households were composed of 697 persons (mean household size of 3.6 persons) and were over 60 percent male. Together with our respondents, nuclear families made up nearly three-quarters of the total membership of these households. An additional one-seventh of the group was composed of other close family members while one also finds small but significant proportions of other relatives and friends.

TABLE 6:2
HOUSEHOLD SIZE, SEX, AND COMPOSITION (SAMPLE III)

Household Size (n=697 persons)	
Mean	3.6 persons[1]
Household Composition (in %)[2]	
Spouses and children of the respondent	46.3
Brothers and sisters of either spouse	10.0
Parents of either spouse	4.3
Other relatives	8.6
Friends	8.1
Boarders	1.3
Other/ No answer	21.3
Total	99.9
Respondent's Relationship to Household Head (in %)	
Self	44.5
Spouse	24.0
Other	31.5
Total	100.0

[1] Size ranged from 1 to 7 persons.

[2] Other than the respondent (192 persons); remaining n=505.

The immigration status of this group of household members is mixed, with undocumented status being the modal category (SeeTable 6:3). Significantly, however, and in a manner which echoes findings on Tables 3:2 and 3:3 on the immigration status of spouses (38.4% permanent residents, 22% citizens -- of whom about two-thirds were Puerto Rican) and children (33% U.S. citizens), only 42.4 percent of the members of these households are undocumented. This proportion is followed, in order of group size, by native citizens (26.8%), permanent residents (23.9%), naturalized citizens (3.3%) and insignificant proportions of parolees, refugees and nonimmigrant visa holders.

Finally, the labor market status of the other members of the respondents' households indicates that effective unemployment rates (i.e. unemployed as a proportion of those who are in the labor force) for these groups are extremely low--about 11 percent--while the labor force participation rate for the entire household approaches two-thirds. This figure is comparable with the rates reported for the six legal immigrant groups on Table 1:3, as is the unemployment figure (See Data Categories 7,8). Finally, as one would expect from the profile of these households, about one-third of the total members are minors, and two-thirds of them are students (See Table 6:4).

These findings highlight again the complex legal, human rights, and moral questions confronting those who must formulate policy in this area. To repatriate these people would violate, at least in terms of general principle, the foundation on which U.S. immigration policy has long rested: the promoting of the reunification of families. The deportation of any members of respondent households who are closely related would in effect impose a cruel choice between family and country for those who are here legally and/or by birthright. It is on the basis of these compelling realities that policymakers should review and reform this nation's immigration laws and not on the basis of false or unreliable information, unwarranted assumptions, noble but abstract appeals to such value- laden concepts as the "national interest" or the need to "regain control of our borders", and the often unsubtantiated claims that undocumented aliens have serious negative effects on this nation's labor market and

TABLE 6:3
HOUSEHOLD COMPOSITION BY IMMIGRATION STATUS (SAMPLE III)

Immigration Status	%
Permanent resident	23.9
Refugee	0.7
Parolee	1.4
Native citizen	26.8
Naturalized citizen	3.3
Undocumented alien	42.4
Non- immigrant visa holder	1.4
Total	99.9

TABLE 6:4
LABOR MARKET STATUS OF HOUSEHOLD MEMBERS
AND
GROSS ANNUAL HOUSELHOLD INCOME (SAMPLE III)

Economic Activity	%
Employed	50.4
Unemployed, looking for a job	5.5
Unemployed, not looking for a job	3.5
Student	22.2
Housewife	4.9
Retired/ Disabled	0.9
Infant	11.4
Other	1.2
Total	100.0

Gross Annual Household Income: $19,574

service infrastructure. These data generally point to the
thoughtfulness of the legalization recommendations of the
Select Commission (1981). The Commission argued that in
view of the moral and legal complexity of the issue of
undocumented immigration, immigration reform must include
a generous legalization component which would wipe the slate
clean and make the nightmares and excesses of such past
enforcement operations as the 1954 "Operation Wetback" a
thing of the past.

CONCLUSION

Data on the probable long-term settlement of
respondents, speculative as they must be by necessity, do
allow for some rather firm generalizations. Although the
remittance behavior of a majority of subjects indicates
continued ties to the home country, few of them report any
plans to return. In fact, over 93 percent of Sample III
respondents reported no plans to leave the U.S. in the near
future except for a short visit home (Table 4:2). What has
become evident from our data is that with **de facto** family
reunification in the U.S. apparently much easier to effect than
many might be willing to acknowledge, many subjects have
increasingly more tenuous ties to their homelands. This, in
turn, increases geometrically the chances that they will
become settlers.

A number of other factors also contribute to make the
stay of respondents in the U.S. more permanent. The
immigration-status profile of undocumented households
probably increases expectations among respondents that they
will be able to adjust their own immigration status and gain
legal residence in the United States. Furthermore, the
extensive media coverage about proposed changes in U.S.
immigration laws, and especially reports that the new law is
likely to include some type of legalization program, further
encourages undocumented aliens to remain here. Finally,
respondents' relative economic success -- which is enormous
by the standards which all migrants initially employ, **i.e.**,
standards reflecting the conditions at home, rather than
destination -- and the frequent reluctance of immigrant
women to return to a social and cultural environment over
which they will again be likely to have little control and in
which they are likely to face substantial reversals in their
enhanced status as mothers, economic beings, and spouses,

further militates against a realistic expectation that the majority of respondents will return to their countries of origin.

Recalling the discussion on the hypothesis about the relationship between remittances and settlement, one must look into another trait common to all immigrants: their preoccupation with the education and future well-being of their children. Those children are clearly thought to have many more opportunities for advancement in the U.S. than they would in the countries of their parents. For all of these reasons, and in view of the effectiveness of the support network which facilitates their transition to the new country, this sample of undocumented aliens have already stayed much longer than they expected and are indeed planning on indefinite stays in the United States. Although few of them have many of the trappings of what Americans may consider the emblems of success (for instance only one in eight own their own homes), their lives are often relatively comfortable (an average household of 3.6 members had apartments which cost an average of $311.00 per month to rent and included three rooms outside of kitchen and bath); they usually have the choice of living among their own countrymen (54.5% choose to do so, although the rest live in areas where few of their countrymen live); and are not averse to moving -- particularly when that move results in the rejoining of family members.

CHAPTER SEVEN

CONCLUSION

During the course of this report, we have attempted to place key findings within the larger context of studies on undocumented aliens in the New York area and elsewhere. One of the studies with which we have made frequent comparisons has been the one by North and Houstoun (1976). This is primarily due to the benchmark character of that work. What remains to be examined briefly here, is whether such comparisons are useful and how much reliance one ought to place on data gleaned from samples of apprehended (detained) undocumented aliens. To obtain some guidelines about the reliability of these data, and assess the wisdom of anchoring the formulation of immigration policy on such data, we have compared each of the two subsamples III with a random sample of detainee profiles made available to us by the Newark and New York INS Offices. The profiles were drawn from the Agency's I-213 (Apprehension) Forms and each sample represents the period during which project interviews were taking place in each of the two areas - spring, summer, and fall of 1984 for Newark, and winter of 1984-85 and spring of 1985 for New York.

Tables 7:1 and 7:2 compare the country of origin profiles of the samples of apprehended undocumented population respectively for Newark and New York with the profiles of the subsamples in each of the two locations. Although the INS samples include substantial contingents of aliens originating from the same countries as the respondents, the differences are substantial. The Newark CCS subsample (Table 7:1) shows a heavy concentration on two groups - Salvadorans and Haitians - followed by substantial numbers of Colombians and Dominicans. The INS sample (n=565) exhibits far less skewing, with Colombians, Haitians, Mexicans and Salvadorans comprising only about 50 percent of the sample, and a number of Asian and European nationalities also represented. The New York comparisons show a similar pattern: this subsample is concentrated on Caribbean region aliens - especially Colombians, Dominicans, Ecuadorians, Salvadorans, and Jamaicans - while the INS group (n=49) is distributed more equally among a number of nationalities, including a high proportion of Salvadorans. Hence, both of the subsamples have only limited comparability with the detained groups in terms of country of origin characteristics.

TABLE 7:1

COUNTRY OF ORIGIN FOR NEWARK CCS CLIENTS WHO ARE RESIDENT ALIENS, FOR
APPREHENDED ALIENS IN THE CUSTODY OF THE NEWARK INS OFFICE, AND FOR
NEW JERSEY SUBSAMPLE III

Country of Origin (in %):	CCS Clients: Resident Aliens (n=91)	Newark INS: Apprehended Aliens (n=565)	New Jersey Subsample III (n=93)
Argentina	1.1	1.6	1.1
Bangladesh	—	1.1	—
Brazil	3.5	—	—
Colombia	12.1	16.8	9.8
Costa Rica	8.8	1.2	1.1
Dominican Rep.	14.3	2.7	6.5
Ecuador	7.7	3.9	2.2
Egypt	—	.5	—
El Salvador	4.4	8.5	25.0
Guatemala	—	2.3	1.1
Haiti	15.4	13.8	33.7
Honduras	3.3	.7	1.1
India	1.1	1.6	—
Iran	—	1.4	—
Italy	8.8	.2	—
Jamaica	—	.7	1.1
Mexico	—	12.2	2.2
Peru	3.3	5.7	3.3
Philippines	—	4.2	—
Poland	1.1	5.0	—
Portugal	5.5	.2	1.1
Uruguay	2.2	1.2	.1
Venezuela	—	1.6	—
Other	7.7	12.3	12.7
Total	100.1	99.9	100.0

TABLE 7:2
COUNTRY AND REGION OF ORIGIN, EMPLOYMENT STATUS, ECONOMIC ACTIVITY,
AND AVERAGE WAGES OF APPREHENDED ALIENS IN NEW YORK CITY[1]

Country and Region of Origin (in %)	Apprehended	N.Y. Subsample III
Salvador	32.7	6.1
Colombia	10.2	28.5
Mexico	8.2	3.0
Haiti	4.1	2.0
Egypt	4.1	—
India	4.1	—
Ecuador	4.1	8.1
Dominica	4.1	—
Other	28.6	52.3
Of whom:		
Caribbean	6.1	30.0
South and Central America	4.1	39.7
Asia	8.2	21.3
Africa	6.1	—
Europe	4.1	1.0
Employment Status (in %)		
Employed	77.6	82.7
Economic Activity in (%)		
Manufacturing, unskilled	4.1	15.2
Manufacturing, semi-skilled	8.2	9.1
Manufacturing, skilled	4.1	2.0
Transportation	8.2	2.0
Hotel/ Restaurants	48.6	5.1
Domestic	4.1	—
Other	—	33.3
Not employed	22.5	32.3
Total	99.9	99.9
Average Hourly Wage	$4.41	$5.75

[1] Information drawn from the randomly picked I-213 forms of 49 undocumented aliens in INS custody at the Brooklyn Detention Center during the Spring of 1985.

The data on the apprehended also permit comparison with a number of other characteristics of these groups with our two groups of respondents. For instance, the study's New York subsample (Table 7:2) exhibited slightly higher employment rates than the detained group but showed an economic activity profile that contrasts sharply with that of our subjects due to its high concentration on low level service jobs, and especially restaurants (over 60% of the sample). While this probably reflects INS enforcement patterns and priorities, it does result in a sharply lower wage profile for the detained group - a finding also observed by Weintraub and Cardenas (1984).

TABLE 7:3
AGE, SEX, MARITAL STATUS, AND LENGTH OF STAY
CHARACTERISTICS OF APPREHENDED AND UNAPPREHENDED
ALIENS IN NEW YORK CITY

	Apprehended[1] (n=49)	Unapprehended: New York Subsample (n=99)
Age		
Percent between 11-20 years old	12.3	7.1
Percent between 21-40 years old	77.6	75.8
Mean Age (in years)	—	31.3
Sex		
Percent Male	65.3	43.4
Marital Status		
Percent Single[2]	69.4	18.4
Average Length of Stay (in months)	27.5	50.5

[1] Information drawn from the randomly picked I-213 forms of 49 undocumented aliens in INS custody at the Brooklyn Detention Center during the Spring of 1985.

[2] Probably inaccurate in order to protect their family.

The comparisons of the profiles of the two New York groups also highlight a number of other significant similarities and differences between them. For instance, the age distribution of the two groups is quite similar but sharp differences emerge in a number of other variables (Table 7:3). The apprehended are almost two-thirds male, while our subsample is nearly 57 percent female. Information on marital status also divulges sharp contrasts with almost 70 percent of the apprehended undocumented aliens reporting single status as compared with only 18 percent for subjects in this study. One should acknowledge, however, that part of the reason for this difference probably lies both with enforcement patterns of INS but also with the desire of those apprehended to protect their families. Finally, the average length of stay for the apprehended group is a little over half that for the New York respondents.

This latter characteristic is also clearly evident with the Newark data comparisons (Tables 7:4 and 7:5). What is emerging, in other words, is a distinct pattern where the likelihood of apprehension decreases substantially with one's length of stay in the United States. In fact, once an undocumented alien manages to go undetected by INS for the first year (**See,** Houstoun, 1983, and INS, Statistical Yearbook, various years, Table ENF 1.4), the chances of apprehension decrease dramatically - although our sample of Newark INS detainee data does not show so dramatic a drop as overall INS data do. The explanation, of course, is simple. As one becomes better acquainted with his/her environment, one is much less likely to work in places which INS often targets or frequent locations which might also be targeted by INS.

Before we attempt to recapitulate and draw some of the tentative policy significance of the data discussed in this report, we thought that it should be emphasized again that almost regardless of immigration status, there is an apparent convergence in the socioeconomic experiences of recent immigrants from the Caribbean area. In fact, and as with the New York comparisons, in comparing our sample III with a sample of legal immigrants assisted by CCS counselors and with a sample of over 500 apprehended aliens in the custody of the Newark INS authorities during the first 10 months of 1984 (Table 7:4), we noticed some not entirely unexpected differences but also many similarities. Legal CCS immigrant clients reported a substantial average wage advantage over all undocumented immigrants - although both groups did better than those in the custody of the INS.

TABLE 7:4
AVERAGE LENGTH OF STAY FOR NEWARK CCS CLIENTS WHO ARE RESIDENT ALIENS,
FOR APPREHENDED ALIENS IN THE CUSTODY OF THE NEWARK INS OFFICE,
AND FOR NEW JERSEY SUBSAMPLE III

	CCS Clients: Resident Aliens (n=91)	Newark INS: Apprehended Aliens (n-565)	New Jersey Subsample III (n=92)
Length of Time in U.S. in months			
0-6	2.2	14.2	1.0
7-12	5.4	25.0	13.0
13-24	6.8	4.6	18.4
25-36	8.0	14.0	25.0
37-48	10.6	14.0	10.0
49-60	4.3	6.6	9.7
61-72	8.1	3.0	3.2
73-84	7.8	1.7	3.2
85-96	15.3	0.5	5.4
97-120	7.7	0.7	2.1
121-132	5.9	2.6	1.0
133-144	8.7	0.7	4.0
145-156	6.5	0.1	4.0
Over 156	3.3	3.0	—
Unknown	0.0	7.3	—
Total	100.1	100.0	100.0

The explanation for the wage difference between legal and undocumented immigrants in these samples is rather simple. Although they perform similar functions in the labor market, the large differences in the national origin composition of the two samples have both a compressing effect on the average wages of the Newark CCS subsample (because of the large representation of recent Haitian and Salvadoran aliens), and an enhancing effect on the average wages of the apprehended (because of the substantial representation of European, Asian, and other South American groups). The fact that the apprehended still report a lower hourly income is due again to their less complete incorporation into the local ethnic communities and labor market. These differences aside, however, the three samples report quite similar sex and age characteristics.

TABLE 7:5

LABOR MARKET STATUS, AVERAGE HOURLY INCOME, SEX AND AGE CHARACTERISTICS FOR NEWARK CCS CLIENTS WHO ARE RESIDENT ALIENS, FOR APPREHENDED ALIENS IN THE CUSTODY OF THE NEWARK INS OFFICE AND FOR NEW JERSEY SUBSAMPLE III

	CCS Clients: Resident Aliens (n=91)	Newark INS: Apprehended Aliens (n=565)	New Jersey Subsample III (n=92)
Total Employed (in %)	32.0	65.0	83.0
Total Average Hourly Income	$5.27	$4.49	$4.62
Sex/ Male (in %)	49.0	62.8	55.9
Average Age (in years)	28.7	29.7	34.0

In all, and with regard both to the Newark and New York comparisons, it appears that unapprehended undocumented aliens do have a distinct wage advantage over apprehended ones - a function of the length of their tenure in the U.S., consequent experience in the U.S. labor market, and type of economic activity. Although the INS data are often incomplete, and we opted for a cross section of detainees, rather than a targeted sample which would resemble the ethnic profile of our own groups, it is still possible to urge extreme caution in extrapolating characteristics of unapprehended undocumented aliens from the characteristics of those in custody of the immigration authorities.

IMMIGRATION AS A NATIONAL ISSUE

Immigration reform is indeed a pressing national issue. Yet, its impacts are by no means uniform. Not only can one not draw a single profile of a hypothetical modal undocumented alien, one must not draw such a profile.

Table 1:3 attempts to paint a national picture of immigration, yet retain as many of the regional and state differences as it is possible within the limits of a single schema. What these "details" show is that the impacts of legal immigration, undocumented immigration, and refugee flows differ from state to state and region to region as the concentration of each of these flows, their sociodemographic and economic profile, and the responses which may be required to address problems generated or exacerbated by their presence differ. Many of these differences are as much a function of history or geography as of international politics, U.S. political and economic involvement in a particular region, superpower competition, and the general internationalization of capital and labor markets.

As we have seen, the economic and many of the social impacts of legal and undocumented aliens co-vary with: their concentration in specific economic sectors, industries, and firms; their role in responding to, facilitating, or initiating the restructuring of local labor markets; their legal or de facto ability to participate fully and on an equal footing in an area's economic, social and cultural life; and the degree to which their economic presence complements, rather than competes with and displaces, other groups. In accordance with these impacts, immigration, in any of its specific forms, will be expected to be beneficial, neutral, largely benign, controversial, or inimical to the interests of populations in different regions or states within the U.S., and to specific groups in these regions or states.

Although it is beyond the current scope of this report to disaggregate these impacts and assess the effect of different types of immigration on targeted regions, states, or social, economic and racial groups, the analysis of these data, and a review of the evidence reported by the many other studies in this research area, do allow us to draw some narrow, tentative and preliminary, if bold, conclusions. We are particularly eager to do so, but careful to point out the preliminary nature of these conclusions.

At this late stage of the report, we wish to reemphasize that it is necessary to recognize that economically, many U.S. industries and most U.S. consumers appear to benefit substantially from the presence of undocumented aliens. What is not nearly so clear is whether specific groups in specific local settings participate in these benefits. Let us take the issue of labor market competition and displacement by undocumented aliens, particularly as it applies to this nation's disadvantaged socioeconomic strata - the blacks and Hispanics who share many but by no means all of the sociodemographic and economic characteristics of undocumented aliens. One recent analysis suggests one potential direction in finding the answers to this question. Muller (1984) found that immigrants (including undocumented aliens) did not reduce the jobs available to nonimmigrants in California during the decade of the 1970s. In fact, by looking at gross economic indicators, Muller was able to show that California experienced consistently lower unemployment rates than the rest of the nation and did not register any drops in labor force participation rates for the decade. In fact, the labor force participation rates for both blacks and whites in the state remained stable for the entire decade and at levels higher than in the rest of the nation. Finally, Muller noticed a negative relationship between changes (increases) in the size of the Mexican immigrant population and black unemployment and found evidence of substantial occupational progress by blacks during the decade. As a result, he concluded that the relationship between (legal and undocumented) immigrants and blacks in the California labor market has been one of complementarity rather than competition.

But how would these arguments fare if one were to disaggregate some of Muller's categories and how generalizable are his findings outside of California. Although we are not at this time prepared to perform the kind of analysis which might confirm or cast doubt on Muller's findings, a number of caveats suggest themselves. Did all blacks benefit from the upward pressures on the job hierarchy brought about by the presence of large supplies of new immigrants? Can the analysis of aggregate data detect otherwise important pockets of competition or displacement between the two groups? Can it be shown whether other traditionally disadvantaged strata, in this case Chicanos, also experienced similar labor market mobility? Might not the upward mobility of blacks as a group hide substantial reduction in opportunities by those blacks or other minorities whose skill structure and education places them in labor market positions identical to those occupied by the new immigrants? Finally, can findings about California, with its vibrant economy and its unique experience in receiving enormous numbers of internal and international immigrants with skill distributions across the entire spectrum of the skill hierarchy be extrapolated into other U.S. settings?

It seems to us that they probably could not. It also seems to us that in view of the fact that the respondents in this study bring with them such substantial amounts of human capital, in labor markets with limited opportunities they would be likely to restrict, rather than expand, opportunities for advancement by an area's disadvantaged groups. New York might be such a labor market. The reasons why these latter groups might be likely to prove unequal to the task of competing successfully with many of our respondents, as well as with recent legal immigrants in general, have become obvious to us during the course of this study and include inferior human capital characteristics and structural and individual discrimination. Some of these reasons have been recently documented in several other studies - including one which compares the socioeconomic attainment of Puerto Ricans with that of "other Hispanics", and especially Dominicans and Colombians, in New York City (Mann and Salvo, 1984).

Recent Caribbean region immigrants, when discounting for the effects of discrimination which cannot be shown to be different than that for other legal immigrant groups but may be different than that for native minorities in the New York area, do possess skills, education, and work experience in their home countries and in the U.S. which allow them to advance economically - although perhaps within often defined boundaries. Data categories 9, 10 and, to a lesser degree, 11 of Table 2:1 profile the attributes of relative economic success by recent legal immigrant groups and the samples from this study share these same characteristics to an extraordinary degree. What this may suggest for the interpretation of Muller's California findings, is that the question of competition can only be addressed in an unbiased fashion when comparing qualitatively equal, rather than unequal, units. To the best of our knowledge, no extant or on-going studies are approaching the level of methodological refinement which would allow for such comparisons.

The remarkable similarities between legal and undocumented aliens along a wide number of crucial social, economic and demographic variables, suggest that with regard to migration, the same selection process appears to operate both at sending and receiving regions and that immigration status is a barrier which can be overcome with the assistance of ethnic networks. After obtaining some language skills and labor market experience in the U.S., the educational and skill preparation of the undocumented serves them well and allows them to gain access to a wide range of U.S. labor market activities in a similar fashion to other operatives in ethnic and native blue collar communities.

This is not to say that undocumented aliens, and recent immigrants in general, can expect equal access to the U.S. labor market with natives, more established ethnics, or native minorities. This project was not designed with this question in mind. Indirect evidence, however, points to the direction of discrimination as being both industry and nationality/race specific. In the first case, it is directed quite indiscriminately at all employees - although because of poor working conditions and low wages it attracts a largely homogeneous group of workers. The garment industry would be an example of this type of discrimination. The second case is much more difficult to establish. Endless studies on the economic hierarchy in New York City consistently point to the Puerto Ricans as the least economically successful group, followed at some distance by blacks (Papademetriou, 1983c). **Vis à vis** both of these groups, respondents, and the members of the legal ethnic communities whose profile they virtually match, fare extraordinarily well. In that sense, they may be seen as occupying an increasingly privileged position in the local labor market. Further analysis of these data may in the future allow us to be more specific in this regard. As it stands now, members of undocumented households appear to be rather successful economic actors who, with increased tenure in the U.S., are able to realize more of a potential which their human capital characteristics might predict.

In the absence of reliable studies on specific undocumented alien groups originating in the Caribbean region, one might be encouraged to look at the 1980 Census results of that immigrant group. There is strong evidence that the two groups are likely to be more similar than dissimilar - at least in the Northeast. Second, the same thing does not hold for the relationship between undocumented aliens who are unapprehended and those who are detained. The two groups are more dissimilar than similar and policy initiatives attain a hit-or-miss quality when they rely on profiles of detainees. Finally, regardless of how well-informed policy may be, its effectiveness can be expected to be blunted and its intent distorted by ethnic networks which have communication channels with sharply different priorities than those utilized by U.S. authorities. Such distortions can be expected to be much more troublesome, however, if policy initiatives betray equivocation about goals and the means and resources necessary to meet these goals.

CONCLUDING REMARKS

One of the more important and controversial assumptions about international migration is that it is often demand-induced, i.e., that exclusive of refugee flows, migration is shaped more by the needs of the receiving industrial societies, than by those of the less developed sending societies (Piore, 1979; Papademetriou, 1983d). This should not be construed, however, as denying the importance of the supply variable in international migration. Data here bear this point out clearly. It becomes important, then, to distinguish between conditions necessary for international migration and conditions sufficient for it. Among the former, one must include an adequate supply of workers who have become alienated from their own country by a combination of structural expulsive forces which include overpopulation, severe un- and underemployment, and extremely restricted opportunities for advancement. One must further include such antecedent factors as international political and economic forces; national government policies (or lack thereof) **vis à vis** fertility, development, and land tenure and distribution patterns; the locus, intensity and type of industrial investment and employment and manpower policies; and the role of history, culture, tradition and politics in providing both the value orientations and the institutional context in which decisions about emigration will be made. Among the latter (sufficient) conditions for migration, one must turn to the social and economic situation in the employment sector of advanced industrial societies which, because of the conditions discussed in Chapter 3:1, are intensely interested in the type of labor readily available in the LDCs.

In the many ways already observed and discussed throughout this report, the U.S. has been able to draw on the human resources of the Caribbean region almost at will - in much the same fashion as with other of the region's resources. The U.S. has in fact been capable of drawing on people whose upbringing, education and training, however commonplace by the standards of certain groups in the U.S., have been paid for by the sending societies. Ingenuous and seductive arguments about opportunity costs, utilities, and "safety valves" notwithstanding, such U.S.-regulated migration is a subsidy of the rich by the poor. Along with committing the ecological fallacy (if the society benefits so will its various components) such arguments disguise many of the possible negative consequences of undocumented migration for this nation's disadvantaged strata and, in the absence of serious efforts to bring it under control, may jeopardize the future social peace of the nation. A close attention to the debate on immigration reform during the past seven years makes clear the underlying currents which threaten to shift the level of the debate to the cultural, social, and racial realms. Few of us would care to speculate on what legislation might emerge then - particularly since the U.S. has had only a brief and uncertain history of confronting openly its own incongruities and divisions, as well as the political instabilities which these forces may be able to release.

Berger and Piore (1980) have shown convincingly that politics are the means by which dominant societal groups seek to escape economic uncertainty and maintain their economic advantage relative to more vulnerable groups. In this scenario, immigration legislation becomes a crucial link in the ability of the dominant groups to address the social and economic tensions associated with a U.S. economy which has been undergoing significant structural transformations. Hence the intense and Byzantine interactions among political parties, employer groups, trade unions, and ethnic and religious actors as they all attempt to protect the interests of their real and presumed constituencies and poise themselves for what will inevitably become the next battleground in this policy area: "reform" of legal immigration.

This report documents that current migration patterns are neither historically unique nor likely to dissipate in the near future. As a result, the challenges that migration flows pose for the U.S. go to the very heart of the sociocultural, economic, and political life not only of this nation but of the entire region. Responding to these challenges by stop-gap and unilateral actions is a patently disingenuous idea. As the Select Commission understood, what are needed are comprehensive initiatives whose mutually reinforcing components can address the multiple dimensions of the problem (SCIRP, 1981). The framework for these responses, however, must also reflect appropriate sensitivity toward the often forgotten victims of the **status quo**: our own disadvantaged citizens and any worker who has contributed to the economic well-being of this country - regardless of legal status.

As a result, policymakers must not continue to treat the symptoms of international migration. Instead, they must come to grips with the structural weaknesses of the U.S. labor market, the equally persistent problems with the economies and societies of the sending countries, and with a regional and global economy which constantly reinforces economic inequalities. A good starting point may be a series of assessments about the sources and dynamics of international migration based on what is already a rich literature on this topic. The motivation for such assessments is already present: immigration policies have become inextricably intertwined with and will increasingly impact on the ability of this nation to articulate and implement even its most basic economic, foreign, and defense policies. The contours of any such assessments have already been suggested in this report.

BIBLIOGRAPHY

Angel, R. and M. Tienda
1985   "Determinants of Extended Household Structure: Cultural Pattern or Economic Need?", **American Journal of Sociology**, 87(6):1360-83.

Arias, A.
1981   "Undocumented Mexicans: A Study in the Social Psychology of Clandestine Migrations to the United States". San Diego: University of California, San Diego. Unpublished Ph.D. Dissertation.

Arizpe, L.
1982a   "The Rural Exodus in Mexico and Mexican Migration to the United States". In **The Border that Joins: Mexican Migrants and U.S. Responsibility.** Edited by P. Brown and H. Shue. Totowa, NJ: Rowman and Littlefield. Pp. 162-83.

1982b   "Women and Development in Latin America and the Caribbean: Lessons from the Seventies and Hopes for the Future". **Development Dialogue 1-2.**

Avante Systems and Cultural Research Associates
1978   "A Survey of the Undocumented Population in Two Texas Border Areas". Report prepared for the Southwestern Regional Office of the U.S. Commission on Civil Rights.

Baca, R. and D. Bryan
1981   "Mexican Undocumented Workers in the Binational Community: A Research Note", **International Migration Review**, 15(4):737-48.

Bach, R.
1985   **Western Hemispheric Immigration to the United States: A Review of Selected Research Trends.** Center for Immigration Policy and Refugee Assistance, Georgetown University, Hemispheric Migration Project. March.

1983   "Emigration from the Spanish-Speaking Caribbean". In **U.S. Immigration and Refugee Policy.** Edited by M. Kritz. Pp. 133-53.

Badillo-Veiga A., et al.
1979   "Undocumented Immigrant Workers in N.Y. City", **The North American Congress on Latin America,** 13(6):2-46.

Bailey, T.
1985   "The Influence of Legal Status on the Labor Market Impact of Immigration", **International Migration Review,** 19(2):220-38.

1984   "Labor Market Structure and Economic Mobility: Implications for Blacks and Immigrants". Columbia University, Conservation of Human Resources. Mimeo.

Bailey T. and M. Freeman
1983   "Immigrant Economic Mobility in an Era of Weakening Employment Relationships: the Role of Social Networks". Columbia University, Conservation of Human Resources. Mimeo.

1981   "Immigrant and Native-Born Workers in the Restaurant Industry". Columbia University, Conservation of Human Resources. Mimeo.

Balmori, D.
1983   "Hispanic Immigrants in the Construction Industry:
        New York City, 1960-1982". New York University,
        Research Program in Inter-American Affairs.

Bean, F., H. Browning and W. Frisbie
1984   "The Sociodemographic Characteristics of Mexican
        Immigrant Status Groups: Implications for Studying
        Undocumented Mexicans", **International Migration
        Review**, 18(3):672-91.

Bean, F., R. Cullen and E. Stephen
1984   "Immigration to the United States: Its Volume,
        Determinants, and Labor Market Implications".
        Report prepared for the U.S. Office of Technology
        Assessment.

Beck, E., P. Horan and C. Tolbert II
1978   "Stratification in a Dual Economy: A Sector Model of
        Earnings Determination", **American Sociological
        Review**, 43(5):704-20.

Belsasso, G.
1981   "Undocumented Mexican Workers in the U.S.: A
        Mexican Perspective". In **Mexico and the United
        States.** Edited by R. McBridge. Englewood Cliffs,
        N.J.: Prentice Hall. Pp. 128-57.

Beranek, W.
1982   "The Illegal Alien Work Force, Demand for Unskilled
        Labor, and the Minimum Wage". **Journal of Labor
        Research,** 3(1):89-99.

Berger, S. and M. Piore
1980   **Dualism and Discontinuity in Industrial Societies.**
        Cambridge: Cambridge University Press.

Birdsall, N. and W. McGreevey
1983   "Women, Poverty and Development". In **Women and Poverty in the Third World**. Edited by Buvinic **et al.** Pp. 3-13.

Black, N. and A. Baker Cottrell, eds.
1981   **Women and World Change: Equity Issues in Development**. Beverly Hills: Sage.

Bonacich, E. and L. Hirata
1981   "International Labor Migration: A Theoretical Orientation". Paper presented at the Conference on New Directions on Immigration and Ethnicity. Duke University. May. Mimeo.

Borjas, G.
1983   "The Labor Supply of Male Hispanic Immigrants in the United States", **International Migration Review,** 17(4):653-71

1982   "The Economic Status of Male Hispanic Migrants and Natives in the U.S.: A Human Capital Approach". University of California, Santa Barbara, Community and Organization Research Institute.

Boserup. E.
1970   **Woman's Role on Economic Development.** London: Allen and Unwin.

Bouvier. L.
1981   **Immigration and Its Impact on U.S. Society.** Washington, D.C.: Population Reference Bureau.

Brana-Shute, R. and G. Brana-Shute
1982   "The Magnitude and Impact of Remittances in The Eastern Caribbean: A Research Note". In **Return Migration and Remittances.** Edited by Stinner **et al.** Pp. 267-89

Briggs, V.
1984a   **Immigration Policy and the American Labor Force.**
         Baltimore: Johns Hopkins.

1984b   "Methods of Analysis of Illegal Immigration into the
         United States", **International Migration Review,**
         18(3):623-44.

1983   "Nonimmigrant Labor Policy". In **The Unavoidable
         Issue.** Edited by Papademetriou and Miller. Pp.
         93-122.

Browning, H. and N. Rodriguez
1982   "The Migration of Mexican Indocumentados as a
         Settlement Process: Implications for Work". Texas
         Population Research Center, Paper Series 4.008.
         University of Texas at Austin.

Bureau of the Census
1981   **1980 Census of Population: Persons of Spanish Origin
         by State, Supplementary Report.** Washington, D.C.:
         Government Printing Office, PC80-S1-7.

Bustamante, J.
1978   "Commodity Migrants: Structural Analysis of Mexican
         Immigration to the United States". In **Views Across
         the Border.** Edited by S. Ross. Albuquerque:
         University of New Mexico Press. Pp. 183-203.

1977   "Undocumented Migration from Mexico: Research
         Report", **International Migration Review,** 11(1):149-77.

Bustamante, Jorge and Geronimo G. Martinez
1979   "Undocumented Immigration from Mexico: Beyond
         Borders but Within Systems", **Journal of International
         Affairs,** 33(2):265-84.

Buvinic, M.
1983   "Women's Issues in Third World Poverty: A Policy
        Analysis". In **Women and Poverty in the Third World.**
        Edited by Buvinic **et al.** Pp. 14-37.

Buvinic, M., M. Lycette and W. McGreevey, eds.
1983   **Women and Poverty in the Third World.** Baltimore:
        Johns Hopkins.

Buvinic, M., N. Youssef, with B. Von Elm
1978   "Women-Headed Households: The Ignored Factor in
        Development   Planning".   Washington,   D.C.:
        International Center for Research on Women. Report
        prepared   for   U.S.   Agency   for   International
        Development, Office of Women in Development.
        March.

Cardenas, G.
1979   "Mexican Illegal Aliens in the San Antonio Labor
        Market", **Texas Business Review,** 53(2): 87-91.

Carruthers, N. and A. Vining
1982   "International Migration: An Application of the Urban
        Location Choice Model", **World Politics,** 35(1):106-20.

Center for the Continuing Study of the California Economy.
1982   **Projections of Hispanic Population for the United
        States, 1990 and 2000.** Palo Alto, California.

Chaney, E.
1985   **Migration from the Caribbean Region: Determinants
        and Effects of Current Movements.** Georgetown
        University, Center for Immigration Policy and
        Refugee Assistance, Hemispheric Migration Project.
        March.

Chapman, M. and M. Prothero
1983   "Themes on Circulation in the Third World," **International Migration Review,** 17(4): 597-632.

Chiswick, B.
1984a   "Human Capital and the Labor Market Adjustment of Immigrants: Testing Alternative Hypotheses." Harvard University, Migration and Development Program, Discussion Paper 7. March.

1984b   "Illegal Aliens in the U.S. Labor Market: Analysis of Occupational Attainment and Earnings", **International Migration Review,** 18(3): 714-32.

1982a   **The Gateway: U.S. Immigration Issues and Policies.** Washington, D.C.: American Enterprise Institute.

1982b   "The Employment and Unemployment Experiences of Immigrants in the United States". Mimeo.

1979   "The Economic Progress of Immigrants: Some Apparently Universal Patterns". In **Contemporary Economic Problems.** Edited by W. Fellner. Washington, D.C.: American Enterprise Institute. Pp. 357-99.

Choldin, H.
1984   "Statistics and Politics: The 'Hispanic Issue' in the 1980 Census". University of Illinois, Department of Sociology. Mimeo. August.

Commission on Population Growth and the American Future
1972   **Population and the American Future.** Washington D.C.: Summary Report.

Community Research Associates
1980   "Undocumented Immigrants: Their Impact on the
        County of San Diego". Report prepared for the
        County of San Diego. May.

Comptroller General, Report to the Congress of the
United States
1980   **Prospects Dim for Effectively Enforcing Immigration
        Laws.** General Accounting Office. November.

Cornelius, W.
1982   Interviewing   Undocumented   Immigrants:
        Methodological Reflections Based on Fieldwork in
        Mexico and the U.S.", **International Migration Review,**
        12(4): 485-501.

1977a   **Mexican Migration to the U.S.: Causes, Consequences,
        and U.S. Responses.** Cambridge, MA: MIT, Center for
        International Studies, Migration and Development
        Group. Monograph c/78-9.

1977b   **Politics and the Migrant Poor in Mexico City.**
        Stanford: Stanford University Press.

Cornelius, W., L. Chavez and J. Castro
1982   "Mexican Immigrants and Southern California: A
        Summary of Current Knowledge". University of
        California at San Diego, Center for U.S. - Mexican
        Studies, Research Report Series, 36.

Cornelius, W., M. Fernandez-Kelly and R. Mines
1984   **The Role of Mexican Labor in the California
        Economy.** La Jolla, California: Center for U.S. -
        Mexican Studies, San Diego.

Cornelius, W., R. Mines, L. Chavez, and J. Castro
1982   "Mexican Immigrants in the San Francisco Bay Area: A Summary of Current Knowledge". University of California at San Diego, Center for U.S. - Mexican Studies, Research Report Series, 40.

Corwin, A., ed.
1978   Immigrants — and Immigrants: Perspectives on Mexican Labor Migration to the United States. Westport, CT.: Greenwood Press.

Crewdson, J.
1983   The Tarnished Door: The New Immigrants and the Transformation of America. New York: Times Books.

Cross, C.
1974   Interviewing and Communication in Social Work. London: Routledge and K. Paul.

Cummings, S.
1980   "White Ethnics, Racial Prejudice, and Labor Market Segmentation", American Journal of Sociology, 84(4): 938-50. January.

Current Population Reports
1980   Persons of Spanish Origin in the United States: March, 1979. Washington, D.C.: U.S. Government Printing Office, No. 354.

Davidson, C.
1981   "Characteristics of Deportable Aliens Located in the Interior of the United States". Immigration and Naturalization Service, Statistical Analysis Branch. March.

Davis, C.,C. Haub and J. Willette
1983   "U.S. Hispanics Changing the Face of America,"
        Population Bulletin, 38(3). June.

Diaz-Briquets, S.
1985   "The Impact of Alternative Development Strategies on
        Migration: A Comparative Analysis". In **Caribbean
        Migration and Development.** Edited by R. Pastor. Pp.
        41-62.

1983   **International Migration Within Latin America and the
        Caribbean: A Review of Available Evidence.** New
        York: Center for Migration Studies.

DiMarzio, N.
1985   "Profiling Undocumented Aliens in the New York
        Metropolitan Area: Social Welfare and Labor Market
        Implications". Rutgers University. Unpublished Ph.D.
        Dissertation.

Dinerman, I.
1982   **Migrants and Stay-at-Homes: A Comparative Study of
        Rural Migration from Michoacan, Mexico.** University
        of California at San Diego, Center for U.S. - Mexican
        Studies, Research Report Series, 5.

1978   "Patterns of Adaptation among Households of
        U.S.-Bound Migrants from Michoacan, Mexico",
        International Migration Review, 12(4): 485-501.

Durham, W.
1979   **Scarcity and Survival in Central America: Ecological
        Origins of the Soccer War.** Stanford: CA: Stanford
        University Press.

Easterlin, R.
1968   Population, Labor Force, and Long Swings in Economic Growth: The American Experience. New York: National Bureau of Economic Research.

Edwards, R.
1979   Contested Terrain: The Transformation of the Workplace in the Twentieth Century. New York: Basic Books.

Ehrlich, P., L. Bilderback and A.H. Ehrlich
1979   The Golden Door: International Migration, Mexican and the United States. New York: Ballantine Books.

Falasco, D. and D. Heer
1984   "Economic and Fertility Differences between Legal and Illegal Migrant Mexican Families: Possible Effects of Immigration Policy Changes", Social Science Quarterly, 65(2): 495-504.

Fenton, R.
1983   "Illegal Immigration to the United States: A Growing Problem for Law Enforcement". Center for Advanced Research, The Naval War College, March.

Findley, S.
1977   Planning for Internal Migration: A Review of Issues and Policies in Developing Countries. Washington, D.C.: U.S. Government Printing Office, ISP-RD-4.

Fitzpatrick, J. and L. Parker
1981   "Hispanic-Americans in the Eastern United States". In America as a Multicultural Society, a special issue of the Annals of the American Academy of Political and Social Science. Edited by M. Gordon, Vol. 454 March Pp. 86-97.

Flores, E.
1984   "Research on Undocumented Immigrants and Public
        Policy: A Study of the Texas School Case".
        International Migration Review, 81(3): 505-23.

‾1‾9‾83   "The Impact of Undocumented Migration on the U.S.
        Labor Market", **Houston Journal of International Law,**
        5(2): 287-321.

Fogel, W.
1983   "Immigrants and the Labor Market: Historical
        Perspectives and Current Issues". In **The Unavoidable
        Issue: U.S. Immigration Policy in the 1980s.** Edited by
        Papademetriou and Miller. Pp. 71-92.

Foner, N.
1982   "Jamaican Migrants: A Comparative Analysis of the
        New York and London Experience". New York: New
        York University, New York Research Program in
        Inter-American Affairs. Mimeo.

Forbes, S.
1981   "The Half-Open Back Door: Illegal Migration to the
        United States". In **U.S. Immigration Policy and the
        National Interest.** Staff Report of the Select
        Commission on Immigration and Refugee Policy.
        April. Pp.457-558.

Ford Foundation
1984   "Hispanics: Challenges and Opportunities". New
        York: Ford Foundation Working Paper. June.

Fox, R.
1983   "Population Growth and Urbanization In Latin
        America". Washington, D.C.: Inter-American
        Development Bank, Reprint Series, 131.

Fox, J. and M. Fox
1978   "Illegal Immigration: A Bibliography, 1968-1978".
        Southern Illinois University, Public Administrative
        Series, P-94. October.

Gallo, V.
1983   "The Construction Industry in New York City:
        Immigrants and Black Entrepreneurs". Columbia
        University, Conservation of Human Resources. Mimeo.

Garcia, V.
1982   Undocumented Mexicans in Two Los Angeles
        Communities: A Social and Economic Profile".
        Working Papers in U.S. - Mexican Studies, No. 4., La
        Jolla, CA: Program in U.S. - Mexican Studies,
        University of California at San Diego.

General Accounting Office
1985a   **Immigration: An Issue Analysis of An Emerging
        Problem.** Washington, D.C.: Program Evaluation and
        Methodology Division. September.

1985b   **The Effects of Illegal Aliens on the American Labor
        Market.** Washington, D.C.: Program Evaluation and
        Methodology Division. December.

1981   **Administrative Changes Needed to Reduce
        Employment of Illegal Aliens.** January.

1980   **Illegal Aliens: Estimating Their Impact On The U.S.**
        March 14, PAD-80-22.

Glaessel-Brown, E.
1984   "The Role of Blue-Collar Migrants from Colombia in
        New England, Labor Markets for Light Manufacturing
        Industry". Cambridge, MA: MIT, Unpublished Ph.D.
        Dissertation in Political Science.

Gorden, R.
1969   **Interviewing: Strategy, Techniques, and Tactics.**
        Homewood, IL: Dorsey Press.

Grasmuck, S.
1984   "Immigration, Ethnic Stratification and Native
        Working Class Discipline: Comparison of Documented
        and Undocumented Dominicans". **International
        Migration Review,** 18(2): 692-713.

Greenwood, M.
1979   "The Economic Consequences of Immigration for the
        U.S.: A Survey of the Findings". In Interagency Task
        Force on Immigration Policy, **Staff Report Companion
        Papers.** Washington, D.C.: Department of Justice,
        Labor and State. August. Pp. 1-108.

Greenwood, M. and J. Lillydahl
1981   "Some Possible Economic Consequences of
        International Migration: A Survey with Special
        Reference to the U.S. and Mexico". University of
        Colorado. Mimeo. November.

Gurak, D.
1982   "Dominicans and Colombians in New York City".
        Fordham University, New York: Hispanic Research
        Center, Research in Progress. Interim Reports.
        Mimeo.

Gurak, D. and M. Kritz
1983   "Kinship Networks and the Settlement Process:
        Dominican and Colombian Immigrants in New York
        City." Fordham University, Hispanic Research
        Center. Mimeo. April.

Hakim, P. and S. Weintraub
1985   Population Trade and Aid: A New Approach for the
        United States".   In   **Caribbean   Migration   and
        Development.** Edited by R. Pastor. Pp. 371-94.

Heer, D.
1979   "What Is the Annual Net Flow of Undocumented
        Mexican   Immigrants   to   the   United   States?",
        Demography, 16(3): 417-23

Heer, D. and D. Falasco
1984   "Determinants of Earnings Among Three Groups of
        Mexican   Americans: Undocumented   Immigrants,
        Legal Immigrants and Native Born".   University of
        Southern California, Population Research Laboratory.
        May.

Higham, J.
1969   **Strangers in the Land: Patterns of American Nativism
        1860-1925.** New York: Atheneum.

Hill, K.
1985   "Illegal Aliens: An Assessment".   In **Immigration
        Statistics.** Edited by Levine **et al.** Pp. 225-50.

Hirschman, A.
1958   **The Strategy of Economic Development.** New Haven:
        Yale.

Hirschman, C.
1978   "Prior U.S. Residence Among Mexican Immigrants",
        Social Forces, 56: 1179-1201.

Hobson, J.A.
1971   **Imperialism.** Ann Arbor: University of Michigan Press.

Holsti, K.
1978   "A New International Politics: Diplomacy in Complex
        Interdependence", **International Organization,** 32(2):
        513-30.

Houstoun, M.
1983   "Aliens in Irregular Status in the United States: A
        Review of Their Numbers, Characteristics and Role in
        the U.S. Labor Market", **International Migration,** 21:
        372-414.

Houstoun, M., R. Kramer and J. Barrett
1984   "Female Predominance of Immigration to the U.S.
        Since 1930: A First Look", **International Migration
        Review,** 18(4): 908-63.

Huddle, D.
1982a   "Illegal Immigrant Workers: Benefits and Costs to the
        Host Country in the Context of the INS Raids --
        Project Jobs". Paper delivered at the American
        Economics and Social Science Meeting. Mimeo.
        December.

1982b   "Undocumented Workers In Houston Non-residential
        and Highway Construction: Local and National
        Implications of a Field Survey". Rice University,
        Department of Economics. June. Mimeo.

Huddle, D., A. Corwin and G. MacDonald
1985   "Illegal Immigration: Job Displacement and Social
        Costs". Alexandria, VA: The American Immigration
        Control Foundation.

Hull, E.
1985   **Without Justice for All: The Constitutional Rights of
        Aliens.** Westport: Greenwood Press.

Hyman, H. and W. Cobb, eds.
1954 **Interviewing in Social Research.** Chicago: University of Chicago Press.

Immigration and Nationality Act (revised)
1980 Committee on the Judiciary, U.S. House of Representatives. Washington, D.C.: Government Printing Office.

Immigration and Naturalization Service
Var.
Years **Statistical Yearbook.** Washington, D.C.: Department of Justice.

Institute for Public Representation
1981 "Illegal Immigration: An Alternative Perspective". Georgetown University Law Center. Mimeo.

Institute for Social Research
1969 **Interviewer's Manual.** Ann Arbor, MI: University of Michigan.

Interagency Task Force on Immigration Policy
1979 **Staff Report.** Washington, D.C.: Departments of Justice, Labor and State. August.

International Bank for Reconstruction and Development (IBRD).
1983 **World Development Report.** Washington, D.C.

Jelin, E.
1982 "Women and the Urban Labour Market". In **Women's Roles and Population Trends in the Third World.** Edited by R. Anker, M. Buvinic and N. Youssef. London: Croom Helm. Pp. 239-67.

Johnson, G.
1980   "The Labor Market Effects on Immigration".
        Industrial and Labor Relations Review, 33(3): 331-41.
        April.

1979   "The Labor Market Effects of Immigration into the
        U.S.: A Summary of the Findings". In Interagency
        Task Force on Immigration Policy, **Staff Report
        Companion Papers.** Washington, D.C.: Departments
        of Justice, Labor and State. August. Pp. 109-62.

Johnson, K. and J. Orr
1981   Labor Shortages and Immigration: A Survey and
        Taxonomy". Washington, D.C.: Bureau of
        International Labor Affairs, U.S. Department of
        Labor, Economic Discussion Paper 13.

Jones, R.
1984a   "Changing Patterns of Undocumented Mexican
        Migration to South Texas"., **Social Science Quarterly,**
        65(2): 465-81.

1984b   "Macro-Patterns of Undocumented Migration Between
        Mexico and the U.S."In **Patterns of Undocumented
        Migration** Edited by Jones. Pp. 3-27.

1984c   **Patterns of Undocumented Migration: Mexico and the
        United States.** Totowa, N.J.: Rowman and Allanheld.

Katz, E. and O. Stark
1985   "The Proposed Immigration Reform in the United
        States: Its Impact on the Employment of Illegal Aliens
        by the Firm". Harvard University, Migration and
        Development Program, Discussion Paper 17. June.

Katzenstein, P.
1976   "International Relations and Domestic Structures: Foreign Economic Policies of Advanced Industrial Societies", **International Organization,** 30(1): 1-29.

Keely, C.
1979   **U.S. Immigration: A Policy Analysis.** New York: The Population Council.

Keely, C., P. Elwell, A. Fragomen and S. Tomasi
1977   **Profiles of Undocumented Aliens in New York City: Haitians and Dominicans.** New York: Center for Migration Studies, Occasional Papers and Documentation.

Keely, C. and E. Kraly
1978   "Recent Net Immigration to the U.S.: Its Impact on Population Growth and Native Fertility". **Demography,** 15(3): 267-83.

Kritz, M.
1981   "International Migration Patterns in the Caribbean Basin: An Overview". In **Global Trends in Migration.** Edited by Kritz, C. Keely and S. Tomasi. New York: Center for Migration Studies. Pp. 208-33.

Kritz, M. and D. Gurak
1984   "Kinship Assistance in the Settlement Process: Dominican and Colombian Cases". Paper presented at the Annual Meetings of the Population Association of America, Minneapolis. May. Mimeo.

Kuhn, T.
1962   **The Structure of Scientific Revolutions.** Chicago: University of Chicago Press.

Levine, D., K. Hill and R. Warren, eds.
1985   **Immigration Statistics: A Story of Neglect.**
Washington, D.C.: National Academy Press.

Lieberson, S. and M. Waters
1985   "Ethnic Mixtures in the United States", **Sociology and Social Research,** 70(1), forthcoming.

Lindauer, D. and D. Kaufmann
1980   **Basic Needs, Inter-household Transfers and the Extended Family.** Washington, D.C.: The World Bank, Urban and Regional Reports, No. 80-5.

Maingot, A.
1985   "The Caribbean: Migration and Social Political Development in an Area of open Borders". In **Caribbean Migration and Development.** Edited by R. Pastor. Pp. 63-90.

Mann, E. and J. Salvo
1984   "Characteristics of New Hispanic Immigrants to New York City: A Comparison of Puerto Rican and Non-Puerto Rican Hispanics". Population Division, Department of City Planning, New York City. May.

Maram, S.
1980   **Hispanic Workers in the Garment and Restaurant Industries in Los Angeles County.** La Jolla, CA: Program in U.S. - Mexican Studies, University of California at San Diego. Working papers in U.S. - Mexican Studies, No. 12.

Maram, S. and S. Long
1981   "The Labor Market Impact of Hispanic Undocumented Workers: An Exploratory Case-Study of the Garment Industry in L.A. County". Report prepared for the Employment and Training Administration, Department of Labor. September.

Marshall, A.
1983   "Immigration in a Surplus Worker Labor Market: The case of New York". New York University, Research Program in Inter-American Affairs.

1985   "Migration and Development in the Eastern Caribbean". In Caribbean Migration and Development. Edited by R. Pastor. Pp. 91-116.

1982   "A Longitudinal Study of Immigrants from the Eastern Caribbean". New York: New York University, New York Research Program in Inter-American Affairs. Research in Progress. Mimeo.

1976   Employment Implications of the International Migration of Workers. Washington, D.C.: National Council on Employment Policy. October.

Martin, P.
1984   "Immigrant Workers and the California Citrus Industry". University of California at Davis, Department of Agricultural Economics. Mimeo. August.

Massey, D.
1985   "The Settlement Process Among Mexican Migrants to the U.S.: New Methods and Findings". In Immigration Statistics. Edited by Levine et al. Pp. 255-92..

Massey, D. and K. Schnabel
1983   "Recent Trends in Hispanic Immigration to the U.S", International Migration Review, 17(2): 212-44.

Massey, D., J. Durand, H. Gonzalez, and R. Alarcon
1983   "The Social Organization of Mexican Migration to the United States". University of Pennsylvania, Department of Sociology. Mimeo.

McCarthy, K. and D. Ronfeldt
1983   "Immigration as an Intrusive Global Flow: A New Perspective". In **U.S. Immigration and Refugee Policy: Global and Domestic Issues.** Edited by M. Kritz. Lexington, MA: D.C. Heath. Pp. 381-99.

McCoy, T.
1984   "The Impact of Seasonal Labor Migration on Caribbean Development: A Case Study". Center for Latin American Studies, University of Florida.

McCullough, D.
1977   **The Path Between the Seas: The Creation of the Panama Canal, 1870-1914.** New York: Simon and Schuster.

McNeill, W.
1984   "Migration in Historical Perspective", **Population and Development Review,** 10(1): 1-18.

McNeill, W. and R. Adams, eds.
1978   **Human Migration: Patterns and Policies.** Bloomington: Indiana University Press.

McPheters, L. and D. Schlagenhauf
1981   "Macroeconomic Determinants of the Flow of Undocumented Aliens in North America". **Growth and Change,** January.

Miller, M. and D. Papademetriou
1983a   "Immigration and U.S. Foreign Policy", In **The Unavoidable Issue.** Edited by Papademetriou and Miller. Pp. 155-84.

1983b   "Immigration Reform: The U.S. and Western Europe Compared". In **The Unavoidable Issue.** Edited by Papademetriou and Miller. Pp. 271-98.

Mines, R.
1985   "Wage Depression and Job Displacement: The Case of California Janitors". Mimeo.

1981   **Developing a Community Tradition of Migration: A Field Study in Rural Racatecas, Mexico and California Settlement Areas.** La Jolla, CA: Program in U.S. - Mexican Studies, University of California at San Diego. Monographs in U.S. - Mexican Studies, No. 13.

Mines, R. and P. Martin
1984   "Immigrant Workers and the California Citrus Industry", **Industrial Relations,** 23(1): 139-49.

Mines, R. and D. Massey
1982   "A Comparison of Patterns of U.S.-Bound Migration in Two Mexican Sending Communities". Mimeo.

Morales, R.
1983   "Transitional Labor: Undocumented Workers in the Los Angeles Automobile Industry", **International Migration Review,** 17(4): 570-96.

Morris, M. and A. Mayio
1980   **Illegal Immigration and United States Foreign Policy.** Washington, D.C.: Brookings. October.

Muller, T.
1984   "The Fourth Wave: California's Newest Immigrants, A Summary". Washington, D.C.: The Urban Institute.

National Council on Employment Policy
1986   **Illegal Aliens: An Assessment of the Issues.** Washington, D.C. October.

North, D.
1975   "Illegal Aliens".   Washington, D.C.:   Linton and
        Company.

North, D. and M. Houstoun
1976   **The Characteristics and Role of Illegal Aliens in the
        U.S. Labor Market: An Exploratory Study.**
        Washington, D.C.: Linton and Company, Inc. March.

North, D. and A. Lebel
1978   **Manpower and Immigration Policies in the United
        States.** Washington, D.C.: National Commission for
        Manpower Policy.

North, D. with the assistance of J. Wagner
1980   **Nonimmigrant Workers in the U.S.: Current Trends
        and Future Implications.** Report prepared for the
        Employment and Training Administration, U.S.
        Department of Labor.

Nye, J. and R. Keohane
1971   "Transnational Relations and World Politics",
        International Organization, 25(3):329-50.

Okada, Y., M. Richards and D. Slesinger
1982   "Migrant Worker Studies: A Critical Review of
        Methodologies". University of Wisconsin at Madison
        Center for Demography and Ecology, Working Paper
        82-33.

Pachon, H. and J. Moore
1981   "Mexican Americans". In **America as a Multicultural
        Society,** a special issue of the **Annals of the American
        Academy of Political and Social Science,** edited by M.
        Gordon, Vol. 454. March. Pp. 98-110.

Palmer, R.
1979   **Caribbean Dependence on the U.S. Economy.** New
            York: Praeger.

1977   "The Migration of Human Resources from the
            Caribbean: Some Economic Implications", **Revista
            Inter-Americans,** 7(2): 242-57.

Papademetriou, D.
1985a   "Emigration and Return in the Mediterranean
            Littoral". **Comparative Politics,** 18(1):21-40.

1985b   "Illegal Caribbean Migration to the United States and
            Caribbean Development". In **Caribbean Migration and
            Development.** Edited by R. Pastor. Pp. 207-36.

1984a   "Dilemmas in International Migration: A Global
            Perspective". **Environment and Planning C:
            Government and Policy,** 2: 383-98.

1984b   "Future Trends: International Migration in a Changing
            World". **International Social Science Journal,** 36(3):
            409-25.

1984c   "Immigration Reform, American Style". **International
            Migration,** 22(4): 265-79.

1983a   "The Foreign Policy Context of U.S. Immigration
            Reform: A Forgotten Dimension". Paper prepared for
            the Council on Foreign Relations, study group on
            Immigration and Refugee Policy. October.

1983b   "International Migration in Western Europe and North
            America". Report to the Population Division,
            UNESCO. June.

1983c   New Immigrants to Brooklyn and Queens. New York: Center for Migration Studies.

1983d   "Rethinking International Migration: A Review and Critique", **Comparative Political Studies,** 15(1): 469-98.

Papademetriou, D. and N. DiMarzio
1985a   **An Exploration into the Social and Labor Market Incorporation of Undocumented Aliens in the New York Metropolitan Area.** New York: Center for Migration Studies, Report to the Tinker Foundation.

1985b   "A Preliminary Profile of Unapprehended Undocumented Aliens in Northern New Jersey", **International Migration Review,** 20(1), forthcoming.

Papademetriou, D. and G. Hopple
1982   "Causal Modelling in International Migration Research: A Methodological Prolegomenon", **Quality and Quantity,** 16: 369-402.

Papademetriou, D., P. Martin and M. Miller
1983   "U.S. Immigration Policy: The Guestworker Option Revisited", **International Migration,** 21(1): 39-55.

Papademetriou, D. and M. Miller, eds.
1983a   **The Unavoidable Issue: United States Immigration Policy in the 1980's.** Philadelphia, PA: Institute for the Study of Human Issues (ISHI).

1983b   "U.S. Immigration Policy: International Context, Theoretical Parameters and Research Priorities". In **The Unavoidable Issue.** Edited by Papademetriou and Miller. Pp. 1-40.

Passel, J. and K. Woodrow

1985 "Growth of the Undocumented Alien Population in the United States, 1979-83, as Measured by the Current Population Survey and the Decennial Census". Population Division, U.S. Bureau of the Census. Mimeo.

——— 1984 "Geographic Distribution of Undocumented Immigrants: Estimates of Undocumented Aliens Counted in the 1980 Census by State", International Migration Review, 18(3): 642-71.

Pastor, R.

1985 Caribbean Migration and Development: The Unexplored Connection. Boulder, Co.: Westview.

——— 1984 "Migration and Development in the Caribbean: The Policy Challenge". School of Public Affairs, University of Maryland. Mimeo.

——— 1982 "Sinking in the Caribbean Basin", Foreign Affairs, 60(5): 1038-58. Summer.

Pessar, P.

1985 "When the Bird s of Passage Want to Roost: An Exploration of the Role of Gender in Dominican Settlement in the United States". In New Directions in Sex and Class in Latin America. Edited by J. Nash and H. Safa. Forthcoming.

——— 1984 "The Constraints Upon and Release of Female Labor Power: Dominican Migration to the United States". Georgetown University, Center for Immigration Policy and Refugee Assistance. Mimeo.

1982a "Kinship Relations of Production in the Migration
       Process: The Case of Dominican Emigration to the
       U.S". New York University, Research Program in
       Inter-American Affairs.

1982b "The Role of Households in International Migration and
       the Case of U.S.-Bound Migration from the Dominican
       Republic". **International Migration Review,** 16(2):
       342-64.

Petras, E.
1982   "Caribbean Labor Migrations in a Global Perspective".
       University of Pennsylvania, Mimeo.

Piore, M.
1979   **Birds of Passage: Migrant Labor in Industrial
       Societies.** Cambridge: Cambridge University Press.

Poitras, G.
1980a "International Migration to the U.S. from Costa Rica
       and El Salvador". San Antonio: Trinity University,
       Border Research Institute. Mimeo.

1980   "The United States Experience of Return Migrants
       from Costa Rica and El Salvador". San Antonio:
       Trinity University, Border Research Institute.
       Mimeo. August.

Polinard, Jr., R. Wrinker and R. de la Garza
1984   "Attitudes of Mexican Americans Toward Irregular
       Mexican Immigration", **International Migration
       Review,** 18(3): 782-99.

Population Reference Bureau
1984   **PRB Occasional Series: The Caribbean.** Washington, D.C.: The Population Bureau. Papers on Barbados, Grenada, St. Lucia, Dominica, Antigua and Barbados, St. Kitts/Nevis, St. Vincent and the Grenadines, and Belize.

Portes, A.
1979   "Illegal Immigration and the International System: Lessons from Recent Legal Mexican Immigrants to the United States", **Social Problems,** 26: 425-38.

1978   "Migration and Underdevelopment., **Politics and Society,** 8: 1-48.

Portes, A. and R. Bach, eds.
1985   **Latin Journey: Cuban and Mexican Immigrants in the United States.** Berkeley: University of California Press, 1984.

Portes, A. and J. Walton
1981   **Labor, Class and the International System.** New York: Academic Press.

Ranney, S. and S. Kossoudji
1984   "The Labor Market Experience of Female Migrants: The Case of Temporary Mexican Migration to the U.S.", **International Migration Review,** 18(4): 1120-43.

1983   "Profiles of Temporary Mexican Labor Migrants to the United States", **Population and Development Review,** 9(3): 475-93.

Reichert, J. and D. Massey
1980   "History and Trends in U.S. -Bound Migration from a Mexican Town", **International Migration Review,** 14(4): 475-91

1979   "Patterns of U.S. Migration from a Mexican Sending
         Community: A   Comparison   of   Legal   and   Illegal
         Migrants", **International Migration Review,** 13(4):
         599-23.

Reimers, C.
1983   "Labor Market Discrimination Against Hispanic and
         Black Men", **Review of Economics and Statistics,**
         65(4): 570-79.

Reimers, D.
1982   "Recent Immigration Policy: An Analysis". In **The
         Gateway: U.S. Immigration Issues and Policies.**
         Edited by B. Chiswick Washington, D.C.: Enterprise
         Institute. Pp. 13-53.

Reubens, E.
1981   "Interpreting Migration: Current Models and a New
         Integration". Occasional Paper No. 29, Center for
         Latin American and Caribbean Studies, New York
         University. Mimeo.

Reubens
1979   "Temporary   Admission   of   Foreign   Workers:
         Dimensions and Policies". Washington, D.C.: National
         Commission for Manpower Policy.

1978   "Aliens, Jobs and Immigration Policy". **The Public
         Interest,** 51:113-34. Spring.

Robinson, G.
1980   "Estimating the Approximate Size of the Illegal Alien
         Population in the U.S. by the Comparative Trend
         Analysis of Age-Specific Death Rates", **Demography,**
         17(2): 159-76.

Rubinstein, H.
1982   "The Impact of Remittances in the Rural English-Speaking Caribbean: Notes on the Literature". In **Return Migration.** Edited by Stinner et al. Pp. 237-66.

Salcido, R.
1982   "Use of Services in Los Angeles County by Undocumented Families: Their Perceptions of Stress and Sources of Support", **California Sociologist,** 5(2): 119-31.

Sassen-Koob, S.
1984   "Direct Foreign Investment: A Migration Push Factor?", **Environment and Planning C: Government and Policy,** 2(3): 399-416.

1981   "Exporting Capital and Importing Labor: The Role of Caribbean Migration to New York City". New York University, Research Program in Inter-American Affairs.

Select Commission on Immigration and Refugee Policy
1981   **U.S. Immigration Policy and the National Interest.** The Final Report and Recommendations of the Select Commission on Immigration and Refugee Policy to the Congress and the President of the United States. March.

Simon, J.
1985   **How Do Immigrants Affect Us Economically?** Washington, D.C.: Georgetown University, Center for Immigration Policy and Refugee Assistance.

1984   "Immigrants, Taxes, and Welfare in the United States", **Population and Development Review,** 10(1):55-70.

1980   "What Immigrants Take From and Give to, the Public Coffers". Final Report Submitted to the Select Commission on Immigration and Refugee Policy, Washington, D.C.. October.

Simon, R. and M. DeLey
1984   "The Work Experience of Undocumented Mexican Women Migrants in Los Angeles, **International Migration Review,** 18(4):1212-29

Sjasstad, L.
1962   "The Costs and Returns of Human Migration", **Journal of Political Economy,** 70(5):80-93.

Smith, B. and R. Newman
1979   "Depressed Wages Along the U.S. - Mexico Border: An Empirical Analysis", **Economic Inquiry,** 15(1):51-66.

Sowell, T.
1981   **Ethnic America: A History.** New York: Basic Books.

Stark, O.
1984   "Discontinuity and the Theory of International Migration". Harvard University, Migration and Development Program, Discussion Paper 6. February.

1983   "Migration, Decision Making: A Review Essay." Harvard University, Migration and Development Program, Discussion Paper 2. October.

Steinberg, S.
1981   **The Ethnic Myth: Race, Ethnicity, and Class in America.** New York: Atheneum.

Stinner, W., K. Albuquerque and R. Bryce-Laporte, eds.
1982   **Return Migration and Remittances: Developing a Caribbean Perspective.** Research Institute on Immigration and Ethnic Studies, Smithsonian Institution, Occasional Paper No. 3.

Stolzenberg, R.
1982   "Occupational Differences Between Hispanics and Non-Hispanics". Santa Monica, CA: A Rand Note, for the National Commission for Employment Policy. July.

Stuart, J. and M. Kearney
1981   **Causes and Effects of Agricultural Labor Migration from the Mixteca of Oaxaca to California.** La Jolla, CA: Program in U.S. - Mexican Studies, University of California at San Diego. Working Papers in U.S. - Mexican Studies, No. 28.

Taylor, J.
1984   "Differential Migration, Networks, Information and Risk". Harvard University, Migration and Development Program, Discussion Paper No. 11. October.

Teitelbaum, M.
1985   **Latin Migration North: The Problem for U.S. Foreign Policy.** New York: Council on Foreign Relations.

1980   "Right Versus Right: Immigration and Refugee Policy in the United States", **Foreign Affairs,** 59(1):21-59.

Tienda, M.
1983a   "Market Characteristics and Hispanic Earnings: A Comparison of Natives and Immigrants", **Social Problems,** 31(1):59-72.

1983b "Nationality and Income Attainment Among Native and Immigrant Hispanic Men in the United States", Sociological Quarterly, 24: 253-72. Spring.

1980 "Segmented Markets and Earnings Inequality of Native and Immigrant Hispanics in the United States". Proceedings of the American Statistical Association, Pp. 72-81.

Tienda, M. and L. Neidert
1982 "Language, Education and the Socioeconomic Achievement of Hispanic Origin Men". University of Wisconsin-Madison: Department of Rural Sociology.

Todaro, M.
1976 International Migration in Developing Countries: A Review of Theory, Evidence, Methodology, and Research Priorities. Geneva: International Labor Office.

Torres-Rivas, E.
1985 Report on the Condition of Central American Refugees and Migrants. Georgetown University, Center for Immigration Policy and Refugee Assistance, Hemispheric Migration Project. July.

Ugalde, A., F. Bean and J. Cardenas
1979 "International Migration from the Dominican Republic: Findings from a National Survey", International Migration Review, 13(2):235-54.

Ugalde, A. and T. Langham
1982 "International Return Migration: Sociodemographic Determinants of Return Migration to the Dominican Republic". In Return Migration and Remittances. Edited by Stinner et al. Pp. 73-95.

United Nations
1982   **International Migration Policies and Programmes: A World Survey.** New York: Population Studies No. 80.

U.S. Commission on Civil Rights
1980   **The Tarnished Golden Door: Civil Rights Issues in Immigration.** September.

U.S. Congress
1985a   "Immigration Reform and Control Act". Washington, D.C.: 99th Congress, U.S. Senate. S. 1200.

1985b   "Immigration Control and Legalization Amendments Act of 1985". Washington, D.C.: 99th Congress, U.S. House of Representatives, H.R. 3080.

1983a   "Immigration Reform and Control Act". Washington, D.C.: 98th Congress, U.S. Senate, S.529.

1983b   "Immigration Reform and Control Act". Washington, D.C.: 98th Congress, U.S. House of Representatives, H.R. 1510.

1982   "Immigration Reform and Control Act of 1982". Washington, D.C.: 97th Congress, House of Representatives, H.R. 6514.

U.S. Department of Justice
1981   **Memorandum on Immigration of the Attorney General to the Secretaries of State, Defense, Education, Labor, Health and Human Services, Transportation, Treasury and to the Director of the Office of Management and Budget.** May 19.

U.S. Department of Labor
1985   **Handbook of Labor Statistics.** Washington, D.C.:
        Government Printing Office. June.

U.S. House of Representatives, Committee on the
Judiciary
1980   "Immigration and Nationality Act with Amendments
        and Notes on Related Laws, 7th Edition". Washington,
        D.C.: Government Printing Office.

1977   **Illegal Aliens: Analysis and Background.** Washington,
        D.C.: Government Printing Office. June.

U.S. Senate, Committee on the Judiciary
1983   "Summary of Hearings Held by the Senate Judiciary
        Subcommittee on Immigration and Refugee Policy,
        July   1981-April   1982",   Washington,   D.C.:
        Congressional Research Service. April.

1979   "U.S. Immigration Law and Policy: 1952-79".
        Washington, D.C.: Congressional Research Service.

Van Arsdol, M., Jr., J. Moore, D. Heer and S. Haynie
1979   **Non-Apprehended and Apprehended Undocumented
        Residents in the Los Angeles Labor Market: An
        Exploratory Study.** University of Southern California
        at Los Angeles, Population Research Laboratory.
        Mimeo.

Vialet, J.
1980   "U.S. Immigration Policy: The Western Hemisphere",
        Congressional Research Service, Report 80-69 EPW.
        April.

Wachter, M.
1979   "The Labor Market and Immigration: The Outlook for the 1980's". In **Interagency Task Force on Immigration, Companion Papers.** Washington, D.C.: U.S. Departments of State, Justice and Labor. Pp. 163-234.

————
1974   "Primary and Secondary Labor Markets: A Critique of the Dual Approach". **Brookings Papers on Economic Activity,** 3:637-80.

Waldinger, R.
1982   "The Sweatshop Labor Market: Immigration and the Dilemmas of Union Regulation in the Garment Industry". Cambridge, MA.: Joint Center for Urban Studies of MIT and Harvard Universities. Unpublished Ph.D. Dissertation.

————
1981   "Immigration and Industrial Change: A Case-Study of Immigrants in the New York City Garment Industry". Joint Center for Urban Studies, MIT and Harvard Universities, Report prepared for the Employment and Training Administration, Department of Labor. May.

Wallerstein, I.
1979   "The Rise and Future Demise of the World Capitalist System: Concepts for Comparative Analysis." In **Capitalist World Economy: Essays by I. Wallerstein.** Edited by Wallerstein. Cambridge: Cambridge University Press. Pp. 1-36.

Warren, R.
1981   "Estimating the Size of the Illegal Alien Population in the United States". Population Division, U.S. Bureau of the Census. October.

Warren, R. and J. Passel
1983   "A Count of the Uncountable: Estimates of Undocumented Aliens Counted in the 1980 U.S. Census". Population Division, U.S. Bureau of the Census. Mimeo.

Weintraub, S.
1982   "Treating the Causes: Immigration and Foreign Policy". In **The Unavoidable Issue: United States Immigration Policy in the 1980s.** Edited by D. Papademetriou and M. Miller. Pp. 185-214.

Weintraub, S. and G. Cardenas
1984   "The Use of Public Services by Undocumented Aliens in Texas". LBJ School of Public Affairs, University of Texas at Austin, Policy Research Project Report 60.

Weintraub, S. and S. Ross
1982   **"Temporary" Alien Workers in the United States.** Boulder: Westview.

Wilson, K. and A. Portes
1980   "Immigration Enclaves: An Analysis of the Labor Market Experiences of Cubans in Miami". **American Journal of Sociology,** 86(2):295-319.

Wood, C.
1982   Equilibrium and Historical-Structural Perspectives on Migration", **International Migration Review,** 16(2):298-319.

Youssef, N., M. Buvinic and A. Kudat
1979   **Women in Migration: A Third World Focus.** Washington, D.C.: International Center for Research on Women. Report prepared for U.S. Agency for International Development Office of Women in Development. June.

Zazueta, C.
1980   "Mexican Workers in the United States: Some Initial Results and Methodological Considerations of the National Household Survey of Emigration". Report on the Encuestra Nacional de Emigracion a la Frontera Norte del Pais y a los Estados Unidos, Centro Nacional de Informacion y Estadistidas del Trabajo (CENIET), Mexican Secretariat for Labor and Social Services.

Zolberg, A.
1984   "Wanted But Not Welcome: Alien Labor in Western Development". New York: New School for Social Research. Mimeo.

APPENDIX I

CENTER FOR MIGRATION STUDIES

AND

CATHOLIC COMMUNITY SERVICES

Profiling Unapprehended Undocumented
Aliens in the New York Metropolitan Area

Questionnaire

 Center for Migration Studies of New York, Inc.

SECTION 1: <u>DEMOGRAPHICS</u>

(INTERVIEWER: WRITE DOWN THE CITY AND STATE WHERE THE RESPONDENT LIVES IF
INTERVIEW CONDUCTED IN RESPONDENT'S HOUSE OR APARTMENT. ASK ZIP CODE IF NOT
KNOWN. THIS INFORMATION MUST <u>ALSO</u> BE RECORDED ON THE COVER PAGE. IF THE
INTERVIEW IS CONDUCTED AWAY FROM THE RESPONDENT'S HOUSE OR APARTMENT, ASK ALL
THE INFORMATION.)

1. Where do you live?

    City _____

    State _____

    Zip Code _____ |__|__|__|__|__|

2. Where were you born?

    Country _____ |__|__|

    Province, State _____ |__|__|

    Village, Town, City _____   _____

3. What is your date of birth? |__|__| |__|__|
                                       MONTH   YEAR

4. How old are you? |__|__|
                                                       AGE

5. SEX: CODE WITHOUT ASKING

    MALE..1

    FEMALE..2

6. In which of the following racial groups do you consider yourself
   to belong?

    White...1

    Black...2

    Mulato..3

    Indian..4

    Mestizo.......................................5

    Oriental/Asian................................6

    HISPANIC......................................7

    OTHER............_____..........8
                        (specify)

    NO ANSWER.....................................9

(INTERVIEWER: DO YOU AGREE WITH THE RESPONDENT'S SELF-IDENTIFICATION? IF YOU
DISAGREE, WHAT SHOULD IT BE?)

    AGREE...1

    DISAGREE......................................2

    (ANSWER SHOULD BE: _____) |__|

7. To which religion do you belong?

NONE...0

ROMAN CATHOLIC.................................1

PROTESTANT........_____.........2
                        (specify)

EASTERN ORTHODOX...............................3

JEWISH...4

ISLAMIC..5

BUDDHIST.......................................6

OTHER.........._____...........7
                        (specify)

NO ANSWER......................................9

8. Did you at any time attend school?

YES..1

NO...............(GO TO Q. 10)................2

9. Which of the following school levels have you attended in your home country?

   FOR EACH LEVEL ATTENDED ASK:

   (a) How many years did you go to school in this level?

   (b) Did you complete this level?

ASK "A" AND "B" FOR LEVELS ATTENDED IN U.S. LEVEL	Home Country			U.S.		
	(a) Number of yrs.	(b) Completed Yes	No	(a) Number of yrs.	(b) Completed Yes	No
NONE	L__I	NA		L__I	NA	
Primary	L__I	1	0	L__I	1	0
Secondary (or equivalency)	L__I	1	0	L__I	1	0
Associate or Technical	L__I	1	0	L__I	1	0
Bachelors	L__I	1	0	L__I	1	0
Masters	L__I	1	0	L__I	1	0
Doctorate	L__I	1	0	L__I	1	0
Other: _____	L__I	1	0	////////	////////	
Other: _____	////////	////////		L__I	1	0
Don't know/No answer						

10. Are you currently attending school?

                  YES...1

                  NO...............(GO TO Q. 12)................2

11. What are you studying? CIRCLE ALL THAT APPLY

                  ENGLISH COURSE................................01

                  BASIC EDUCATION FOR ADULTS....................02

                  SECONDARY (YEAR: _____)....................04

                  TECHNICAL COURSE (YEAR: _____).............08

                  UNIVERSITY
                            (Undergraduate - year: _____)
                            (Graduate -   year: _____)...........16

                  JOB TRAINING PROGRAM..........................32

                  OTHER..........._____..........64
                                (specify)

                  NO ANSWER.....................................99

12. What is your present marital status?

                  NEVER MARRIED (GO TO Q. 22)....................1

                  MARRIED (FORMALLY OR LEGALLY)..................2

                  CONSENSUAL UNION...............................3

                  WIDOWED (GO TO Q. 22).........................4

                  SEPARATED (GO TO Q. 22).......................5

                  DIVORCED (GO TO Q. 22).......................6

                  NO ANSWER.....................................9

13. Where was your spouse born?

                  Country_____ |__|__|

                  Province, State _____ |__|__|

                  Village, Town, City _____

14. Is your spouse currently living with you?

                  YES...............(GO TO Q. 17)...............1

                  NO..2

15. Where is your spouse living?

                  HOME COUNTRY...........(GO TO Q. 18)...........1

                  ANOTHER PLACE IN THE U.S......................2

                  OTHER......_____ (GO TO Q. 18).......3
                      (specify)

16. How long has your spouse been in the U.S.?

CIRCLE "NA" IF SPOUSE WAS BORN IN ANY OF THE FIFTY STATES, THE DISTRICT OF
COLUMBIA, PUERTO RICO OR THE VIRGIN ISLANDS).

|___,___| |___,___| BORN IN U.S......(GO TO Q. 19).....NA
   YEARS   MONTHS

17. Is this separation...

        Temporary due to migration........................1
        Temporary for other reasons.......................2
        Permanent..............Verify Q. 12..............3

18. What is your spouse's immigration status?

        PERMANENT RESIDENT ALIEN..........................1
        REFUGEE...2
        PAROLEE/ENTRANT...................................3
        PUERTO RICAN MIGRANT..............................4
        CITIZEN (NATURALIZED).............................5
        UNDOCUMENTED......................................6
        NON-IMMIGRANT (VISA-CLASS)........................7

19. Which of the following school levels has your spouse attended in his/her home country?

FOR EACH LEVEL ASK:

(a) How many years did he/she go to school in this level?

(b) Did he/she complete this level?

ASK "A" AND "B" FOR LEVELS ATTENDED IN U.S.	Home Country			U.S.		
	(a) Number of yrs.	(b) Completed Yes	No	(a) Number of yrs.	(b) Completed Yes	No
LEVEL						
NONE	L__I	NA		L__I	NA	
Primary	L__I	1	0	L__I	1	0
Secondary (or equivalency)	L__I	1	0	L__I	1	0
Associate or Technical	L__I	1	0	L__I	1	0
Bachelors	L__I	1	0	L__I	1	0
Masters	L__I	1	0	L__I	1	0
Doctorate	L__I	1	0	L__I	1	0
Other: _____	L__I	1	0			
Other: _____				L__I	1	0
Don't know/No answer						

20. Is your spouse currently working?

YES.................(GO TO Q. 22)..................1

NO..2

21. What does your spouse do?

LOOKING FOR A JOB...............................1

STUDYING.......................................2

HOMEMAKER......................................3

OTHER_____.....................4
            (specify)

UNABLE TO WORK: PHYSICAL/MENTAL INCOMPETENCE.......5

NO ANSWER.......................................9

22. How many children have you had (own and/or adopted)?

   NO. OF CHILDREN ⟶ | INTERVIEWER, IF NO CHILDREN, GO TO Q. 28 |

23. How many children under the age of 18 do you have?

   NO. OF CHILDREN ⟶ | INTERVIEWER, IF NO CHILDREN UNDER 18, GO TO Q. 28 |

(INTERVIEWER: ASK THE FOLLOWING QUESTIONS FOR EACH CHILD UNDER 18 BEGIN-NING WITH THE OLDEST ONE. FILL IN THE INFORMATION ON THE TABLE BELOW USING THE APPROPRIATE CODES. VERIFY THAT YOU OBTAIN INFORMATION FOR THE NUMBER OF CHILDREN SPECIFIED IN QUESTION #23).

24. How old is the child?

   |___,___| Age in years

25. Where is the child currently living?

   WITH RESPONDENT...................................1

   WITH SPOUSE BUT NOT WITH RESPONDENT IN U.S.......2

   WITH SPOUSE NOT IN U.S...........................3

   WITH OTHER RELATIVES IN U.S......................4

   WITH OTHER RELATIVES NOT IN U.S..................5

   LIVES ON OWN IN U.S..............................6

   LIVES ON OWN NOT IN U.S..........................7

   OTHER_____..........................8
                (specify)

26. Where was this child born?

   U.S..1

   HOME COUNTRY.....................................2

   OTHER _____.........................3
                (specify)

27. If this child is studying, where does he/she go to school?

```
                    U.S................................................1
                    HOME COUNTRY.......................................2
                    OTHER_____.............................3
                    DOES NOT GO TO SCHOOL..............................8
```

How old is the child? (Q. 24)	Where does the child live? (Q. 25)	Where was the child born? (Q. 26)	Where does child go to school? (Q. 27)
|_|_|	|_| _____	|_| _____	|_| _____
|_|_|	|_| _____	|_| _____	|_| _____
|_|_|	|_| _____	|_| _____	|_| _____
|_|_|	|_| _____	|_| _____	|_| _____
|_|_|	|_| _____	|_| _____	|_| _____
|_|_|	|_| _____	|_| _____	|_| _____
|_|_|	|_| _____	|_| _____	|_| _____
|_|_|	|_| _____	|_| _____	|_| _____

SECTION 2: <u>REGION OF ORIGIN</u>

28. Where did your mother usually live at the time of your birth?

Country_____ |_|_|_|

Province, State_____ |_|_|_|

Village, Town, City_____

29. Is this where you were actually born?

YES...1

NO..2

30. Where did you usually live during the first 15 years of your life?

PLACE OF BIRTH..1

ANOTHER PLACE...2

Country   _____ |_|_|_|

Province, State _____ |_|_|_|

Village, Town, City _____

31. Before you reached the age of 15, did you ever live in a place other than _____ for a period of 6 months or more?
     (ANSWER TO Q. 30)
                         YES...1
                         NO..2

32. During the first 15 years of your life would you say you lived most of the time in a (an):

Urban area...1

Rural area or farm...................................2

33. When you were 15 years old, where did you live?

Country_____ |_|_|_|

Province, State_____ |_|_|_|

Village, Town, City _____

34. Since you were 15 years old and up to your first trip to the U.S., did you ever live in a place other than _____ for a period of 6 months or more?   (PLACE FROM Q. 33)

YES...1

NO..................(GO TO Q. 38)....................2

(INTERVIEWER: IF RESPONDENT ANSWERED "YES" TO QUESTION #34, ASK THE FOLLOW-ING QUESTIONS FILLING THE TABLE WITH THE ANSWERS. BE SURE TO OBTAIN INFORM-ATION FOR EACH MOVE OF 6 MONTHS OR MORE UNTIL THE RESPONDENT'S FIRST TRIP TO THE U.S. AGES ARE PROVIDED IN THE TABLE SO THAT YOU CAN RECORD THE INFORMATION. FIRST, FILL IN THE INFORMATION OF THE FIRST TRIP TO THE U.S. IN THE LINE WHICH CORRESPONDS TO THE AGE OF HIS/HER ARRIVAL. ALSO, FILL IN THE PLACE AND COUNTRY WHERE RESPONDENT LIVED AT 15 (FROM QUESTION #33). FOR EACH MOVE ASK:

Q. 35 At what age did you move?	Q. 36 To where? COUNTRY	PLACE	Q. 37 Until what age did you live in that place?
15			
16			
17			
18			
19			
20			
21			
22			
23			
24			
25			
26			
27			
28			
29			
30			
31			
32			
33			
34			
35			
36			
37			
38			
39			
40			
41			
42			
43			
44			
45			
46			
47			
48			
49			
50			

(INTERVIEWER: IF RESPONDENT CAME TO THE U.S. AFTER HE HAD REACHED THE AGE OF 50 AND LIVED AT ANOTHER PLACE FOR 6 MONTHS OR MORE AFTER THAT AGE, DETAIL THE INFORMATION IN THE SPACE PROVIDED BELOW):

_____

_____

_____

_____

_____

38. Before you came to the U.S. for the first time, where did you live?

Country _____ |__|__|

Province, State _____ |__|__|

Village, Town, City _____

39. Was this place a (an):

Urban area...1

Rural area or farm...................................2

(INTERVIEWER: ASK THIS QUESTION ABOUT THE PLACE RESPONDENT LIVED IN FOR LONGEST PERIOD SINCE AGE 15):

40. About how many people lived in your (HOMETOWN/OTHER PLACE_____) in your (HOME COUNTRY/OTHER COUNTRY_____) at that time?

POPULATION............................._____

(INTERVIEWER: SKIP QUESTION 41 AND CIRCLE N.A. IF RESPONDENT LIVED IN ONE OF THE LARGEST CITIES).

41. Approximately how many people lived in the largest city closest to your home town?

POPULATION............................._____

NOT APPLICABLE.......................................NA

42. What was your father's main occupation or work? The one in which he dedicated the most time:

_____ |__|__|

43. Did your father ever come and work in the U.S.?

YES..1

NO...2

44. What was your mother's main occupation or work? The one in which she dedicated the most time:

_____ |__|__|

45. Did your mother ever come and work in the U.S.?

    YES...1

    NO..2

46. Do you (or your family) own a house or an apartment in your home country?

    YES................... (GO TO Q. 48)...................1

    NO..2

47. Do you pay (or help pay) rent for a place where you (and/or your family or relatives with whom you lived) live in your home country?

    YES...1

    NO..2

48. How much do you (or your family or relatives with whom you lived) pay every month for that place?

    DOLLARS.......................................|___|___|___|

    OWN OUTRIGHT.......................................NA

(INTERVIEWER: TRY TO OBTAIN THE FIGURES IN DOLLARS. IF NOT POSSIBLE, GIVE FIGURE IN LOCAL CURRENCY AND SPECIFY CURRENCY).

49. How many people live in that household?

    NUMBER OF PERSONS..................................|___|___|

50. How many in that household are employed?

    |___|___| ⟶ | INTERVIEWER: IF NO PERSONS ARE
    NUMBER   EMPLOYED GO TO Q. 53 |

51. Do they help pay the rent (or mortgage)?

    YES...1

    NO..2

    HOME RENTED...3

    OWN OUTRIGHT..4

52. Do they help with other expenses in the house?

    YES...1

    NO..2

53. Is there any other relative who contributes to the household expenses?

    YES...1

    NO................... (GO TO Q. 55)...................2

54. Who?

    _____

    _____

    _____

55. Do they receive any other help from persons outside the family or agencies?

        YES...1

        NO....................(GO TO Q. 58).....................2

56. From whom?

_____

_____

_____

57. What kind of help do they receive?

_____

_____

_____

_____

58. Do you own a farm or land in your home country (other than the home you have already told me about)

        YES...1

        NO..2

59. Do you own (fully or partly) a business (store, agency, etc.) in your home country?

        YES...1

        NO..2

60. Has any other member in your household ever lived in the U.S. for 6 months or more?

        YES...1

        NO..2

61. Has any other member of your household ever lived in a place other than that where he/she was born (not including U.S.) for 6 months or more?

        YES...1

        NO....................(GO TO Q. 64).....................2

62. Was it in another country?

        YES...1

        NO..2

63. Where?

_____

_____

64. Before you came to the U.S. for the first time, had you worked in your home country?

YES..1

NO....................(GO TO Q. 66)....................2

65. What kind of work did you usually do?

_____ |__,__|

_____

_____

66. Were you employed during the 12 months before your first trip to the U.S.?

YES..1

NO....................(GO TO Q. 72)....................2

67. How many months did you work?

MONTHS |__,__|

68. What kind of work did you do?

SAME AS ABOVE...1

OTHER_____

_____..2

69. What were your main tasks or duties?

_____

_____

_____

_____

70. Did you supervise anyone?

YES..1

NO...2

71. How much did you earn in the last year before coming to the U.S.?

(INTERVIEWER: WRITE DOWN THE INFORMATION IN THE LINE CORRESPONDING TO THE PERIOD THEY GIVE. TRY TO OBTAIN THE FIGURES IN DOLLARS, BUT INSTRUCT THE RESPONDENT TO CONVERT USING THE RATE OF CHANGE AT THAT TIME. IF NOT POSSIBLE, GIVE FIGURE IN LOCAL CURRENCY AND SPECIFY THE CURRENCY).

|__,__,__| Weekly..1

|__,__,__| Monthly.......................................2

|__,__,__,__| Annually......................................3

********(GO TO Q. 73)********

72. Were you looking for a job?

        YES...1

        NO..2

73. Were you studying?

        YES...1

        NO..2

SECTION 3: <u>HOW/WHY CAME</u>

74. Which is your country of citizenship?

_____ |__|__|

75. How many times did you arrive in the U.S. in the last 10 years?

TIMES |__|

(<u>INTERVIEWER</u>: IF ONLY ONE TRIP TO THE U.S., GO TO Q. 81.)

76. When did you <u>first</u> come to the U.S.?   MONTH |__| YEAR |__|

77. When you first came to the U.S., did you enter with a visa?

YES...1

NO....................(GO TO Q. 79).....................2

78. What kind of visa?

GOVERNMENT OFFICIALS (A-1)..01
GOVERNMENT OFFICIALS FAMILY (A-2)...................................02
GOVERNMENT OFFICIALS EMPLOYEES AND FAMILIES (A-3)..................03
VISITORS FOR BUSINESS (B-1)...04
VISITORS FOR PLEASURE (B-2)...05
ALIENS IN TRANSIT THROUGH THE U.S. (C-1, 3).......................06
ALIENS IN TRANSIT TO U.N. HEADQUARTERS (C-2)......................07
TRANSIT WITHOUT VISA (TROV)...08
CREWMEN REMAINING WITH VESSEL OR AIRCRAFT (D-1)...................09
CREWMEN DISCHARGED FROM VESSEL OR AIRCRAFT (D-2)..................10
TREATY TRADERS (E-1, 2)...11
STUDENTS (F-1)..12
STUDENTS' FAMILIES (F-2)..13
REPRESENTATIVES OF INTERNATIONAL ORGANIZATIONS AND THEIR
    FAMILIES (G-1, 2, 3, 4)..14
EMPLOYEES OF REPRESENTATIVES OF INTERNATIONAL ORGANIZATIONS
    AND FAMILIES (G-5)...15
TEMPORARY WORKERS (H-1, 2, 3).......................................16
SPOUSE AND MINOR CHILDREN OF TEMPORARY WORKERS (H-4).............17
FOREIGN INFORMATION REPRESENTATIVES AND FAMILIES (I).............18
EXCHANGE VISITORS (J-1)...19
FAMILIES OF EXCHANGE VISITORS (J-2)................................20
FIANCEES AND FIANCES (K-1)..21
CHILDREN OF FIANCEES AND FIANCES (K-2).............................22
INTRA-COMPANY TRANSFEREES (L-1).....................................23
SPOUSE AND MINOR CHILDREN OF INTRA-COMPANY TRANSFEREES (L-2).....24
NATO REPRESENTATIVES AND FAMILIES (NATO-1, 2).....................25
NATO EMPLOYEES AND FAMILIES (NATO-5, 6, 7)........................26
NON-RESIDENT ALIEN CANADIAN BOARDING CROSSING CARD (1-185).......27
NON-RESIDENT ALIEN MEXICAN BOARDING CROSSING CARD (1-186)........28
NO ANSWER...99

      ********GO TO Q. 80********

79. If you did not have a visa, how did you enter?

    FALSE DOCUMENTS...1
    FALSE STATEMENT TO BOARDER GUARD..2
    ENTERED WITHOUT INSPECTION: - CROSSED BORDER ILLICITLY..........3
                             - SMUGGLED OR STOWED AWAY............4
                             - JUMPED SHIP.......................5
    OTHER_____..............................6
               SPECIFY)
    NO ANSWER..9

80. When you first came to the U.S., how long did you stay?

               MONTHS |__| YEARS |__|

81. When did you last enter the U.S.?   MONTH |__| YEAR |__|

82. The last time you entered the U.S., did you have a visa?

    YES..1
    NO...................(GO TO Q. 84)....................2

83. What kind of visa?

    GOVERNMENT OFFICIALS (A-1)...01
    GOVERNMENT OFFICIALS FAMILY (A-2)......................................02
    GOVERNMENT OFFICIALS EMPLOYEES AND FAMILIES (A-3)...............03
    VISITORS FOR BUSINESS (B-1)...04
    VISITORS FOR PLEASURE (B-2)...05
    ALIENS IN TRANSIT THROUGH THE U.S. (C-1, 3).....................06
    ALIENS IN TRANSIT TO U.N. HEADQUARTERS (C-2)...................07
    TRANSIT WITHOUT VISA (TROV)...08
    CREWMEN REMAINING WITH VESSEL OR AIRCRAFT (D-1)...............09
    CREWMEN DISCHARGED FROM VESSEL OR AIRCRAFT (D-2)..............10
    TREATY TRADERS (E-1, 2)...11
    STUDENTS (F-1)..12
    STUDENTS' FAMILIES (F-2)..13
    REPRESENTATIVES OF INTERNATIONAL ORGANIZATIONS AND THEIR
       FAMILIES (G-1, 2, 3, 4)..14
    EMPLOYEES OF REPRESENTATIVES OF INTERNATIONAL ORGANIZATIONS
       AND FAMILIES (G-5)..15
    TEMPORARY WORKERS (H-1, 2, 3)...16
    SPOUSE AND MINOR CHILDREN OF TEMPORARY WORKERS (H-4)..........17
    FOREIGN INFORMATION REPRESENTATIVES AND FAMILIES (I)..........18
    EXCHANGE VISITORS (J-1)...19
    FAMILIES OF EXCHANGE VISITORS (J-2)...................................20
    FIANCEES AND FIANCES (K-1)..21
    CHILDREN OF FIANCEES AND FIANCES (K-2)................................22
    INTRA-COMPANY TRANSFEREES (L-1).......................................23
    SPOUSE AND MINOR CHILDREN OF INTRA-COMPANY TRANSFEREES (L-2)....24
    NATO REPRESENTATIVES AND FAMILIES (NATO-1, 2).................25
    NATO EMPLOYEES AND FAMILIES (NATO-5, 6, 7)....................26
    NON-RESIDENT ALIEN CANADIAN BOARDING CROSSING CARD (I-185)......27
    NON-RESIDENT ALIEN MEXICAN BOARDING CROSSING CARD (I-186).......28
    NO ANSWER...99

        ********GO TO Q. 88********

84. If you did not have a visa, how did you enter?

```
     FALSE DOCUMENTS..................(GO TO Q. 88)...................1
     FALSE STATEMENT TO BORDER GUARD..........(GO TO Q. 88)...........2
     ENTERED WITHOUT INSPECTION:
        - CROSSED BORDER ILLICITLY............(GO TO Q. 88)............3
        - JUMPED SHIP..................(GO TO Q. 88)...................4
        - SMUGGLED OR STOWED AWAY    ...................................5
     OTHER_____.........(GO TO Q. 88)........6
                        (specify)
     NO ANSWER.....................................................9
```

85. Did you pay someone to smuggle you into the U.S. the last time you came?

```
          YES........................................................1
          NO...................(GO TO Q. 87)......................2
```

86. How much did you pay?   DOLLARS |___|___|___|

        ********GO TO Q. 88********

87. Were you recruited and smuggled for work purposes?

```
          YES........................................................1
          NO.........................................................2
```

88. Where did you last enter?

        City: _____ |__|__|

        State: _____ |__|__|

89. How did you come?

```
          BY AIR.....................................................1
          BY SEA.....................................................2
          BY LAND....................................................3
```

90. How long have you been in the U.S. since you came the last time?

              MONTHS |__|__| YEARS |__|__|

91. Have you ever been apprehended by the immigration authorities (INS)?

```
          YES........................................................1
          NO....................(GO TO Q. 99)....................2
```

92. How many times have you been apprehended by the INS?   TIMES |__|__|

93. In what city and state were you apprehended? (THE LAST TIME IF MORE THAN ONCE).

        City: _____ |__|__|

        State: _____ |__|__|

94. Where were you when you were apprehended? (THE LAST TIME)

```
          HOME.......................................................1
          STREET.....................................................2
          WORK.......................................................3
          OTHER_____.....................4
                        (specify)
          NO ANSWER..................................................9
```

95. Were you incarcerated? (THE LAST TIME)

        YES..1

        NO...................(GO TO Q. 97)......................2

96. How long?   DAYS |___|___|

97. (If you were not incarcerated) what was the result of the apprehension?

        VOLUNTARY DEPARTURE......................................1

        DEPORTED..2

        RELEASED..3

        OTHER_____......................4
                            (specify)

        NO ANSWER...9

98. When were you last apprehended?   MONTH |___|___|-   YEAR |___|___|

(INTERVIEWER: ASK QUESTIONS #99-111 FOR THE FIRST TRIP TO THE U.S., IF MORE
THAN ONE TRIP. IF ONLY ONE TRIP TO THE U.S., ASK THE QUESTIONS FOR THAT TRIP).

99. What were the main reasons for coming to the U.S. the first time you came?
(MARK UP TO TWO ANSWERS).

	Main Reason	Second Reason
TO REJOIN FAMILY MEMBERS	1	1
PERSONAL/FAMILY EMERGENCY	2	2
DID NOT HAVE A JOB (UNEMPLOYED)	3	3
THERE WAS NOT ENOUGH WORK AT HOME	4	4
MY JOB THERE DID NOT PROVIDE ENOUGH INCOME	5	5
FOR POLITICAL REASONS	6	6
TO STUDY	7	7
FOR HEALTH CARE	8	8
OTHER _____ (specify)	0	0
NO ANSWER	9	9

100. Who were the main persons who influenced you to move to the U.S. the
first time you came? (MARK UP TO TWO ANSWERS)

	Main Person	Second Person
YOU	1	1
SPOUSE	2	2
CHILDREN	3	3
PARENTS	4	4
BROTHERS OR SISTERS	5	5
PARENTS-, BROTHERS-, OR SISTERS-IN-LAW	6	6
OTHER RELATIVES	7	7
OTHER_____ (specify)	8	8
NO ANSWER	9	9

101. Was the person most responsible for your coming to the U.S. already in the U.S. at that time?

YES...1

NO..2

NOT APPLICABLE...NA

102. During your <u>first</u> <u>trip</u> to the U.S., who accompanied you?   (MARK ALL THAT APPLY)

NOBODY..001

SPOUSE..002

CHILDREN..004

PARENTS...008

BROTHERS OR SISTERS...................................016

IN-LAWS...032

OTHER RELATIVES_____.........064
(specify)

FRIENDS...128

OTHER_____..................256
(specify)

NO ANSWER...999

103. Who paid for your <u>first</u> <u>trip</u> to the U.S.)   (MARK ALL THAT APPLY)

YOURSELF, FROM SAVINGS.......(GO TO Q. 105)..........001

YOURSELF, BORROWING MONEY........(GO TO Q. 105).......002

YOURSELF, SELLING PROPERTY.......(GO TO Q. 105).......004

SPOUSE..008

PARENTS...016

BROTHERS OR SISTERS...................................032

IN-LAWS...064

OTHER RELATIVES_____.........128
(specify)

OTHER_____..................256
(specify)

NO ANSWER...999

104. Was this person(s) already in the U.S.?

YES...1

NO..2

105. Who among your relatives were already living in the U.S. at the time of your arrival?   (MARK ALL THAT APPLY)

        NONE...01

        SPOUSE...02

        CHILDREN...04

        PARENTS...08

        BROTHERS OR SISTERS.................................16

        IN-LAWS...32

        OTHER RELATIVES_____..........64
                            (specify)

106. How many of these relatives lived in the U.S. at that time?

   |__,__| (INTERVIEWER: IF NONE, GO TO Q. 109)

107. Did any of your relatives who lived in the U.S. assist you in settling here?

        YES...1

        NO.................... (GO TO Q. 109).................2

108. What kind of assistance did you get from them?   (MARK ALL THAT APPLY)

        HOUSING...01

        FOOD AND/OR CLOTHES.................................02

        FINDING EMPLOYMENT.................................04

        GIVING OR LENDING MONEY.............................08

        EMOTIONAL AND/OR GENERAL GUIDANCE..................16

        OTHER_____...............32
                   (specify)

        NO ANSWER...99

109. Did any of your friends from your home country live in the U.S. at that time?

        YES...1

        NO.................... (GO TO Q. 112).................2

110. Did any of your friends assist you in settling here?

        YES...1

        NO.................... (GO TO Q. 112).................2

111. What kind of assistance did you get from them?   (MARK ALL THAT APPLY)

        HOUSING...01
        FOOD AND/OR CLOTHES.................................02
        FINDING EMPLOYMENT.................................04
        GIVING OR LENDING MONEY.............................08
        EMOTIONAL AND/OR GENERAL GUIDANCE..................16
        OTHER_____...............32
                   (specify)
        NO ANSWER...99

112. If after coming to the U.S. for the first time you returned to your home country, why did you return home?

        HAD PROBLEMS ADAPTING.....................................1

        NEEDED TO REJOIN FAMILY MEMBERS..........................2

        DID NOT FIND A JOB.......................................3

        HAD PROBLEMS WITH THE INS................................4

        PERSONAL/FAMILY EMERGENCY................................5

        OTHER _____ 6
                     (specify)

        N.A. - DID NOT GO BACK.........(GO TO Q. 114)..........8

        NO ANSWER.................(GO TO Q. 114).................9

113. If returned to home country, why did you come back to the U.S.? (MARK UP TO TWO ANSWERS)

	Main Reason	Second Reason
TO REJOIN FAMILY MEMBERS................................	01	01
PERSONAL/FAMILY EMERGENCY................................	02	02
WAS STILL UNEMPLOYED.....................................	03	03
WAS UNDEREMPLOYED..	04	04
JOB THERE DID NOT PROVIDE ENOUGH INCOME.................	05	05
FOR POLITICAL REASONS....................................	06	06
TO STUDY..	07	07
FOR HEALTH CARE...	08	08
SITUATION WHICH PROMPTED TRIP BACK HOME WAS SOLVED.....	09	09
OTHER_____	10	10
(specify)		
NO ANSWER...	99	99

114. If you were apprehended by INS and deported would you return to the U.S.?

        YES..1

        NO...................(GO TO Q. 116)....................2

115. Why?

        TO VISIT RELATIVES.......................................1

        TO WORK..2

        TO STUDY...3

        OTHER_____ 4
                   (specify)

        ********GO TO Q. 117********

116. Why not?

      AFRAID YOU WILL BE CAUGHT BY INS AGAIN.............................1

      AFRAID OF GETTING YOUR RELATIVES HERE IN TROUBLE.................2

      IT COSTS TOO MUCH MONEY TO COME BACK.............................3

      IT IS TOO MUCH TROUBLE TO COME BACK..............................4

      OTHER_____..............................5
                       (specify)

117. Would you reveal your status in order to accept amnesty?

            YES..1

            NO...2

            DON'T KNOW...9

118. Would you reveal your status in order to accept temporary legal status (less than full amnesty)?

            YES..1

            NO...2

            DON'T KNOW...9

SECTION 4: <u>SETTLEMENT</u>

119. When you first came to the U.S., how long did you think you were going to stay?

```
                    LESS THAN ONE YEAR.................................1
                    ONE TO TWO YEARS..................................2
                    THREE TO FIVE YEARS..............................3
                    MORE THAN FIVE YEARS.............................4
                    WAS NOT SURE...........(GO TO Q. 124).............5
```

120. Have you changed your plans?

```
                    YES...............................................1
                    NO...................(GO TO Q. 124)...............2
```

121. Have you decided to:

```
                    STAY LONGER.............(GO TO Q. 123).............1
                    LEAVE EARLIER.....................................2
```

122. If you now believe that you will depart the U.S. after a shorter stay than originally expected, what are the principal reasons for this? (MARK UP TO TWO RESPONSES).

	FIRST ALTERNATIVE	SECOND ALTERNATIVE
PROBLEMS ADAPTING	01	01
NEED TO REJOIN FAMILY MEMBERS	02	02
FAMILY MEMBERS HERE WANT TO LEAVE	03	03
WAS MORE SUCCESSFUL ECONOMICALLY THAN EXPECTED	04	04
WAS LESS SUCCESSFUL ECONOMICALLY THAN EXPECTED	05	05
ECONOMIC CONDITIONS HAVE CHANGED IN HOMELAND	06	06
ECONOMIC CONDITIONS HAVE CHANGED HERE	07	07
POLITICAL CONDITIONS HAVE CHANGED IN HOMELAND	08	08
POLITICAL CONDITIONS HAVE CHANGED HERE	09	09
HAVE PROBLEMS WITH INS	10	10
JUST PREFER HOMELAND	11	11
OTHER_____	12	12
(specify)		

********GO TO Q. 124********

123. If you have stayed longer or now believe it probable you will stay
     longer than originally expected, what are the reasons for this change?
     (MARK UP TO TWO RESPONSES).

	FIRST ALTERNATIVE	SECOND ALTERNATIVE
ADAPTED BETTER THAN EXPECTED	01	01
JOINED BY FAMILY MEMBERS	02	02
STARTED A FAMILY HERE	03	03
WAS MORE SUCCESSFUL ECONOMICALLY THAN EXPECTED	04	04
WAS LESS SUCCESSFUL ECONOMICALLY THAN EXPECTED	05	05
ECONOMIC CONDITIONS HAVE NOT IMPROVED IN HOMELAND	06	06
ECONOMIC CONDITIONS CHANGED HERE	07	07
POLITICAL CONDITIONS HAVE NOT IMPROVED IN HOMELAND	08	08
POLITICAL CONDITIONS CHANGED IN HOMELAND	09	09
POLITICAL CONDITIONS CHANGED HERE	10	10
APPLIED FOR REGULARIZATION OF STATUS	11	11
JUST BECAME MORE INVOLVED HERE	12	12
OTHER _____	13	13
(specify)		

124. Evaluating your current situation and that of your family in terms of factors such as employment prospects, quality of life, and whatever else seems important to you, how probable is it that you will be living here in the U.S....(MARK ONE RESPONSE FOR EACH ALTERNATIVE).

	VERY UNLIKELY	NOT PROBABLE	50/50	PROBABLE	VERY PROBABLE
One year from now	1	2	3	4	5
Three years from now	1	2	3	4	5
Five years from now	1	2	3	4	5
Ten years from now	1	2	3	4	5
Fifteen years from now	1	2	3	4	5

125. What are the factors/reasons that are most important in your reaching this judgement concerning the future? (MARK UP TO TWO RESPONSES).

	FIRST ALTERNATIVE	SECOND ALTERNATIVE
ECONOMIC OPPORTUNITIES IN U.S.	01	01
ECONOMIC OPPORTUNITIES IN HOME COUNTRY	02	02
GOALS FOR CHILDREN	03	03
RESTRICTIVE POLITICAL CONDITIONS IN HOME COUNTRY	04	04
RESTRICTIVE POLITICAL CONDITIONS IN U.S.	05	05
GENERAL QUALITY OF LIFE IN U.S. IS WORSE	06	06
GENERAL QUALITY OF LIFE IN U.S. IS BETTER	07	07
NEVER INTENDED TO STAY BEYOND THAT TIME	08	08
PROBLEMS WITH OR FEAR OF INS	09	09
OTHER_____	10	10
(specify)		

126. If you were offered a job in your home country like the one you have here and with the same salary, would you accept it and go back?

```
YES.................................................1
NO..................................................2
NOT APPLICABLE..........(GO TO Q. 128)..............9
```

127. Why?/Why not?

_____ |_↓_|
_____
_____

128. Do you have any specific plans for leaving the U.S. other than to visit abroad?

```
YES.................................................1
NO....................(GO TO Q. 131)...............2
```

129. Do you know when you will leave?

        YES...1
        NO.................. (GO TO Q. 131).................2

130. When?

                        MONTH |__,__| YEAR |__,__|

131. Do you plan to move to some place else ,in the U.S.?

        YES...1
        NO.................. (GO TO Q. 133).................2
        NOT SURE............ (GO TO Q. 133).................9

132. Where in the U.S. do you think you will move to?

        Place_____ |__,__|
        State_____ |__,__|

133. Where do you want to be living 5 years from now?

        Place_____ |__,__|
        Province/State_____ |__,__|
        Country_____

134. If you plan or would like to stay in the U.S., would you consider be-
     coming a citizen of the U.S.?

        YES.................. (GO TO Q. 136)...............1
        NO...2
        NOT SURE............ (GO TO Q. 136)................9

135. Why not? Would it not be convenient for you?

        _____ |__,__|
        _____
        _____
        _____

SECTION 5: <u>SUBJECTIVE EVALUATION</u>

136. During the first months after your arrival in the U.S., what were the main difficulties you faced? (MARK UP TO TWO ANSWERS)

	MAIN DIFFICULTY	SECOND DIFFICULTY
HOME SICKNESS.....................	1	1
NOT FINDING WORK..................	2	2
NOT FINDING ADEQUATE HOUSING.....	3	3
ADJUSTING TO FOOD/CULTURE........	4	4
LANGUAGE.........................	5	5
CLIMATE..........................	6	6
PROBLEMS WITH INS................	7	7
OTHER_____........	8	8
(specify)		
NO ANSWER/DON'T KNOW.............	9	9

137. What are the main difficulties you are facing now? (MARK UP TO TWO ANSWERS)

	MAIN DIFFICULTY	SECOND DIFFICULTY
HOME SICKNESS.....................	1	1
NOT FINDING WORK..................	2	2
NOT FINDING ADEQUATE HOUSING.....	3	3
ADJUSTING TO FOOD/CULTURE........	4	4
LANGUAGE.........................	5	5
CLIMATE..........................	6	6
PROBLEMS WITH INS................	7	7
OTHER_____........	8	8
(specify)		
DON'T KNOW/NO ANSWER.............	9	9

138. Does the fact that you do not have documents to work or live in the U.S. prevent you from enjoying certain activities or going certain places?

            YES.................,..1
            NO..................(GO TO Q. 140)................2

139. How? What activities or places?

       _____ |__|__|
       _____
       _____

140. What do you like most about living in the U.S.?

       _____ |__|__|
       _____
       _____

141. What do you like least about living in the U.S.?

_____

_____

_____

142. Do you feel that you have been treated differently by anybody because of your immigration status?

                    YES...1
                    NO..............(GO TO Q. 144)...................2

143. By whom?

                    EMPLOYER...1
                    CO-WORKERS...2
                    NEIGHBORS..3
                    FELLOW COUNTRYMEN..................................4
                    PUBLIC AGENCIES_____.............5
                                         (specify)
                    OTHER_____.....................6
                              (specify)
                    NO ANSWER..9

144. Would you say that everyone with a given level of education and train-ing and some knowledge of English in this city has about the same probability of getting a particular job? Or do members of certain groups have a better chance?

                    EQUAL CHANCE.......... (GO TO Q. 146).............1
                    UNEQUAL CHANCE......................................2

145. Which groups have a better chance?

(INTERVIEWER: TRY TO OBTAIN A SPECIFIC GROUP IN THE ANSWER. FOR EXAMPLE, IF THE ANSWER IS "AMERICANS", ASK: WHICH SPECIFIC GROUP OF AMERICANS, WHITES, BLACKS, PUERTO RICANS OR OTHER? IF ANSWER IS "HISPANIC", ASK: WHICH SPECIFIC GROUP? FROM WHICH COUNTRY?

_____   └─┴─┘

_____

_____

_____

(INTERVIEWER: GET THE FOLLOWING INFORMATION FROM THE CURRENT JOB OR THE PREVIOUS ONE IF RESPONDENT HAS NO JOB AT PRESENT (BUT ONLY IF THE PREVIOUS JOB WAS HELD IN THE U.S.). ASK THE QUESTIONS SELECTING THE APPROPRIATE PHRASE.)

In the place where you work (used to work in the U.S.), do (did) people without papers tend to have certain kinds of jobs?

YES..1
NO...................(GO TO Q. 146)...................2
NO ANSWER, DON'T KNOW OR DOES NOT APPLY
                              (GO TO Q. 146)....9

What jobs are (were) those?

_____

_____

_____

SECTION 6: <u>ENGLISH SPEAKING ABILITY</u>

146. Can you read English?

              YES..1
              A LITTLE..2
              NO..................(GO TO Q. 148)..................3

147. Well enough to read job applications?

              YES, WITHOUT PROBLEMS...............................1
              YES, WITH DIFFICULTY................................2
              NO...3

148. Do you understand English?

              YES..1
              A LITTLE..2
              NO..................(GO TO Q. 150)..................3

149. Well enough to understand T.V. and radio programs in English?

              YES, WITHOUT PROBLEMS...............................1
              YES, WITH DIFFICULTY................................2
              NO...3

150. Can you speak English?

              YES..1
              A LITTLE..2
              NO..................(GO TO Q. 152)..................3

151. Well enough to converse with someone who does not speak or understand your native language?

              YES, WITHOUT PROBLEMS...............................1
              YES, WITH DIFFICULTY................................2
              NO...3

152. What language or languages do you use when you talk to members of your family?

              _____(SPECIFY LANGUAGES)   _____

153. What language or languages do you use when you talk to your neighbors?

              _____(SPECIFY LANGUAGES)   _____

154. What language or languages do you use when you talk to your co-workers?

(<u>INTERVIEWER</u>: WRITE N.A. IF RESPONDENT HAS NO CO-WORKERS)

              _____(SPECIFY LANGUAGES)   _____

155. What language or languages do you use when you talk to your close
     friends?

     _____(SPECIFY LANGUAGES)   _____

156. What language or languages do you use when you go shopping?

     _____(SPECIFY LANGUAGES)   _____

157. Taking all things into consideration, how would you evaluate your abil-
     ity to: (CIRCLE ONE RESPONSE FOR EACH ALTERNATIVE).

	VERY POOR	POOR	AVERAGE	GOOD	VERY GOOD
A. Speak English	1	2	3	4	5
B. Write English	1	2	3	4	5
C. Read English	1	2	3	4	5
D. Understand English spoken by others	1	2	3	4	5

(INTERVIEWER: ASK THE FOLLOWING QUESTIONS IF THE RESPONDENT ANSWERED "YES" TO
ANY OF THE ABOVE QUESTIONS OR REPORTED IN ANY WAY KNOWLEDGE OF ENGLISH).

158. Did you learn to speak English in your home country before you came to
     the U.S.?

                    YES...1
                    NO..................(GO TO Q. 160)..................2

159. Did you learn in school?

                    YES...1
                    NO..2

160. Did you study English in a U.S. school?

                    YES...1
                    NO..2

SECTION 7: <u>REMITTANCES/INCOME TRANSFER</u>

161. Which relatives are living in your home country?   (MARK ALL THAT APPLY).

        NONE...001
        SPOUSE...002
        MOTHER...004
        FATHER...008
        SON(S) OR DAUGHTER(S).............................016
        BROTHER(S) OR SISTERS(S).........................032
        PARENTS-, BROTHERS-, SISTERS-IN-LAW..............064
        GRANDPARENTS......................................128
        OTHER RELATIVES_____..............256
                (specify)

162. During the past 12 months, have you or any member of your household sent or delivered currency or goods to any of your relatives living outside of the U.S.?

        YES..1
        NO.................(GO TO Q. 171).................2

163. Approximately what is the total dollar value of this money and/or goods which you or other household members have sent during the past year?

                      DOLLARS |__|__|__|

164. How often did you usually send money home?

        EVERY WEEK...1
        TWICE A MONTH......................................2
        ONCE A MONTH.......................................3
        EVERY TWO MONTHS...................................4
        EVERY THREE MONTHS.................................5
        OTHER_____..........................6
            (specify)

165. About how much money did you send home each time?

                      DOLLARS |__|__|__|

166. When you sent money back to your home country, how did you usually send it?

        POSTAL MONEY ORDER.................................1
        MONEY ORDER BOUGHT AT A BANK.......................2
        MONEY ORDER BOUGHT ELSEWHERE.......................3
        CASH SENT BY MAIL..................................4
        CASH SENT BY A FRIEND..............................5
        PERSONAL CHECK.....................................6
        OTHER_____..........................7
            (specify)

167. To which relatives or friends are money or goods being sent?   (MARK
     ALL THAT APPLY).

                    SPOUSE..001
                    PARENTS...002
                    CHILDREN..004
                    BROTHERS OR SISTERS.............................008
                    IN-LAWS...016
                    GRANDPARENTS....................................032
                    OTHER RELATIVES.................................064
                    FRIENDS...128

168. How many relatives living in your home country do you help support?

                                            NUMBER |__|__|

169. How much of that support do you provide?

                    Less than half their living expenses..............1
                    About half..2
                    More than half....................................3
                    All...4

170. How important would you say that these monies and/or goods are to those
     who receive them?

                    Very necessary....................................1
                    Helpful but not crucial...........................2
                    Appreciated but only marginally useful............3
                    Considered as tokens/gifts rather than assistance.4
                    Other_____....................5
                              (specify)
                    Don't Know..9

171. Are you sending money to your relatives in your home country at this
     time?
                    YES...1
                    NO...................(GO TO Q. 174)................2

172. Has the amount you send:

                    Remained the same.........(GO TO Q. 175)..........1
                    [Increased..2
                    [Decreased..3

173. Why?
                    _____ |__._|

                    _____

                    _____

                ********(GO TO Q. 175)********

174. Why not?

_____   └─┴─┘
_____
_____

175. Does any other member of your family living in the U.S. but not in your
household help your relatives in your home country?

                    YES..1
                    NO...2
                    DON'T KNOW...9

(INTERVIEWER: ASK Q. 176 to Q. 179 ONLY IF RESPONDENT ANSWERED YES TO Q. 162
OR #171 OR #175).

176. How is the money your relatives receive from abroad used?   (MARK ALL
THAT APPLY).

                    PAY RENT..0001
                    BUY FOOD..0002
                    BUY CLOTHING....................................0004
                    PAY SCHOOLS.....................................0008
                    PAY MEDICAL SERVICES............................0016
                    BUY LAND..0032
                    BUILT HOUSE (OR BUY)............................0064
                    PAY DEBTS.......................................0128
                    OPEN SMALL BUSINESS.............................0256
                    OTHER_____..........................0512
                              (specify)
                    DON'T KNOW......................................9999

177. How long have you or other members in your family been sending money to
your relatives?

                    MONTHS |_,_| YEARS |_,_| DON'T KNOW.......DK

178. Has the money been used always for the same purpose?

                    YES..................(GO TO Q. 180)................1
                    NO...2
                    DON'T KNOW...9

179. How was the money used before?   (MARK ALL THAT APPLY).

                    PAY RENT..0001
                    BUY FOOD..0002
                    BUY CLOTHING....................................0004
                    PAY SCHOOLS.....................................0008
                    PAY MEDICAL SERVICES............................0016
                    BUY LAND..0032
                    BUILT HOUSE (OR BUY)............................0064
                    PAY DEBTS.......................................0128
                    OPEN SMALL BUSINESS.............................0257
                    OTHER_____..........................0512
                              (specify)
                    DON'T KNOW......................................9999

180. Do you have a bank account?

                    YES...1
                    NO................(GO TO Q. 182)................2

181. Is it a:

                    Checking Account....................................1
                    Savings Account.....................................2
                    Checking and Savings..............................3
                    Other_____........................4
                              (specify)

182. Are you receiving (or have you received) any type of assistance from
     Governmental or State sources:

                    YES...1
                    NO................(GO TO Q. 186)................2

(INTERVIEWER: FILL IN THE TABLE WITH THE INFORMATION ABOUT THE FOLLOWING
QUESTIONS:

183. What kind of help?: Mark all types of help received, with a circle around
     the number. Then, for each type of help received ask the following
     questions:

184. Since when?: State month and year when person began to receive help or
     duration of the period the person has been receiving it. Fill in this
     information in the "past" column if the person is not receiving the help
     any longer or in the "present" column if currently receiving it.

185. How much?: Specify the monthly amount in dollars. If does not apply,
     write N.A.

TYPE OF HELP	PRESENT		PAST	
	DATE STARTED RECEIVING ASSISTANCE	AMOUNT (MONTHLY)	DATE/DURATION	AMOUNT (MONTHLY)
1. Social Security-Old Age				
2. Social Security-Survivors				
3. Social Security-Disability Insurance				
4. SSI-Supplemental Security Income				
5. Medicare A or B				
6. AFDC-Aid to Families with Dependent Children				
7. Refugee Cash Assistance				
8. Food Stamps				
9. Unemployment Compensation				
10. Worker's Compensation				
11. General Assistance/Welfare				
12. Temporary Disability Insurance				
13. Medicaid				
14. Veterans				
15. Other _____ (Specify Source)				

186. Is there a social security system in your home country or any system
     that will provide income to the old people when they retire?

                    YES..1
                    NO...................(GO TO Q. 188)................2
                    DON'T KNOW..........(GO TO Q. 188)................9

187. In your home country, did you or your employer ever pay money to be
     entitled to those benefits?

                    YES..1
                    NO...2

188. Have your employers in the U.S. at any time deducted social security/
     withholding tax from your wages:

                    YES..1
                    NO...................(GO TO Q. 190)................2
                    NOT APPLICABLE (HAS NOT WORKED IN U.S.)...........
                    ....(GO TO Q. 190)......9

189. Are you paying social security now?

                    YES..1
                    NO...2
                    N.A. (NOT WORKING)...................................9

190. Do you have a U.S. Social Security card?

                    YES..1
                    NO...................(GO TO Q. 196)................2

191. Is it on your name?

                    YES..1
                    NO...................(GO TO Q. 196)................2

192. What kind of social security card to you have?

                    FOR EMPLOYMENT AUTHORIZED PURPOSES................1
                    FOR BANKING PURPOSES...............................2
                    FOR STUDENT REGISTRATION PURPOSES.................3
                    FOR OTHER PURPOSES (E.G., TAX PAYMENT)...........4

193. How did you get your social security card?

                    APPLIED FOR IT FROM THE GOVERNMENT................1
                    BOUGHT IT..............GO TO Q. 195)..............2
                    OTHER_____(GO TO Q. 195)........3

                    _____
                              (explain)

194. What documents did you present in order to obtain it?

```
NONE...............................................0
BIRTH CERTIFICATE..................................1
INS AUTHORIZATION FOR EMPLOYMENT
    (I-91) STAMPED.................................2
ALIEN REGISTRATION CARD/PASSPORT/PROOF
    OF CITIZENSHIP................................3
```

195. When (year) did you get your social security card?

YEAR ⌊_,_⌋

196. Have you ever filed a Federal Income Tax Return with the U.S. Government?

```
YES................................................1
NO..................(GO TO Q. 198)................2
```

197. Did you file this year?

```
YES................................................1
NO.................................................2
```

198. In the last 12 months, did you or any member of your family go to a U.S. hospital or public clinic for any medical care?

```
YES................................................1
NO..................(GO TO Q. 201)................2
```

199. How many times?

TIMES ⌊_,_⌋

200. How was that medical care usually paid for?

```
YOU PAID BY CASH OR CHECK..........................1
YOUR OWN HEALTH INSURANCE..........................2
MEDICAID OR MEDICARE...............................3
MEDICAL INSURANCE PROVIDED FOR BY YOUR
       (OR SPOUSE'S) EMPLOYER......................4
THE TREATMENT WAS FREE.............................5
OTHER_____.......................6
            (specify)
```

SECTION 8: <u>WORK EXPERIENCE IN U.S.</u>

201. Since you arrived in the U.S. for the first time, have you worked for pay?

                    YES...1
                    NO...................(GO TO Q. 311)................2

202. How long have you worked in the U.S.?

                    MONTHS | , | YEARS | , |

203. How many jobs have you had in the U.S.?

                    ONE...1
                    TWO...2
                    THREE...3
                    MORE THAN THREE...................................4

204. Are you working now?

                    YES...1
                    NO...................(GO TO Q. 235A)...............2

     Now, I want to ask you some questions about your <u>current</u> job:

205. When did you start?

                    MONTH | , | YEAR | , |

206. What is your occupation? What do you do?

     _____ | ,   , |
     _____
     _____

207. In your job, what are your specific tasks or duties?

     _____   _____
     _____
     _____

208. Do you supervise anyone?

                    YES...1
                    NO..2

209. What is the principal product or service of this industry, agency or place?

     _____ | , |
     _____
     _____

210. How did you find out about this job?

```
FRIENDS OR RELATIVES IN THE U.S...................1
FRIENDS OR RELATIVES IN YOUR HOME COUNTRY.........2
YOU ASKED EMPLOYER DIRECTLY.......................3
EMPLOYER (OR LABOR CONTRACTOR) RECRUITED YOU......4
NEWSPAPERS........................................5
EMPLOYMENT AGENCY.................................6
OTHER_____.....................7
            (specify)
DOES NOT RECALL...................................9
```

211. When you found this job, were you asked to show any form of identification?

```
YES...............................................1
NO..................(GO TO Q. 213)................2
```

212. What type?

```
INS PAPERS (GREEN CARD, ETC.).....................1
SOCIAL SECURITY CARD..............................2
UNION CARD........................................3
SCHOOL DIPLOMA....................................4
LETTER OF RECOMMENDATION..........................5
DRIVERS LICENSE...................................6
OTHER_____.....................7
            (specify)
DON'T KNOW, DOES NOT REMEMBER.....................9
```

213. Were you asked for your Social Security number?

```
YES...............................................1
NO................................................2
```

214. Who held your job before you got it?

```
An American citizen...............................1
An immigrant with papers .........................2
An immigrant without papers.......................3
DON'T KNOW........................................9
```

215. Where is this job located?

```
City_____     |__.__|

State_____     |____|

Zip Code_____  |__.__.__.__|
```

216. How many days a week do you usually work?

                                    DAYS PER WEEK |__|

217. How many hours a day do you usually work?

                                    HOURS PER DAY |__.__|

218. How much do you earn?

(INTERVIEWER: FILL IN ONLY ONE WAGE RATE: FOR EXAMPLE, IF RESPONDENT KNOWS
HOURLY WAGE, FILL IN PER HOUR WAGE ONLY).

    _____ PER HOUR.......... (GO TO Q. 220)................1
    _____ PER DAY........... (GO TO Q. 220)................2
    _____ PER WEEK.......... (GO TO Q. 220)................3
    _____ PER TWO WEEKS..... (GO TO Q. 220)................4
    _____ PER MONTH......... (GO TO Q. 220)................5
    _____ PER INDIVIDUAL JOB CONTRACT... (GO TO Q. 222)...6
    _____ PER PIECE.....................................7

219. How much money do you usually earn a day?   PER DAY |__|__|

********GO TO Q. 222********

220. In addition to your base pay, do you also earn commission or tips?

        YES..1
        NO.................. (GO TO Q. 222)................2

221. How much money do you usually earn in commission or tips per week?

                       PER WEEK |__|__|

222. If you work more than 40 hours per week, are you paid a premium note
for overtime?

        YES..1
        NO...2

223. How does your employer pay you?

        Cash 01
        Check...02
        Cash and room 03
        Cash and board 04
        Check and room.....................................05
        Check and board....................................06
        Room and board only 07
        Cash, room and board 08
        Check, room and board..............................09
        Other _____....................10
                 (specify)

224. Does your employer make any withholding from your wages?

	YES	NO
U.S. Income Tax	1	2
State Income Tax	1	2
City Income Tax	1	2
Social Security	1	2
Other _____	1	2
(specify)		

225. Which of the following benefits do you receive and who pays for them?

(FOR EACH ALTERNATIVE MARK ONE ANSWER IN THE COLUMN OF "BENEFITS RE-CEIVED" AND ONE ANSWER IN THE COLUMN OF "PAYMENT" WHEN IT APPLIES).

	Benefits Received		Payment		
	Yes	No	Paid by Employer	Deducted From Pay	D.N.A.
A. Medical Insurance	1	2	1	2	9
B. Life Insurance	1	2	1	2	9
C. Retirement Plan	1	2	1	2	9
D. Sick Leave	1	2	1	N.A.	N.A.
E. Vacations	1	2	1	N.A.	N.A.
F. Maternity Leave	1	2	1	N.A.	N.A.

226. If you have paid vacations, how many days do you receive annually?

DAYS _____   NOT APPLICABLE.....................NA

227. Is your place of work union organized?

YES..1
NO...................(GO TO Q. 229).................2
DON'T KNOW..........(GO TO Q. 229).................9

228. Are you a member of that union?

YES..1
NO...2

229. Did you ever belong to a labor union in your home country?

YES..1
NO...2

230. Approximately, how many people work at the place where you work?

NUMBER   _____

231. Approximately, how many persons working there: (GIVE AN ANSWER FOR EACH ALTERNATIVE) (INTERVIEWER: THIS TOTAL SHOULD EQUAL ANSWER TO QUESTION #230).

Came from your country...................... |__|__|
Are Hispanics.................................. |__|__|
Are Whites (non-Hispanics).................... |__|__|
Are Blacks (American) .... |__|__|
Belong to another group_____ ... |__|__|
(specify)
TOTAL   _____

232. How many of your co-workers would you say are here without papers (not including yourself)?

NUMBER |⎯,⎯,⎯|

233. Were you hired specifically for a limited period of time?

YES..1
NO...2

234. Is there some form of job security where you work? That is, are you laid off according to seniority?

YES..1
NO...2
DON'T KNOW...9

235. If you were laid off, would you be called back first in a call-back?

YES..1
NO...2
DON'T KNOW...9

235A. (INTERVIEWER: CHECK THE BOX WHICH SUMMARIZES RESPONDENT'S WORK HISTORY)

Is not working now but has had two or more jobs in the U.S.; or, ☐ (GO TO Q. 236)

Is currently working and has had three or more jobs in the U.S.; ☐ (GO TO Q. 236)

Is not working now and has had only one job in the U.S.; or, ☐ (GO TO Q. 270)

Is currently working and has had two jobs in the U.S. ☐ (GO TO Q. 270)

Is currently working and has had only one job in the U.S. ☐ (GO TO Q. 304)

236. Now, I'd like to ask you some questions about your previous job. When did you start?

MONTH |⎯,⎯| YEAR |⎯,⎯|

237. What was your occupation? What did you do?

_____ |⎯,⎯|
_____
_____

238. In your job, what were your specific tasks or duties?

_____ |⎯,⎯|
_____
_____

239. Did you supervise anyone?

                    YES...1
                    NO..2

240. What was the principal product or service of this industry, agency or place?

                    _____
                    _____
                    _____

241. How did you find out about that job?

                    FRIENDS OR RELATIVES IN THE U.S.....................1
                    FRIENDS OR RELATIVES IN YOUR HOME COUNTRY...........2
                    YOU ASKED EMPLOYER DIRECTLY.........................3
                    EMPLOYER (OR LABOR CONTRACTOR) RECRUITED YOU........4
                    NEWSPAPERS..5
                    EMPLOYMENT AGENCY...................................6
                    OTHER_____........................7
                            (specify)
                    DOES NOT RECALL.....................................9

242. When you found this job, were you asked to show any form of identification?

                    YES...1
                    NO.................(GO TO Q. 244).................2

243. What type?

                    INS PAPERS (GREEN CARD, ETC.).......................1
                    SOCIAL SECURITY CARD................................2
                    UNION CARD..3
                    SCHOOL DIPLOMA......................................4
                    LETTER OF RECOMMENDATION............................5
                    DRIVERS LICENSE.....................................6
                    OTHER_____........................7
                            (specify)
                    DON'T KNOW, DOES NOT REMEMBER.......................9

244. Were you asked for your social security number?

                    YES...1
                    NO..2

(INTERVIEWER: ASK QUESTION #245 ONLY IF NOT ASKED BEFORE - IF RESPONDENT IS
NOT CURRENTLY WORKING)

245. Who held your job before you got it?

                        An American citizen...................................1
                        An immigrant with papers...........................2
                        An immigrant without papers.......................3
                        Don't know...9

246. Where was that job located?

                        City _____ |__|__|
                        State _____ |__|__|
                        Zip Code _____ |__|__|__|__|

247. How many days a week did you usually work?

                                  DAYS PER WEEK |__|

248. How many hours a day did you usually work?

                                HOURS PER DAY |__|__|

249. How much did you earn?

(INTERVIEWER: FILL IN ONLY ONE WAGE RATE: FOR EXAMPLE, IF RESPONDENT KNOWS
HOURLY WAGE, FILL IN PER HOUR WAGE ONLY).

          _____ PER HOUR ....(GO TO Q. 251)................1
          _____ PER DAY...............(GO TO Q. 251)...............2
          _____ PER WEEK..............(GO TO Q. 251)...............3
          _____ PER TWO WEEKS........(GO TO Q. 251)...............4
          _____ PER MONTH............(GO TO Q. 251)...............5
          _____ PER INDIVIDUAL JOB CONTRACT...(GO TO Q. 253).....6
          _____ PER PIECE...7

250. How much money did you usually earn a day?   PER DAY |__|__|

        ********GO TO Q. 253********

251. In addition to your base pay, did you also earn commissions or tips?

                        YES..1
                        NO.................(GO TO Q. 253)................2

252. How much money did you usually earn in commissions or tips per week?

                                PER WEEK |__|__|

253. If you worked more than 40 hours per week, were you paid a premium note
    for overtime?

                        YES..1
                        NO...2

254. How did your employer pay you?

```
CASH...............................................01
CHECK..............................................02
CASH AND ROOM......................................03
CASH AND BOARD.....................................04
CHECK AND ROOM.....................................05
CHECK AND BOARD....................................06
ROOM AND BOARD ONLY................................07
CASH, ROOM, AND BOARD..............................08
CHECK, ROOM AND BOARD..............................09
OTHER _____..............................10
           (specify)
```

255. Did your employer make any withholdings from your wages?

	YES	NO
U.S. Income Tax	1	2
State Income Tax	1	2
City Income Tax	1	2
Social Security	1	2
Other_____	1	2
(specify)		

256. Which of the following benefits did you receive and who paid for them? (FOR EACH ALTERNATIVE MARK ONE ANSWER IN THE COLUMN OF "BENEFITS RECEIVED" AND ONE ANSWER IN THE COLUMN OF "PAYMENT", WHEN IT APPLIES).

	Benefits Received		Payment		
	Yes	NO	Paid by Employer	Deducted From Pay	D.N.A.
A. Medical Insurance	1	2	1	2	9
B. Life Insurance	1	2	1	2	9
C. Retirement Plan	1	2	1	2	9
D. Sick Leave	1	2	1	N.A.	N.A.
E. Vacations	1	2	1	N.A.	N.A.
F. Maternity Leave	1	2	1	N.A.	N.A.

257. If you had paid vacations, how many days did you receive annually?

DAYS |__,__| NOT APPLICABLE......................NA

258. Was your place of work union-organized?

```
YES...............................................1
NO.................(GO TO Q. 260)..................2
DON'T KNOW.........(GO TO Q. 260)..................9
```

259. Were you a member of that union?

```
YES...............................................1
NO................................................2
```

(<u>INTERVIEWER</u>: ASK QUESTION #260 <u>ONLY</u> IF RESPONDENT IS NOT CURRENTLY WORKING)

260. Did you ever belong to a labor union in your home country?

            YES...................................1
            NO....................................2

261. Approximately, how many people worked at the place where you worked?

            NUMBER | |

262. Approximately, how many persons working there: (GIVE AN ANSWER FOR <u>EACH</u> ALTERNATIVE)

        CAME FROM YOUR COUNTRY..............................1
        WERE HISPANICS......................................2
        WERE WHITES (NON-HISPANICS)........................3
        WERE BLACKS (AMERICAN).............................4
        BELONGED TO ANOTHER GROUP_____.......5
                             (specify)

            TOTAL | |

(<u>INTERVIEWER</u>: THIS TOTAL SHOULD EQUAL ANSWER TO QUESTION #261)

263. How many of your co-workers would you say are here without papers (not including yourself)?

            NUMBER | |

264. Were you hired specifically for a limited period of time?

            YES...................................1
            NO....................................2

265. Was there some form of job security where you worked? That is, were you laid off according to seniority?

            YES...................................1
            NO....................................2
            DON'T KNOW............................9

266. If you were laid off, were you called back first in a call-back?

            YES...................................1
            NO....................................2
            DON'T KNOW............................9

267. Was the decision to leave that job:

        Your own...1
        Your employer's...........(GO TO Q. 269)...........2
        Other _____ (SKIP QUESTIONS #268 AND
              (specify)   #269 AND CONTINUE WHERE
                            APPLICABLE).............3

268. Which of the following was your main reason for deciding to leave?

```
                  Pregnancy.........................................1
                  To stay at home with family.....................2
                  To go to school.................................3
                  To move to another place in U.S.................4
                  Personal Health.................................5
                  No longer needed money..........................6
                  Something disagreeable about the job...........7


                  _____
                            (specify)
                  To look for a better job.......................8
                  To return to your home country voluntarily.....9
                  Other_____.................10
                            (specify)
```

(SKIP QUESTION #269 AND CONTINUE)

269. What was the reason?

```
                  LAID OFF BECAUSE BUSINESS WAS BAD..............1
                  FIRED..........................................2
                  THE SEASON FOR THAT JOB ENDED..................3
                  JOB WAS TEMPORARY AND WAS FINISHED.............4
                  PROBLEMS WITH INS..............................5
                  SOME OTHER REASON_____.............6
                                    (specify)
                  NO ANSWER......................................9
```

270. Now, I'd like to ask you some questions about your first job in the U.S. When did you start?

MONTH |___,___| YEAR |___,___|

271. What was your occupation? What did you do?

_____

_____

_____

272. In your job, what were your specific tasks or duties?

_____

_____

_____

273. Did you supervise anyone?

```
                  YES............................................1
                  NO.............................................2
```

274. What was the principal product or service of this industry, agency or place?

_____

_____

_____

275. How did you find out about that job?

```
FRIENDS OR RELATIVES IN THE U.S..................1
FRIENDS OR RELATIVES IN YOUR HOME COUNTRY.........2
YOU ASKED EMPLOYER DIRECTLY.......................3
EMPLOYER (OR LABOR CONTRACTOR) RECRUITED YOU......4
NEWSPAPERS........................................5
EMPLOYMENT AGENCY.................................6
OTHER_____.....................7
          (specify)
DOES NOT RECALL...................................9
```

276. When you found this job, were you asked to show any form of identification?

```
YES...............................................1
NO.................(GO TO Q. 278)...............2
```

277. What type?

```
INS PAPERS (GREEN CARD, ETC.).....................1
SOCIAL SECURITY CARD..............................2
UNION CARD........................................3
SCHOOL DIPLOMA....................................4
LETTER OF RECOMMENDATION..........................5
DRIVERS LICENSE...................................6
OTHER_____.....................7
          (specify)
DON'T KNOW, DOES NOT REMEMBER.....................9
```

278. Were you asked for your social security number?

```
YES...............................................1
NO................................................2
```

(INTERVIEWER: ASK QUESTION #279 ONLY IF NOT ASKED BEFORE - RESPONDENT NOT CURRENTLY WORKING AND WITH ONLY ONE JOB HELD IN THE U.S.)

279. Who held your job before you got it?

```
An American citizen...............................1
An immigrant with papers .........................2
An immigrant without papers.......................3
Don't know........................................9
```

280. Where was this job located?

City_____ |_|_ _|

State_____ |_|_ _|

Zip Code_____ |_|_ _ _ _|

281. How many days a week did you usually work?

DAYS PER WEEK |_|

282. How many hours a day did you usually work?

HOURS PER DAY |_ _|_|

283. How much did you earn?

(INTERVIEWER: FILL IN ONLY ONE WAGE RATE: FOR EXAMPLE, IF RESPONDENT KNOWS HOURLY WAGE, FILL IN PER HOUR WAGE ONLY).

_____ PER HOUR............(GO TO Q. 285)............1
_____ PER DAY.............(GO TO Q. 285)............2
_____ PER WEEK............(GO TO Q. 285)............3
_____ PER TWO WEEKS.......(GO TO Q. 285)............4
_____ PER MONTH...........(GO TO Q. 285)............5
_____ PER INDIVIDUAL JOB CONTRACT...(GO TO Q. 287)....6
_____ PER PIECE...................................7

284. How much money did you usually earn a day?   PER DAY |_ _|_ _|

********GO TO Q. 287********

295. In addition to your base pay, did you also earn commissions or tips?

YES...1
NO..................(GO TO Q. 287)................2

286. How much money did you usually earn in commissions or tips per week?

PER WEEK |_ _|_ _|

287. If you worked more than 40 hours per week, were you paid a premium note for overtime?

YES...1
NO..2

288. How did your employer pay you?

CASH...01
CHECK..02
CASH AND ROOM....................................03
CASH AND BOARD...................................04
CHECK AND ROOM...................................05
CHECK AND BOARD..................................06
ROOM AND BOARD ONLY..............................07
CASH, ROOM, AND BOARD............................08
CHECK, ROOM AND BOARD............................09
OTHER_____ 10
(specify)

289. Did your employer make any withholdings from your wages?

	YES	NO
U.S. Income Tax	1	2
State Income Tax	1	2
City Income Tax	1	2
Social Security	1	2
Other _____	1	2

(specify)

290. Which of the following benefits did you receive and who paid for them? (FOR EACH ALTERNATIVE MARK ONE ANSWER IN THE COLUMN OF "BENEFITS RECEIVED" AND ONE ANSWER IN THE COLUMN OF "PAYMENT", WHEN IT APPLIES).

	Benefits Received		Payment		
	Yes	No	Paid by Employer	Deducted From Pay	D.N.A.
A. Medical Insurance	1	2	1	2	9
B. Life Insurance	1	2	1	2	9
C. Retirement Plan	1	2	1	2	9
D. Sick Leave	1	2	N.A.	N.A.	N.A.
E. Vacations	1	2	N.A.	N.A.	N.A.
F. Maternity Leave	1	2	N.A.	N.A.	N.A.

291. If you had paid vacations, how many days did you receive annually?

DAYS _____   NOT APPLICABLE......................NA

292. Was your place of work union-organized?

YES..1
NO...................(GO TO Q. 294)...........2
DON'T KNOW..........(GO TO Q. 294)...........9

293. Were you a member of that union?

YES..1
NO...2

(INTERVIEWER: ASK QUESTION #294 ONLY IF SAME QUESTION WAS NOT ASKED BEFORE)

294. Did you ever belong to a labor union in your home country?

YES..1
NO...2

295. Approximately, how many people worked at the place where you worked?

NUMBER |__,__|

296. Approximately, how many persons working there: (GIVE AN ANSWER FOR EACH ALTERNATIVE).

CAME FROM YOUR COUNTRY...........................1
WERE HISPANICS...................................2
WERE WHITES (NON-HISPANICS)......................3
WERE BLACKS (AMERICAN)...........................4
BELONGED TO ANOTHER GROUP_____......5
                              (specify)

                                   TOTAL _____

(INTERVIEWER: THIS TOTAL SHOULD EQUAL ANSWER TO QUESTION #295)

297. How many of your co-workers would you say were here without papers (not including yourself)?

                              NUMBER |___|___|___|

298. Were you hired specifically for a limited period of time?

YES..1
NO...2

299. Was there some form of job security where you worked? That is, were you laid off according to seniority?

YES..1
NO...2
DON'T KNOW.......................................9

300. If you were laid off, were you called back first in a call-back?

YES..1
NO...2
DON'T KNOW.......................................9

301. Was the decision to leave that job:

Your own...1
Your employer's..............(GO TO Q. 303)........2
Other_____(SKIP QUESTIONS #302
         (specify)   AND #303 AND CONTINUE
                        WHERE APPLICABLE)........3

302. Which of the following was your main reason for deciding to leave:

```
                    Pregnancy.......................................1
                    To stay at home with family....................2
                    To go to school...............................3
                    To move to another place in U.S...............4
                    Personal health...............................5
                    No longer needed money........................6
                    Something disagreeable about the job..........7

                    _____
                              (specify)

                    To look for a better job......................8
                    To return to your home country voluntarily....9
                    Other_____.................10
                              (specify)
                    (SKIP QUESTION #303 AND CONTINUE)
```

303. What was the reason?

```
                    LAID OFF BECAUSE BUSINESS WAS BAD..............1
                    FIRED.........................................2
                    THE SEASON FOR THAT JOB ENDED.................3
                    JOB WAS TEMPORARY AND WAS FINISHED............4
                    PROBLEMS WITH INS............................5
                    SOME OTHER REASON_____.........6
                              (specify)
                    NO ANSWER....................................9
```

(INTERVIEWER: GET THE FOLLOWING INFORMATION FROM THE CURRENT JOB OR THE PREVIOUS ONE IF RESPONDENT HAS NO JOB AT PRESENT (BUT ONLY IF THE PREVIOUS JOB WAS HELD IN THE U.S.). ASK THE QUESTIONS SELECTING THE APPROPRIATE PHRASE.

304. In the place where you work (used to work in the U.S.), do (did) people without papers or with inadequate tend to have certain kinds of jobs?

```
                    YES...........................................1
                    NO..............(SKIP QUESTIONS #305 TO #309)......2
                    NO ANSWER, DON'T KNOW OR DOES NOT APPLY (SKIP
                              QUESTIONS #305 TO #309)..........3
```

305. What jobs are (were) those?

```
          _____            ⌐ ⌐
          _____            └─┴─┘
          _____
```

306. Do (did) those jobs pay better, the same, or worse than jobs held by those with papers?

```
                    BETTER........................................1
                    THE SAME......................................2
                    WORSE.........................................3
                    DON'T KNOW/NO ANSWER..........................9
```

307. Are (were) the working conditions on those jobs better, the same, or worse than on jobs held by those with papers?

    BETTER...1
    THE SAME...2
    WORSE..3
    DON'T KNOW/NO ANSWER.................................9

308. Are (were) the chances for promotion better, the same, or worse than on jobs held by those with papers?

    BETTER...1
    THE SAME...2
    WORSE..3
    DON'T KNOW/NO ANSWER.................................9

309. How often do (did) workers with no papers or inadequate papers move up to better jobs at the place where you work (used to work)?

    Hardly ever..1
    Sometimes..2
    Often..3
    Don't know/no answer.................................9

(INTERVIEWER: IF RESPONDENT IS CURRENTLY EMPLOYED GO TO Q. 315.)

310. How long have you been without work? (Fill whatever applies)

    DAYS |___|___| 1
    WEEKS |___|___| 2
    MONTHS |___|___| 3

311. Are you looking for work now?

    YES..1
    NO.................(GO TO Q. 314).................2

312. How long have you been looking? (Fill whatever applies)

    DAYS |___|___| 1
    WEEKS |___|___| 2
    MONTHS |___|___| 3

313. What are you doing to find a job? (MARK ALL THAT APPLY)

    GOING TO EMPLOYMENT AGENCIES........................1
    ANSWERING WANT ADS IN PAPERS........................2
    WALKING THE STREETS AND MAKING INQUIRIES...........4
    TALKING WITH FRIENDS AND RELATIVES.................8
    SENDING OUT RESUMES................................16
    USING A SOCIAL SERVICE AGENCY......................32
    OTHER_____......................64
                 (specify)

314. Which of the following best describes why you are not looking for work?

Pregnant...1
Wants to (or has to) stay home to care
    for family...................................2
Going to school to learn English..................3
Going to school to learn skills...................4
Health reasons preclude working...................5
Does not need the money...........................6
Just does not like to work........................7
Has been unable to find work in the past..........8
Self-employed.....................................9
Other_____....................10
                 (specify)

315. How many weeks did you work in the U.S. in the last twelve months?

(INTERVIEWER: IF RESPONDENT HAS BEEN IN THE U.S. LESS THAN 12 MONTHS, ESTI-
MATE THE PERCENTAGE OF TIME THAT THE RESPONDENT WAS EMPLOYED IN THE U.S.   FOR
EXAMPLE, IF RESPONDENT HAS BEEN IN THE U.S. FOR 6 MONTHS AND HAS BEEN WORKING
HERE FOR THREE MONTHS, INDICATE 50% IN THE APPROPRIATE SPACE)

WEEKS | , | (OR)   PERCENT OF TIME | , , |%

316. Do you (or have you) work(ed) on your own (self-employed) in the U.S.?

YES..1
NO...................(GO TO Q. 324)...................2

317. In what kind of business?

_____ | , |

_____

_____

318. When did you start this business?

MONTH | , | YEAR | , |

319. How long have you had (or did you have) this business? (Fill whatever applies)

MONTHS | , | YEARS | , |

320. Is (was) this:

FULL TIME (35-40 HOURS PER WEEK)....................1
PART TIME (LESS THAN 35 HOURS PER WEEK).............2

321. Approximately how much are (were) you earning in this business?   (Fill
     <u>only</u> <u>one</u> alternative).

	Gross	Net
PER DAY		
PER WEEK		
PER MONTH		
PER YEAR		

322. When did you finish your business?

(<u>INTERVIEWER</u>: IF BUSINESS IS FINISHED FILL IN THE DATES AND GO TO QUESTION
#324. IF NOT, CONTINUE AFTER MARKING 99).

MONTH |___|___| YEAR |___|___|

DOES NOT APPLY: STILL HAVE BUSINESS..............99

323. Do you see this as a long term enterprise, or as something you will no
     longer be doing within a short period of time (say one year)?

LONG TERM...1
SHORT TERM..2
OTHER_____......................3
              (specify)
NOT SURE, DON'T KNOW................................9

SECTION 9: HOUSEHOLD IN U.S.

A - Composition

324. Who is the head of this (your) household?

```
                RESPONDENT..........................................1
                SPOUSE OF RESPONDENT................................2
                CHILD OF RESPONDENT.................................3
                PARENT OF RESPONDENT...............................4
                OTHER RELATIVE OF RESPONDENT_____.....5
                                          (specify)
                FRIEND OF RESPONDENT...............................6
                NO HEAD INDICATED..................................7
                OTHER_____.....................8
                      (specify)
```

325. How many persons (including yourself) live in this household?

```
                                      NUMBER   |___|___|
```

Now, I want to ask you a few questions about the persons who live with you in this household.

(INTERVIEWER: ASK QUESTIONS #326 TO #331 FOR EACH MEMBER OF THE HOUSEHOLD. FILL IN THE TABLE WITH THE CORRESPONDING INFORMATION, USING THE APPROPRIATE CODES).

326. What is the relationship of each person to you?

```
                SPOUSE..............................................01
                CHILD...............................................02
                PARENT..............................................03
                GODPARENT...........................................04
                GRANDCHILD..........................................05
                GRANDPARENT.........................................06
                MOTHER-, FATHER-IN-LAW..............................07
                BROTHER OR SISTER...................................08
                BROTHER-, SISTER-IN-LAW.............................09
                OTHER RELATIVE......................................10
                OTHER RELATIVE OF SPOUSE............................11
                FRIEND..............................................12
                BOARDER.............................................13
                OTHER_____.......................14
                      (specify)
```

327. What is the relationship of each person to the head of the household?

(INTERVIEWER: SKIP THIS QUESTION IF RESPONDENT IS THE HEAD OF THE HOUSEHOLD)

                SPOUSE...01
                CHILD..02
                PARENT...03
                GODPARENT..04
                GRANDCHILD...05
                GRANDPARENT..06
                MOTHER-, FATHER-IN-LAW.................................07
                BROTHER OR SISTER......................................08
                BROTHER-, SISTER-IN-LAW................................09
                OTHER RELATIVE...10
                OTHER RELATIVE OF SPOUSE...............................11
                FRIEND...12
                BOARDER..13
                OTHER_____.....................14
                          (specify)

328. What is the immigration status of each person in the household?

                PERMANENT RESIDENT ALIEN..............................1
                REFUGEE...2
                PAROLEE/ENTRANT.......................................3
                CITIZEN (NATIVE)......................................4
                CITIZEN (NATURALIZED).................................5
                UNDOCUMENTED..6
                NON-IMMIGRANT (VISA)..................................7

329. What is the sex of each person in the household?

                MALE..1
                FEMALE..2

330. What is the age of each person in the household? (Age in completed years)

331. What is the principal activity of each person in the household?

                EMPLOYED..1
                UNEMPLOYED, LOOKING FOR JOB...........................2
                UNEMPLOYED, NOT LOOKING FOR JOB.......................3
                STUDYING..4
                HOUSEWIFE...5
                RETIRED/DISABLED......................................6
                INFANT..7
                OTHER_____....................8
                          (specify)

Relationship to Respondent (Q. 326)	Relationship to Head (Q. 327)	Migration Status (Q. 328)	Sex (Q. 329)	Age (Q. 330)	Principal Activity (Q. 331)
RESPONDENT |__|	|_0_|	___ |_|	M F	|_|_|	___ |_|
_____|_|	_____|_|	___ |_|	1 2	|_|_|	___ |_|
_____|_|	_____|_|	___ |_|	1 2	|_|_|	___ |_|
_____|_|	_____|_|	___ |_|	1 2	|_|_|	___ |_|
_____|_|	_____|_|	___ |_|	1 2	|_|_|	___ |_|
_____|_|	_____|_|	___ |_|	1 2	|_|_|	___ |_|
_____|_|	_____|_|	___ |_|	1 2	|_|_|	___ |_|
_____|_|	_____|_|	___ |_|	1 2	|_|_|	___ |_|
_____|_|	_____|_|	___ |_|	1 2	|_|_|	___ |_|
_____|_|	_____|_|	___ |_|	1 2	|_|_|	___ |_|
_____|_|	_____|_|	___ |_|	1 2	|_|_|	___ |_|
_____|_|	_____|_|	___ |_|	1 2	|_|_|	___ |_|
_____|_|	_____|_|	___ |_|	1 2	|_|_|	___ |_|
_____|_|	_____|_|	___ |_|	1 2	|_|_|	___ |_|
_____|_|	_____|_|	___ |_|	1 2	|_|_|	___ |_|
_____|_|	_____|_|	___ |_|	1 2	|_|_|	___ |_|

332. How many persons, in total, are employed in the household?

                 NUMBER   \|__,__\|

(INTERVIEWER: VERIFY THAT THE INFORMATION GIVEN IN QUESTION #332 CORRESPONDS TO THAT GIVEN IN QUESTION #331).

333. How many persons, in total, receive any income in the household (including social security, pension, public assistance, etc.)?

                 NUMBER   \|__,__\|

334. How many persons in the household help pay the rent (or mortgage)?

                 NUMBER   \|__,__\|

335. How many persons in the household contribute to other living expenses?

                 NUMBER   \|__,__\|

336. What is the total annual household income?   (Select one of the alternatives)

GROSS |_|_|_|_|_| 1

NET |_|_|_|_|_| 2

337. Do you receive economic help from relatives in your home country?

YES..1
NO..................(GO TO Q. 339)................2

338. How much support do you get from relatives in your home country?

LESS THAN HALF YOUR LIVING EXPENSES...............1
ABOUT HALF..2
MORE THAN HALF....................................3
ALL....`..4
NO SUPPORT..5
NO ANSWER...9

B - Ownership

339. Is the house or apartment where you live your own or rented?

OWN.................(GO TO Q. 343)..................1
RENTED..............(GO TO Q. 340)..................2
OWNED BY SOMEONE ELSE IN THE HOUSEHOLD............
                          (GO TO Q. 344).....3

340. What is the approximate monthly rent?

DOLLARS |_|_|_|_|

341. Does that include utilities?

YES..1
NO.................(GO TO Q. 344)................2

342. Which ones?   (MARK ALL THAT APPLY)

ELECTRICITY.......................................1
GAS (INCLUDING GAS HEAT)..........................2
WATER...3
OIL HEAT..4

(GO TO QUESTION #344)

343. What is the monthly mortgage or maintenance payment and taxes?

DOLLARS |_|_|_|

344. How many rooms are there in the apartment or house excluding the kitchen and bathroom?

ROOMS |_|_|

345. What is the means of transportation you use most frequently?

PUBLIC TRANSPORTATION.................................1
OWN CAR...2
SOMEONE ELSE'S CAR....................................3
OTHER _____.......................4
(specify)

C - Neighborhood Composition

346. While in the U.S., have you usually lived in a neighborhood where other people of your own nationality also live?

YES...1
NO..2
NOT SURE..3

347. How many other people of your own nationality live in your neighborhood now?

Almost all of the people in the neighborhood........1
Most of the people in the neighborhood..............2
About half the people...............................3
Less than half......................................4
Very few..5
None..6
Don't know/no answer................................9

348. Would you say that all, most, about half, a few or none of your friends are: (Circle one response for each alternative)

	All	Most	About Half	Few	None
A. From same country	1	2	3	4	5
B. Immigrants of a similar culture	1	2	3	4	5
C. Immigrants of a different culture	1	2	3	4	5
D. Native Americans	1	2	3	4	5
E. Other _____	1	2	3	4	5
(specify)					

349. Do you know other persons from your home town who live in the U.S.?

YES...1
NO..................(GO TO Q. 352)...................2

350. Are those persons:

Relatives only..1
Friends only..2
Relatives and Friends 3
Other _____.......................4
(specify)

351. How many people do you know from your home town who are or who have been in the U.S. without papers (or working without papers) at any time in the last 5 years?

NUMBER |___|___|

352. How many of your relatives live in your neighborhood?

NUMBER |___|___|

353. Which relatives live in your neighborhood?   (Circle all that apply)

```
NONE...................................................0
SPOUSE.................................................1
MOTHER.................................................2
FATHER.................................................4
SON(S) OR DAUGHTER(S)..................................8
BROTHER(S) OR SISTER(S)...............................16
PARENTS-, BROTHER-, SISTERS-IN-LAW...................32
GRANDPARENTS.........................................64
OTHER RELATIVES_____.............128
                    (specify)
```

354. How many of your relatives in the U.S. are permanent resident aliens in the U.S.?

```
All....................................................1
Most...................................................2
Half...................................................3
Few....................................................4
None...................................................5
No relatives in U.S....................................6
```

355. How many of your relatives in the U.S. are U.S. citizens?

```
All....................................................1
Most...................................................2
Half...................................................3
Few....................................................4
None...................................................5
No relatives in U.S....................................6
```

356. How many of your relatives live outside your neighborhood in the U.S.?

```
All....................................................1
Most...................................................2
Half...................................................3
Few....................................................4
None...................................................5
No relatives in U.S....................................6
```

(INTERVIEWER: GO BACK TO QUESTION #352 AND VERIFY IF ANSWER IS ALL)

D - <u>Mobility in the U.S.</u>

357. Have you lived in another place in the U.S. outside of the place where you live now?

YES..1
NO..............(END QUESTIONNAIRE HERE)..............2

(INTERVIEWER: IF RESPONDENT ANSWERED "YES" TO QUESTION #357, ALL QUESTIONS #358 TO #363 FOR <u>EACH</u> MOVE <u>WITHIN</u> THE U.S. FILL IN THE TABLE ON PAGE 60 WITH THE INFORMATION USING CODES WHEN APPLICABLE).

358. Was it in a:

DIFFERENT STATE.......................................1
SAME STATE, DIFFERENT COUNTY..........................2
SAME COUNTY, DIFFERENT PLACE..........................3

(INTERVIEWER: IF RESPONDENT DOES NOT KNOW THE ANSWER TO QUESTION #358, SKIP IT AND FILL OUT QUESTION #359 WITH THE AVAILABLE INFORMATION)

359. Where?

PLACE _____ _____

COUNTY _____

STATE _____

360. Why did you move to that place?

LOOK FOR WORK...1
REJOIN FAMILY MEMBERS.................................2
OTHER_____.....................3
(specify)

361. How long did you live in that place?

MONTHS _____   YEARS _____

362. When (in what year) did you live in that place?

YEAR _____

363. Why did you leave that place?

COULD NOT FIND A JOB.................................1
RELATIVES/FAMILY MEMBERS MOVED......................2
OTHER _____.....................3
(specify)

Move	Was It At A: (Q. #358)	Where (Q. #359)	Why Moved In (Q. #360)	For How Long (Q. #361)	When (Q. #362)	Why Moved Out (Q. #363)
1						
2						
3						
4						
5						

DESIGN, METHODOLOGY AND TRAINING PROCEDURES

I.   QUESTIONNAIRE ISSUES

A. Translation

The questionnaire was translated into two languages: French, with Creole annotations, and Spanish. The translation into French was done by a former French teacher and now full-time immigration counselor who had worked with French Creole speaking Haitians for many years. That translation was pretested with seven respondents. The Creole annotations were again obtained from two native Haitian priests who also are counselors at the Newark CCS Offices. These annotations reflected the experience of the "pretesters" with those items and questions which are likely to pose a problem for a patois-speaking Haitian.

The Spanish translation was done by the project's bilingual and bicultural research coordinator with the assistance of a Spanish (Colombian) interviewer who is a graduate student in economics and who eventually did almost half of the interviews.

B. Pretesting

The pretest was conducted among clients of the CCS offices in the Newark Diocese. These interviews were conducted between July and October, 1983. A total of 36 interviews were completed, and in each case, the respondent was randomly selected and was interviewed in his/her native language. The interviews were conducted by three CCS counselors who had been with the project since its inception and were thus extensively trained prior to administering the questionnaire. Twenty-nine of the interviews were conducted in Spanish; seven were conducted in French/Creole.

The pretesting of the questionnnaire helped identify places throughout the instrument where problems were encountered by the interviewer and the respondent. These problems were generally of the following types:

* imprecise or ambiguous question wording;

* incorrect or insufficient skip logic; and,

* unclear interviewer instruction (Institute for Social Research, 1969).

The necessary adjustments in the questionnaire were then made without altering any substantive aspects of the instrument.' Finally, the pretest helped identify those sections of the questionnaire which needed to receive special attention in interviewer training.

C. Substantive Survey Design and Execution Problems

The pretest among CCS clients also helped bring into focus a number of issues which might impact on the usefulness of the instrument and aspects of the planned analysis. In this context a particular concern involved the following issues:

* the threatening or sensitive nature of the questions;

* respondent fatigue;

* the completeness of response categories; and,

* high item non-response or lack of useful respondent information.

None of these issues proved to be a major factor in the pretest. Although much of the information collected can be considered sensitive or potentially threatening to respondents, there was minimal item non-response. This is attributed to the fact that the pretest was conducted by well-trained counselors who had the full confidence of the respondents. Respondents seemed to find the different measures sufficiently distinct and relevant. Respondent fatigue was also not a major issue. Although the length of the pretest interview was quite substantial (one-and-one-half to two hours) we noticed that with additional training the process could be made less burdensome for the respondents. The results justified this decision and toward the end of the pretest period the length of administration time was reduced to approximately one to one-and-one-half hours. In addition, the technical and format changes made as a result of the pretest effectively reduced the burden for both interviewer and respondent.

After the pre-test, certain basic decisions were made with regard to the administration of the survey instrument in the following areas: method of administration, appropriate interviewer characteristics, and location of administration. These decisions built on one another in two ways: they were all linked to similar concerns that the quality of the data and design choices in one area might constrain those in another.

The survey instrument for this study touched on topics that are personally sensitive to respondents, that have normative expectations associated with certain responses, and that cause concern about possible repercussions of the information. Many of the questions about personal experiences, for instance, have negative connotations associated with them (for example, apprehensions by INS); others, such as household income, while perhaps more positive, may be felt to be personal. Other questions, particularly when dealing with reasons for migration, may call forth standard responses based on what is considered socially desirable. Finally, since we were asking respondents to describe instances of illegal behavior, issues of confidentiality and anonymity may have been related to concerns about possible repercussions of making these reports. Respondents may have feared that their on-going relationship with CCS may be affected or jeopardized by their refusal to participate. They may have perceived possible consequences such as poor service or outright refusal of needed assistance. In addition, ongoing developments with the Immigration Reform and Control Act may have acted as incentives or disincentives for some to participate in the survey.

The way respondents deal with personally sensitive, normatively constrained or potentially harmful topics can affect data quality in two ways. Respondents may either refuse to participate in the study entirely, or they may refuse to answer certain questions (Hyman and Cobb, 1954; Cross, 1974). We encountered many examples of both dilemmas. In some cases, respondents may provide inaccurate information because they wish to hide information, present an attractive "face" to the researchers and/or interviewer, or are fearful for their status with the agency. Biased responses are even more troublesome than non-responses. However, with no external source against which to check answers, the extent of response bias will remain unknown. Because of the potential for either missing or invalid data on key items of interest, great care was taken in designing comprehensive instrument administration procedures.

At the outset, it was decided that in-person interviews would be conducted with the respondents. In-person interviews have one major disadvantage - respondents are more likely to be careful about presenting positive information about themselves or revealing sensitive information or unpopular attitudes (Gorden, 1969). However, the advantages of the in-person interview far outweigh the disadvantages. Interviewers can exert more control over the stimuli presented to the respondents. They can motivate responses to difficult questions, guide respondents through skip patterns, provide definitions or alternative wording if necessary, or probe inadequate or incomplete responses. Given this decision, the other design choices became relevant: choice of interviewer and place of administration (Hyman and Cobb, 1954).

There were two key questions with regard to the choice of interviewer: 1) Should we attempt to match interviewers and respondents on relevant social characteristics such as ethnicity and race? 2) Should CCS clients be interviewed exclusively by their counselors? The relevant methodological concerns here were the willingness of respondents to reveal private information or reveal socially disapproved behavior or attitudes to a stranger in a face-to-face situation. Where issues involve racially sensitive matters where there is a possibility of a socially desirable response, there appear to be normative constraints on what one is willing to discuss depending on the characteristics of the interviewer. This effect may be due to suppression of negative information in the presence of the interviewer of the different race, or exaggeration of responses in the presence of an interviewer of the same race (Hyman and Cobb, 1954; Cross, 1974).

Interviewers with characteristics different from those of the respondents may also have less empathy with their experiences and feelings and use less effective probes or non-verbal cues. It is also possible, however, that excessive rapport between interviewer and respondent may be associated with biased responses. There is no external criterion that can be used to assess the direction of the possible bias caused by the interaction between interviewer and respondent characteristics (Hyman and Cobb, 1954). This posed a difficulty in deciding on the best survey strategy.

Based on our own experience and that of others with similar surveys, and our pre-testing, we decided to reduce interviewer interaction effects by keeping the survey team as small as possible. We also decided to hire experienced interviewers - persons who have interviewed undocumented aliens successfully for other survey projects - while continuing to utilize the Newark counselors who participated in the pretest. The remaining counselors in the other offices would be used for refusal conversions, and if item non-response was high for key items.

With regard to location, several options were available for the in-person interviews: at the respondent's home, at the CCS offices, or at some other "neutral" ground. The most important consideration raised by location was the effect on anonymity and confidentiality. Issues of convenience, time and space also affect schedule logistics and perhaps ultimately the response rate.

Administration in the CCS offices lessened fears of unfavorable consequences of participation in the study. At the same time, however, it may have conceivably also increased social pressure to provide certain answers - either responses favorable to CCS or those playing up their actual situation. Furthermore, it may have been at times more difficult to schedule interviews in the CCS offices if respondents were working and were unable or unwilling to take time off to participate in the survey. Finally, agency interviews may have also involved increased cost to the respondent because of respondent travel time and expense.

Scheduling interviews in some other "neutral" environment might give the respondent a sense of confidentiality and removal from potential agency pressure. However, without the legitimizing effect of the agency, client refusal to participate in the survey might increase geometrically - as it did in the Archdiocese of New York component of the study. Again, a major drawback involved the ease of scheduling and respondent burden in terms of travel time and expense.

Although the most convenient location for the respondent may appear to be in his/her home, it is here where the respondent may feel the greatest pressure to modify his/her answers in certain ways. We offered each of the respondents a choice in the location for the interview, the place where she/he feels most comfortable: at home, at the CCS offices or in a "neutral" place. Virtually all respondents chose the agency offices. The options were clearly described in the advance letter that each designated respondent received.

D. Survey Operation

In view of the fact that each of the agencies participating in the study had its own administrative structure and its own system for handling external projects, the following steps were taken:

* providing additional information to these agencies about the study - its purpose, objectives, overall design and schedule;

* reviewing the planned data collection procedures and tailoring these procedures to particular situations;

* making arrangements for space and other facilities;

* making arrangements for the cooperation of counselors in setting up appointments and performing refusal-conversion work.

Interviewers were carefully screened to ensure that they were able to relate to and interview a broad range of people; protect the anonymity and confidentiality of the respondents; and be sensitive to the delicate nature of the project.

After the interviews were completed and checked, the data reduction process was begun. The quality and productivity objectives included:

* 20 percent verification of each interviewer's work;

* monitoring of scheduling and resolving appointment conflicts;

* editing of interviews; and,

* ensuring a smooth flow of project documents.

Interviewers were trained with the assistance of a specifically designed training manual, describing procedures for administering the questionnaire and containing instructions for individual questions.

Training began with a full orientation about the objectives of the study. The confidential nature of the study was stressed, and general procedures to be used for the duration of the survey were explained. Interviewers were required to participate in mock interviews to ensure familiarity with the questionnaire and to identify problem areas and procedures for handling these problems. Round-table discussions were held after the mock interviews to discuss particular problems. The first five interviews of each interviewer were fully edited by and discussed with a member of the research team before further assignments were made.

The main purpose of interviewer training was to ensure that interviewers understood both general interviewing techniques and the specific tasks necessary for this survey. Training was designed to cover the following topics:

* Roles of the interviewer and the respondents;

* Use of non-directive probes;

* Interviewing techniques;

* How to record responses;

* A discussion of the purpose of the survey;

* Description and illustration of each part or section of the questionnaire;

* A question-by-question explanation specifying probes to use or other special features of the question;

* Exercises (mock interviews, group completion of

questions/sections) to familiarize interviewers with question patterns and wordings;

*   The procedures to be followed during the survey;

*   Explanation of the use of contact sheets and any other supplementary forms;

*   Explanation of personnel matters, expense reports, and interviewer productivity reports.

During the training sessions, there were ample opportunities to ask questions and discuss the topics covered. At the end of the session, each interviewer was given a small initial assignment. After interviewing their first respondent, each interviewer had his/her first questionnaire reviewed in detail. Full assignments were not made until the initial assignment was completed and reviewed.

The most useful part of training seemed to be the technical component of it, whereby interviewers were taught how to create an environment which encourages the respondent to give valid and precise answers. In the next few pages, we outline briefly some of the procedures and conventions followed in the training regiment of the project interviews with particular emphasis on the first three training topics outlined above. Interviews require a friendly but impersonal attitude on the interviewer's part. Questions must be asked exactly as written, answers elicited without the creation of biases, and responses recorded accurately and completely (Institute for Social Research, 1969). Interviewers were trained to expect and react to different respondent personalities. A small number of respondents may be suspicious; others may require some encouragement or persuasion. Interviewers were trained to offer reassurance and encouragement, without being impolite or aggressive, and answer all legitimate questions honestly but without offering information or modifying questions which may influence the respondent's answers.

In view of the fact that the questionnaire is a data collection tool, interviewers were asked to adhere to the following procedures:

* Ask all questions exactly as worded; do not add or leave out anything.

* Ask questions as they are numbered in the questionnnaire following all interviewer instructions.

* Ask every question unless otherwise instructed to skip. Do not assume any answers.

* Ask questions in a relaxed manner. Do not make it sound like a test or cross-examination; on the other hand, show confidence in the study and do not apologize for asking the questions.

* Do not attempt to explain or define questions unless you have been provided with a specific definition.

* Be sure you enter the answers clearly and thoroughly - illegible or ambiguous responses are useless.

* Note places when you had to reassure the respondent or probe for answers.

* Note any interruptions.

Interviewers were also trained in the art of probing in order to:

* encourage the respondent to elaborate;

* encourage the respondent to clarify;

* encourage the respondent to explain;

* encourage the respondent to give a more exact figure instead of a range;

* encourage the respondent to focus on the specific question.

When probing, however, care had to be exercised not to "lead" the respondent or indicate in any way that one expects a particular answer. Avoiding biasing of the respondent's

answer (known as "nondirective probing") was highlighted as a
key ingredient of the art of interviewing and the interviewers
received training in:

* pausing;

* rereading the question;

* asking for more information;

* stressing generality;

* stressing subjectivity;

* zeroing-in; and

* repeating the response.

Interviewers were also trained to avoid biases. Of all
the sources of error in interviewing, interviewer bias (any
influence that changes a result from what it would have been
without that influence) remains the most difficult to control.
Even after successful training and field experience, the
day-to-day demands of interviewing often tempt even
experienced interviewers to neglect once-mastered
fundamental skills of the interviewer's role.

To ensure the quality of the interviews, arrangements
were made in each of the sample locations to have access to
private areas to conduct the interviews. An advance letter
was sent to each designated respondent requesting their
cooperation in the survey. Respondents were then contacted
after five days to set up appointments for the interviews.
Appointments were verified two days before the interview.
Each interviewer was required to log any contacts with sample
members. This included last-minute changes in appointments,
refusals, and related information.

In all, five interviewers were utilized, three of whom
were CCS counselors. The Newark interviews took place
during the spring, summer, and early fall of 1984. The New
York interviews took place during the fall of 1984 and winter
of 1984-85. In addition to the locations identified earlier, five
interviews took place at the offices of the Migration Office of
the Archdiocese of New York in Manhattan.

II. RECORDING CONVENTIONS

A. Questionnaire Format

There was a specific questionnaire format for these interviews.

1. Capital and lower case letters.

   Sentences and phrases written in lower case should be read to the respondent. Sentences, phrases, or words in capital letters are instructions or answer categories for the interviewer's use only, and are not to be read aloud.

   Capitals can also indicate the substitution of a more relevant word. For example, a question may read, "Did you complete (LEVEL)?"

2. Parentheses:

   These indicate a choice of wording in which you would read the more relevant word or phrase. Parentheses are also used around additional wording which might, in some cases, be needed.

3. Skips:

   Because we are interviewing respondents with different characteristics, some questions are relevant to one respondent but not relevant to another respondent - that is, some questions are relevant to only a subset of the sample. Therefore, throughout the interview you will find interviewer instructions (IN CAPITAL LETTERS) which will guide you to the appropriate question. If there are no skip instructions, proceed to the next question.

4. Answer Categories:

   The majority of responses will be entered into the questionnaire by circling either a number code:

YES......................1

NO......................2

or filling boxes:

| | | |

In a few places in the interview it may be necessary that you write in a response. This only appears when the respondent's answer does not fit any of the precoded answers, and there is a space provided for an "OTHER" (SPECIFY), or when lines are provided to write in the answer.

5. Right-justifying Numbers:

In all cases, where a number is to be entered in boxes, enter only one digit per box. You should always right-justify an answer entered in boxes. That is, if the number is a single digit, enter it in the right-hand box, and enter "O" in the left box(es).

EXAMPLES:

| 0 | 9 | | 9 | 0 |

If a person's age is 9 years old, then the correct way to enter the response would be as above, on the left-hand side of the page. If the answer was entered as it appears on the right, then the coder would enter 90 years of age on the data entry machine.

6. Corrections:

If you circle the wrong response or if the respondent changes his/her mind, make the correction and mark through the entire incorrect answer. After you have done this, the respondent or you may determine that the first answer is the correct answer. See examples on the following page.

EXAMPLES:

YES	1
NO	2
YES	1
NO	2

B.   Recording the Responses

All answers are to be recorded in the questionnnaire using a black or blue ball point pen.

Many interviewer errors occur when recording responses. Take your time. Be careful and always take a moment to recheck your work. If necessary, do not hesitate to ask a respondent to repeat an answer. This will help you to get an accurate answer and will also let the respondent know that you are interested in recording his/her answer completely and accurately.

If you have probed to the fullest and the answer still seems unclear, note all your comments in the margin and discuss it later with your supervisor for resolution. For questions that require you to write in answers rather than circling precoded response categories, record these answers in the respondent's own words. Do not paraphrase or summarize in one word.

If the respondent gives you an answer which requires some mathematical calculations, try to work it out at that time, if possible, and check the answer with the respondent. If this is not possible, calculate it when you edit the interview.

"Don't Know" responses should always be probed by letting the respondent know that we need his/her opinion, that there are no right or wrong answers or, if applicable, that a best guess or estimate would be all right.

If a respondent really doesn't know, and cannot give an estimate, put a DK next to the provided answer space.

If a respondent refuses to answer a specific question and your probing cannot elicit a response, enter an RF next to the provided answer space.

III. PROFESSIONAL BEHAVIOR

You are the study's representative. Accordingly, your behavior must be beyond reproach. Please remember that although you should create a comfortable atmosphere while interviewing, your involvement with the respondent is an impersonal one. It must stay that way. Be pleasant, be polite, but do not become involved. Please keep your own views to yourself at all times. We are interested in respondents' opinions during the interview situation and want to ensure that they do not feel uncomfortable expressing their opinions. Some of the respondents may ask you to help them regarding their immigration status. Be sympathetic but do not mislead them. Suggest that they contact their counselor at the CCS offices. Explain that we are taking a survey but are not involved, personally, in the CCS program, and that you are prevented by the rules of the study from actively helping anyone.

Please be aware, be patient and courteous and conduct yourself in a manner which will give the least offense and which will help make the interview a pleasant experience for each respondent.

A. Establishing Rapport

1. General Suggestions

   A good interviewer/respondent rapport is essential for obtaining accurate and valid data. It is important that the respondent feels that you are a capable, interested interviewer who will keep the information confidential and who is able to respond to his/her questions. The following are some suggestions to help you develop good rapport.

   a. Be friendly and relaxed but professional
   b. Be a good listener
   c. Maintain a neutral attitude
   d. Be confident of your ability to obtain an accurate and valid interview
   e. Understand and be able to convey in a few sentences the purpose of the study.

B. Introducing Yourself

How you present yourself during your first contact with the respondent will usually determine success or failure in obtaining an interview. Since this is your first opportunity to describe the survey in such a way that the respondent's interest is stimulated sufficiently to participate in the interview, it is very important that the introduction be positive and friendly. If you can communicate your interest and enthusiasm about the survey and the interview, the respondent will view it as a pleasant and worthwhile experience.

A brief introduction will suffice. However, you must immediately establish the following items with the respondent:

* Who you are;

* What you are doing;

* What you want.

An advance letter has been sent to all respondents informing them that an interviewer will be contacting them. In most cases, you will be scheduling appointments by telephone. However, some respondents who do not have telephones may have to first be contacted in-person to schedule an appointment. Details of these procedures are outlined below.

C. Answering Respondents' Questions

Although the advance letter is all that is required in most cases, there will be times when you need to answer questions before you can begin the interview. Each respondent has the right to ask questions and you should be prepared to answer them.

Listen to the respondent's questions/concerns and answer by providing only the information he/she needs to remove any doubt he or she has about you or the survey. In other words, your answers should be brief and to the point. Do not volunteer any extra information. Unasked-for information may be misunderstood and confuse the respondent. You should be familiar with the advance letter so that you can show the respondent and use it to answer his/her questions.

If you don't know the answer to a question, admit that you don't know. Continue with the interview, but volunteer to have your supervisor call with the information if · the respondent wants you to.

D.   Confidentiality

One of the most important duties of the project staff is to protect the confidentiality of data gathered during this survey. The responsibility starts with interviewers,but other project participants are just as involved.

We have a legal and a moral obligation to assure respondents that both the names and any information gathered about individuals will be kept in the strictest confidence, and will be used only for the purposes of this study, and will never be released in a form where individuals could be identified.

The principles guiding our confidentiality procedures and the elements of the system implementing those principles are described below. Knowledge about the confidentiality safeguards we employ will be critical in helping you to alleviate respondents' concerns about privacy.

1.   **Restrict Access to the Data.** Data on individuals are not made available to anyone outside the immediate research project. Within the research effort, access to all data is limited to those who must have it; safeguards exist that protect these restrictions. In particular, the identifying information is limited to those whose administrative role demand it and only for the period of time they need it.

2.   **Raw Data.** (Original information as recorded, for example, by interviewers). Information is kept in its most vulnerable form (raw data) for the shortest amount of time possible.

3.   **Key elements of the System of Protection.**

   a.   Separation of identifying information from the questionnaire prior to being assembled for data entry.

   b.   Rapid movement of all completed questionnaires to data entry with a minimum of delay.

c.   Physical safeguards to protect data and prevent unauthorized access to the data files.

d.   Rapid conversion of data to machine form. (for example, a computer tape) and entry into the research data base where confidentiality can be securely protected.

e.   Limited access to research records and other individual information to project staff.

f.   A confidentiality pledge signed by all project staff to emphasize the importance of confidentiality and to affirm that you accept your legal responsibility to protect confidentiality.

By following these guidelines we can all be sure that no confidential information is improperly used.

IV.   SURVEY PROCEDURES

A.   Receiving Assignments

You will be given your first assignment at the end of the training session. After you have successfully completed your first interviews and returned them to the CCS offices, you will receive your subsequent assignments.

The assignment packets that you will receive will contain the contact sheets and an Interviewer Assignment List. Report any discrepancies between the contact sheet and the assignment list to your supervisor.

B.   Organizing Your Assignments

While an attempt will be made to make assignments in similar geographical areas, this will not always be possible. Upon receipt of your assignments, you should spend some time organizing them so that you can spend your time efficiently. Respondents will be given the option to choose the interview site. They may be interviewed at a CCS office, at their homes or at some other location of their choice. You should obtain an area street map, and mark the interview location at the time the appointment is scheduled. Attempt to get as many interviews as possible within the same geographical area; this way you will be able to cut down on travel time while boosting your productivity.

1. Scheduling Your Time

The amount of time you allow between each interview will depend partly on whether you must travel and how far you need to travel between each interview. It is best to allow yourself some flexibility when you are scheduling appointments with respondents, especially for any which are scheduled after your first appointment of the day; for example, set the appointment for between 2 and 4 rather than at 3 PM sharp when you have agreed to meet the respondents at a place other than the CCS office. In this way, if a respondent breaks an appointment, you will not have to waste time waiting for your next appointment.

C. Contacting CCS Clients

1. **Advance Letter.** Before we assign you a contact sheet, an advance letter will be sent from the Newark office to each sample member, signed by the appropriate CCS office director. This letter will describe the purpose of the survey and request their cooperation.

Every effort must be made to schedule interviews in advance. If you can reach the respondent by phone, you will set the appointment by telephone. If the respondent cannot be reached by telephone you should make an in-person visit for the purpose of scheduling an appointment.

2. **Telephone Call to Respondent.** The contact sheet may or may not contain a telephone number along with the name and address of the potential respondent. If it does not, attempt to obtain a telephone number, first by looking in the phone book, then by dialing directory assistance.

Ask to speak to the person whose name is on the contact sheet. Identify yourself and briefly describe the study before scheduling the interview. The introduction below may be used as a guide in contacting potential respondents:

Hello, my name is_____ , and I am working on a research project for the Catholic Community Services of (OFFICE LOCATION). You should have received a letter from_____ of_____ letting you know about the study. In order to do this project, we must talk with people like yourself who are undocumented. I need to set up a time convenient with you to ask you some questions. When will be best for you?

Remember to document each attempt to contact the respondent under the "RECORD OF ATTEMPTS" on your contact sheet.

D. Entering the Field

Once assignments are made, it is up to the interviewer to make the best use of the information and material at his/her disposal to locate sample members and to complete the interview. To accomplish this, be sure you carry sufficient materials in the field. The following is a checklist of the materials needed:

1. Contact sheets
2. One questionnaire booklet for each contact sheet
3. Sample advance letter which was mailed to sample member
4. Interviewer manual
5. Ball point pens
6. Large envelopes to keep completed interviews together
7. Timepiece
8. Street map

E. Contact Sheets

You will fill out one contact sheet for each respondent you try to contact, whether or not it results in a completed interview. The contact sheet will have the ID number, name, address and phone number (if any) of the sample member (potential respondent).

1. Record of Attempts

You will fill out one line across each time you attempt to contact a respondent whether by phone or in person. For each attempt you should fill out the date, the time, and the result of the attempt, which we call the status.

2. Status Codes

The following are definitions of status codes to be used. Codes from 1 to 11 are final status codes, while those 21 and above are interim status codes to be used when more attempts will be made.

01 COMPLETE   This means you have gone through the entire interview, asking all necessary questions. An interview would be considered complete even if the respondent refused to answer a few questions in the interview, as long as the questions were actually asked and the majority of the applicable questions were answered.

02 REFUSAL   This code is used if the respondent refused to be interviewed at all; if the refusal came after you had started the questionnaire and gotten some answers, the status would be considered a "partial" rather than a "refusal". Note the reason for refusal under "NOTES", and whether another try is advisable.

03 PARTIAL   Use this code if the interview was started but terminated before it could be completed either due to a refusal to continue or some other reason, like a family emergency. Record the reason under "NOTES" and note whether a reattempt is advisable.

04 INELIGIBLE/
    DOCUMENTED
    AT TIME OF
    FIRST CONTACT
    WITH CCS

If the respondent was documented at the time of his first contact with CCS use this code

05 INELIGIBLE/
    NOW DOCUMENTED

If the person was undocumented at the time the sample was drawn but is now documented, and refuses to participate in the survey, use this code

06 NOT LOCATED

This code is used when a respondent cannot be located. Under "NOTES" record the searching procedures you used to locate the respondent.

07 LANGUAGE/
    BARRIER DOES
    NOT SPEAK
    ENGLISH OR
    SPANISH OR
    FRENCH/PATOIS

This code is used if the respondent does not speak English, Spanish or French/Patois

8   PHYSICAL/MENTAL
    INCOMPETENCE

This code describes respondents who are physically or mentally incapable of completing the interview. Under "NOTES" fully describe the circumstances which caused you to use this code.

09 DEAD

The respondent has died. Record the name and address of the person who gave you this information.

10 RETIRED

Do not use this code. Your supervisor is the only person who can use this category.

11 OTHER/
    (SPECIFY
    IN
    NOTES)

Use this for any other final status category not previously mentioned. Describe the circumstances fully under "NOTES".

21 NO ANSWER/   Record this code when a telephone
   TELEPHONE   attempt to contact the respondent
                       results in a busy signal or a no answer.
                       Remember to stagger phone calls
                       during different days of the week and
                       different hours of the day.

22 NOT HOME/   Use this code if you attempted to
   IN-PERSON   to reach the respondent in-person
   ATTEMPT   and no one was home.

23 CALLBACK/   This code is used if the repondent
   TELEPHONE   or someone else in the household tells
                       you to call back at a later date or time
                       to set up an appointment.

24 CALLBACK   Use this code if an in-person attempt
   IN-PERSON   is made but the respondent or someone
                       else in the household tells you to come
                       back at a later time to set up an
                       appointment.

25 APPOINTMENT   If an actual appointment is made, code
                       this number. Record date and time
                       under "NOTES".

26 REASSIGN TO   This is used if, for some reason, the
   A DIFFERENT   contact sheet is to be reassigned to
                       another interviewer. For example, the
                       respondent speaks only Patois and the
                       contact sheet needs to be reassigned to
                       a Patois-speaking interviewer. Contact
                       your supervisor regarding the use of
                       this code.

F. Interviewer Edit

You will be responsible for pinpointing and correcting your own errors. Before you return the materials to the Newark office, you should read through the questionnaire thoroughly, checking the following points.

a. The RESPONDENT ID number from the contact sheet must be recorded on the questionnaire. The importance of correctly recording the ID numbers cannot be overstated.

b. All answers must be recorded clearly and legibly for reading by quality controller and keypunch operator. Circles should be clear and should not overrun response codes. Open-ended responses should be written out clearly. Any marginal notes should be detailed and descriptive.

c. All required questions have been asked. Every question that should be asked must have an answer recorded in it (or an indication of a refusal or "don't know" response). All questions must conform to the skip directions in the questionnaire. If you find that a question was missed, recontact the respondent for the missing information as soon as possible. Be sure the skip logic is carefully followed and that the necessary corrections, if any, are made to questions previously recorded incorrectly in subsequent sections.

d. Open-ended questions. Be sure these questions are answered fully. Your answers must be presented in sufficient detail for readers to interpret them easily.

e. Right-justifying numbers. All numerical answers must be right-justified.

f. Inconsistencies. The interview makes sense only when viewed in its entirety. The questionnaire was designed to follow a logical pattern with each question and series of questions being interrelated. In reviewing the interview, make sure the information from questions makes sense logically. Interviewer training will point out the specific areas within the questionnaire which are cross-referenced.

Sometimes, respondents will have seemingly inconsistent but real responses. If you cannot clear up apparent inconsistencies through neutral probing, do not force the respondent to conform to your perceptions of what makes sense, but describe the probes you used in notes to your supervisor.

G. Communication With Your Supervisor

You will be reporting directly to the research coordinator with whom you will be talking on the phone on a calling schedule of times when you will be available for a call from Newark. At the time of these calls you will discuss the status of your assigned work; have ready your contact sheets and assignment lists, so that you can report the ID numbers of your completed assignments, and the status of your other work. This is also the time for you to ask any questions you may have, and discuss any problems which may have come up. In addition, your supervisor will be giving you feedback on the quality of the work you have been performing.

1. Returning Materials to Newark

Upon completion and editing of the questionnaire, you should remove the contact sheet and keep it separate from the interview. The contact sheet, which contains personal identifying information should, under no circumstances, be kept with the interview. Completed questionnaires and contact sheets should be returned to the Newark office on a weekly basis. When completed interviews are returned, fresh samples will be assigned to the interviewer.

It is important that you keep an accurate account of what you return to Newark and when, so that you provide this information to project staff in claiming your salary. This will be your only record of what you have completed and returned.

2. Verification on Field Interviews

A percentage of each interviewer's work will be verified by phone and in-person. Respondents will be called, and a few questions from the interview will be reasked.

H. Computation of Salary and Expenses

Each Friday, interviewers will return their completed questionnaires to the Newark office. The payroll requests will be hand-carried to the CMS office on Staten Island, and the checks will be issued the following Monday. Checks can be mailed to the interviewers, or if they so desire, special arrangements can be made with the supervisor.

Interviewers may be compensated for expenses incurred while doing field work. If the interview is completed at a CCS office in your own geographical location, we will consider travel and expenses to get to that offfice as a normal expense anyone who has a job has to incur. If, however, interviews are to be conducted at the respondent's home or at a place of his/her choosing, interviewers will be reimbursed for their expenses. We will pay tolls, parking, mileage and phone calls. Any other expense will not be paid unless it has first been cleared by your supervisor. Meals are not a reimbursable expense. To be reimbursed for phone calls, you must submit a copy of the phone bill with the reimbursable calls underlined. Try to keep these to an absolute minimum. We have made arrangements to have desk and phone facilities at the CCS offices.

Interviewer Time and Productivity Report

This form is necessary for the management of the data collection effort. It should be completed and submitted each week along with your interviews. Instructions for completing this form will be provided during training.

V.   QUESTION-BY-QUESTION REVIEW

The following should be read along with an open copy of the questionnaire.

Introduction

The undocumented, unapprehended aliens survey questionnaire is designed to collect data about:

* demographic characteristics

* migration patterns

* reasons for migrating

* settlement in the U.S.

* subjective evaluation of U.S. immigration experience

* English-speaking ability

* remittances/income transfer to home country

* social service program utilization

* work experience in the U.S.

* U.S. household composition

* ownership and mobility

The following are some terms you will need to understand fully before administering the questionnaire.

"UNDOCUMENTED" An undocumented alien is one who is in the United States in violation of the immigration laws; that is, a person who comes to the United States illegally, or who came legally and is now out of status in reference to the original visa, e.g., persons who overstay B-2 visitor's visas, or E.W.I. (Entry Without Inspection) or persons who are out of status in any other manner. A more thorough discussion of undocumented and documented statuses will be provided during training.

"CASE MEMBER" This is the person whose name is on the contact sheet - the person you are to interview. In some rare instances, there may be cases where the name on the contact sheet is not an undocumented person. An example of this might be a person who is documented, but who has sought out assistance for a family member. However, wishing to protect the anonymity of the undocumented relative, our case member name, is the name of the documented sponsor. We anticipate that this will be a very rare situation if it comes up at all. If this occurs, report the case immediately to your supervisor for instructions on how to proceed with that case (sample) member.

SECTION I

Overview

The first section requests demographic characteristics such as age, sex, religion, and racial/ethnic identification. In addition we will be asking about educational background, and family characteristics such as the immigration status of the spouse and their children's characteristics.

Q. 9   For the educational roster, ask the respondent about levels attended, number of years attended at each level and whether or not the level was completed. Read all of the levels to the respondent. Do not assume that if they stopped school at one point they did not resume it at a much higher level later in life. First ask these questions about school levels attended in their home country, then ask about levels attended in the United States. Always probe responses with: Any other levels or educational courses completed?

Q. 19   Same as Q. 9

Q. 24- Ask each of these questions for all children under
   27   18. Check that the chart contains information for the total number of children mentioned in Q. 23.

SECTION 2: Region of Origin

Overview

The second section contains information about the region of origin and migration patterns of the respondent. In this section we are essentially tracking the respondent's movement (geographical) until the time that he/she first arrived in the United States.

Q. 35- Note that we are interested in a person's movement
   37   after the time that that person completed their 15th birthday. Also, we will be recording the migratory "stops" only if the stop lasted six months or more. We have provided spaces from ages 15-50. If a person migrated to the U.S. after the 50th

birthday, we have provided blank spaces for you to detail the information immediately following the migration chart. We are interested in collecting the same information that we are gathering in the chart. The age at which the respondent moved, the place he moved to, country and place, and the age until the person moved from that site.

Q. 40   Here we are interested in the place that the respondent spent the largest share of his/her life after age 15. Please note the city/town referred to in answering this question in a marginal note.

SECTION 3: How/Why Came

Overview

The third module focuses on the immigration experience. Essentially we are interested in how a person came into the U.S., with or without a visa. We also want to know about their experiences with INS, whether or not they have ever been apprehended. In addition, we explore the reasons that motivated them to come and stay in the U.S.

The questions for this section are fairly straightforward. However, if any interviewer has any problems with this section, we will discuss it during the training session.

SECTION 4: Settlement

The fourth section focuses on their settlement experience in the U.S. Their expectations, their evaluation of their current situation and the impact that this has on the expected length of their stay in this country. Here again, the questions are straightforward. Do not hesitate to ask questions, if you have any, during the training session.

SESSION 5: Subjective Evaluation

Overview

This section is entirely subjective in nature. We ask them

their perceptions of their life in the U.S. Specifically, we are interested in the kinds of problems that they first had in adapting to life in the United States, and in the evolution of those problems. Note that these questions may require careful probing. Take great care in ensuring that your probes do not bias responses.

SECTION 6: English-Speaking Ability

Overview

Here we ask respondents to rate their ability to use English effectively. First we ask them if they can read English, understand English, speak English. Later we ask them to evaluate each of these components individually. If during the course of the interview you have an opportunity to evaluate the respondent's English-speaking ability, and if that ability conflicts with the self-evaluation, make a note in the margin of this section. However, you should be aware that the purpose of these questions is not to test their English language ability.

SECTION 7: Remittances/Income Transfer

Overview

In section seven, we are interested in finding out about the transfer of income or other remittances to their home country. In particular, we'd like to know if they send money home, how much and how often they send these amounts, and for what purpose this money is used by their relatives in their home country. In this section we are also interested about the respondent's participation in U.S. governmental social programs such as unemployment compensation, social security benefits, food stamps etc.

Q. 183-   We need to know the kinds of governmental assist-
  185   ance received and whether they are currently
              receiving it. If a person is currently receiving
              public assistance, write the information in under
              the PRESENT column; if a person received
              assistance in the past, and is no longer currently
              receiving it, write the information in under the
              PAST column.

SECTION 8: Work Experiences in the U.S.

Overview

In section eight we'd like to capture a snapshot of a person's work history/experience in the U.S. If a person is currently working, we'd like to know more about his/her current job. If a person is working two jobs, ask the questions about the job at which she/he spends most of the working time. Secondly, we'd also like to get some information about the job the person had immediately before he/she got the current job. Finally, we'd like to get comparable information about the person's first job. Become familiar with the skip patterns in this Section. It will save a lot of time in the administration of the instrument for persons who have only held one job.

SECTION 9: Household in U.S.

Overview

Here we focus on the respondent's U.S. household composition. We ask about the head of household, the relationship of persons in household to the head of household, income, household expenditures, ownership and neighborhood composition. We are also interested in examining a person's migration sequence in the U.S. and ask a series of questions on moves within the U.S. Please note that we are not interested in changes of address, if the change involves moves within the same city.

APPENDIX III

CONTACTS WITH OTHER AGENCIES

1. American Council for Nationalities Service (New York).

2. Board of Home Missions of the Congregational and Christian Churches (New York).

3. Board of Social Missions of the United Lutheran Church in America (New York).

4. Central Department of the Church World Service (New York).

5. Church World Service, Inc. (New York).

6. Commission on Ecumenical Mission and Relation of the United Presbyterian Church in the U.S. (New York).

7. Community Action for Legal Services (Brooklyn).

8. Comite Nuestra Senora de Loreto Sobre Asuntos de Imigracion Hispana (Brooklyn).

9. International Rescue Committee (New York).

10. MFY League (New York).

11. Nassau County Hispanic Foundation (Hempstead).

12. Northeastern Conference of Seventh Day Adventists (New York).

13. The Salvation Army (New York).

14. Unidad Civica Hispano Americana (Hempstead).

15. United Refugee Council Corp. (Brooklyn).

16. World Council of Churches (New York).

17. Community Service Society (New York).